DIGITAL 2025

Advances on Societal Digital Transformation

July 6th– 10th, 2025

Venice, Italy

DIGITAL 2025 Editors

Claudia Heß, IU Internationale Hochschule, Germany

Sibylle Kunz, IU Internationale Hochschule, Germany

Printed from e-media with permission by:

Curran Associates, Inc.
57 Morehouse Lane
Red Hook, NY 12571

International Academy, Research, and Industry Association (IARIA)
412 Derby Way
Wilmington, DE 19810

Phone: (408) 893-6407
Fax: (408) 527-6351

petre@iaria.org

Additional copies of this publication are available from:

Curran Associates, Inc.
57 Morehouse Lane
Red Hook, NY 12571 USA
Phone: 845-758-0400
Fax: 845-758-2633
Email: curran@proceedings.com
Web: www.proceedings.com

DIGITAL 2025

Forward

The Advances on Societal Digital Transformation 2025 (DIGITAL 2025), held between July 6th -10th, 2025, continued a series of international events covering a large spectrum of topics related to digital transformation of our society.

The society is continuously changing at a rapid pace under digital transformation. Taking advantage of a solid transformation of digital communication and infrastructures, and with great progress in AI (Artificial Intelligence), IoT (Internet of Thinks), ML (Machine Learning), Deep Learning, Big Data, Knowledge acquisition and Cognitive technologies, almost all societal areas are redefined.

Transportation, Buildings, Factories, and Agriculture are now a combination of traditional and advanced technological features. Digital citizen-centric services, including health, well-being, community participation, learning and culture are now well-established and set to advance further on.

As counter-effects of digital transformation, notably fake news, digital identity risks and digital divide are also progressing in a dangerous rhythm, there is a major need for digital education, fake news awareness, and legal aspects mitigating sensitive cases.

We take here the opportunity to warmly thank all the members of the DIGITAL 2025 technical program committee, as well as all the reviewers. The creation of such a high-quality conference program would not have been possible without their involvement. We also kindly thank all the authors who dedicated much of their time and effort to contribute to DIGITAL 2025 We truly believe that, thanks to all these efforts, the final conference program consisted of top-quality contributions. We also thank the members of the DIGITAL 2025 organizing committee for their help in handling the logistics of this event.

We hope that DIGITAL 2025 was a successful international forum for the exchange of ideas and results between academia and industry and for the promotion of progress in the field of societal digital transformation. We also hope that Venice provided a pleasant environment during the conference and everyone saved some time to enjoy the historic charm of the city.

DIGITAL 2025 Chairs

DIGITAL 2025 Steering Committee

Sibylle Kunz, IU Internationale Hochschule, Germany
Fernando Joaquim Lopes Moreira, Universidade Portucalense, Portugal
Júlio Monteiro Teixeira, Universidade Federal de Santa Catarina, Brazil
Claudia Heß, IU Internationale Hochschule, Germany
Christelle Scharff, Pace University, USA

DIGITAL 2025 Publicity Chairs

Laura Garcia, Universidad Politécnica de Cartagena, Spain
Lorena Parra Boronat, Universitat Politecnica de Madrid, Spain
José Miguel Jiménez, Universitat Politecnica de Valencia, Spain

DIGITAL 2025

Committee

DIGITAL 2025 Steering Committee

Sibylle Kunz, IU Internationale Hochschule, Germany
Fernando Joaquim Lopes Moreira, Universidade Portucalense, Portugal
Júlio Monteiro Teixeira, Universidade Federal de Santa Catarina, Brazil
Claudia Heß, IU Internationale Hochschule, Germany
Christelle Scharff, Pace University, USA

DIGITAL 2025 Publicity Chairs

Laura Garcia, Universidad Politécnica de Cartagena, Spain
Lorena Parra Boronat, Universitat Politecnica de Madrid, Spain
José Miguel Jiménez, Universitat Politecnica de Valencia, Spain

DIGITAL 2025 Technical Program Committee

Qammer Abbasi, University of Glasgow, UK
Aaroud Abdessadek, Chouaib Doukkali University, Morocco
Kawiwat Amnatchotiphan, Thai-Nichi Institute of Technology, Thailand
Daniel Amo Filvà, La Salle, Ramon Llull University, Spain
Mariia Andriyiivna Nazarkevych, Lviv Polytechnic National University, Ukraine
Mohamed Basel Almourad, Zayed University, United Arab Emirates
Faouzi Benzarti, Engineering School of Tunis (ENSIT), Tunisia
Louiza Bouallouche-Medjkoune, University of Bejaia, Algeria
An Braeken, Vrije Universiteit Brussel, Belgium
Roberta Calegari, University of Bologna, Italy
Sayali Chavan, Ulster University, UK
Jundong Chen, Dickinson State University, USA
Siming Chen, Fudan University, China
Marta Chinnici, ENEA, Rome, Italy
Javier Cifuentes-Faura, University of Murcia, Spain
María Elicia Cortés Cediel, Universidad Complutense de Madrid, Spain
José Paulo Cravino, Universidade de Trás-os-Montes e Alto Douro, Portugal
Mohamed Dahmane, CRIM – Computer Research Institute of Montreal, Canada
Babu R. Dawadi, Tribhuvan University, Nepal
Burcu Demirdöven, Pamukkale University, Turkey
Noella Edelmann, University for Continuing Education Krems, Austria
Birgitta Dresp-Langley, Centre National de la Recherche Scientifique UMR 7357, France
Zakaria Abou El Houda, University of Montreal, Canada

Clausthal University of Technology, Germany
Marcelo Iury S. Oliveira, Federal Rural University of Pernambuco, Brazil
Amizan Omar, University of Bradford School of Management, UK
Nicola Orio, University of Padova, Italy
Nuria Ortigosa, Universitat Politècnica de València, Spain
Hamza Ouarnoughi, INSA Hauts-de-France, Valenciennes, France
Pedro R. Palos-Sanchez, University of Sevilla, Spain
Giovanni Pau, Kore University of Enna, Italy
Sandra Milena Pérez Buitrago, Pontificia Universidad Católica del Perú, Lima, Perú
Paulo Pinto, Universidade Nova de Lisboa, Portugal
Filipe Portela, University of Minho, Portugal
Rui Quaresma, Universidade de Évora, Portugal
Achim Rettberg, University of Applied Sciences Hamm-Lippstadt / Carl von Ossietzky University Oldenburg, Germany
Manuel Pedro Rodríguez Bolívar, University of Granada, Spain
Amirreza Rouhi, Drillmec SPA / Politecnico di Milano, Italy
Christelle Scharff, Pace University, USA
Razak Seidu, Norwegian University of Science and Technology (NTNU), Norway
Atriya Sen, University of New Orleans, USA
Ecem Buse Sevinç Çubuk, Adnan Menderes University, Turkey
Pietro Siciliano, Institute for Microelectronics and Microsystems (IMM-CNR), Lecce, Italy
Anthony Simonofski, Namur Digital Institute | Université de Namur, Belgium
Rosario Soria, IAG Finance, New Zealand
Abel Suing, Universidad Técnica Particular de Loja, Ecuador
Do Duy Tan, Ho Chi Minh City University of Technology and Education (HCMUTE), Vietnam
Camel Tanougast, University of Lorraine, Metz, France
Evelyne Tauchnitz, University of Lucerne, Switzerland
Giacomo Valente, University of L'Aquila, Italy
Washington Velasquez Vargas, Escuela Superior Politécnica del Litoral, Ecuador
Massimo Villari, University of Messina, Italy
Ke Wang, University of North Carolina at Charlotte, USA
Li Wang, University of North Carolina at Chapel Hill, USA
Olaf Witkowski, Cross Labs | University of Tokyo | Tokyo Institute of Technology, Japan
Marcin Wozniak, Silesian University of Technology, Poland
Seyed Yahya Nikouei, Kar Global, USA
Guillaume Zambrano, Nimes University, France
Tengchan Zeng, Virginia Tech, USA
Chi Zhang, The University of Glasgow, UK
Zheng Zhao, Synopsys Inc., USA

Copyright Information

Table of Contents

Artifical Intelligence – Myth or Measurable?

A systematic framework to determine AI-induced productivity gains

Sibylle Kunz, Claudia Hess
IT & Engineering
IU International University of Applied Sciences
Erfurt, Germany
e-mail: sibylle.kunz@iu.org; claudia.hess@iu.org

Abstract—**Many companies using Analytical and Generative Artifical Intelligence (AI) are proclaiming productivity gains, but there is still no structured approach how to calculate the real values. This article shows a set of dimensions to classify use cases with regard to savings in time/ cost or rises in quality and suggests a way of calculating results based on the relationship between productivity and profitability. To estimate the costs, a Total-Cost-of-Ownership (TCO) approach for AI systems is introduced, covering the whole system lifecycle. Comparing both structures, estimations of AI benefits can be calculated more efficiently. A set of AI projects from different branches is used to demonstrate the appropriateness of the framework.**

Keywords-artificial intelligence; productivity; profitability; cost of ownership.

I. Introduction

Productivity gains resulting from analytical Artificial Intelligence (AI), such as in medical diagnosis or fraud detection, have been discussed for several years now. AI can solve complex problems that would otherwise need much more time, resources or would be intractable due to the sheer volume of data involved. Since the introduction of Open AI's Large Language Model (LLM) GPT3.5 to the general public in November 2022 and the emergence of many competing models, the number of news articles and publications that postulate even higher expectations concerning the use of Generative AI (GenAI) in the form of LLMs has multiplied.

For example, a McKinsey study conducted in 2023 [1] proclaimed an estimated world-wide productivity gain induced by GenAI of 2.6 to 4.4 billion dollars and a rise in working productivity of 0.1% to 0.6% per year. According to this study, branches benefitting the most from GenAI will be finance, high-tech, media and bioscience. 75% of this potential can be found in the field of customer service, sales and distribution, software development and research & development. The study evaluated 850 different jobs and 2.100 different job tasks. The study also distinguished between three clusters of task types: Physical work (foreseeable or unforeseeable) with productivity gains of 70% rsp. 34% (slightly more than using analytic AI only), data collection (79%, 65% by analytical AI only) and data management (92%, 75% by analytical AI only) and decision making and collaboration (management, stakeholder communication and interaction, knowledge application) with an increase of 50-55% in productivity – almost three times as much as with analytical AI only. That the amount of productivity gains seems correlated with the level of education comes as a surprise – employees with lower qualifications saw less possibilities to raise their productivity.

There are further national and international studies that aim to quantify the economic effects of AI and its impact on functions and job profiles. In 2024, a study conducted by ifo among German companies [2] revealed that almost 84% of them expected productivity gains for the national economy within five years, estimating an average increase of 12%. But 70% of all managers predicted productivity gains of averagely 8% for their own company, thereby estimating lower values for their company than nationwide.

Hammermann et al. [3] report that 45% of all employees in the 815 companies included in their study, who have used AI in their daily work between 2022 and 2024, claim productivity gains in their own job. On the other hand, 15% of the employees using AI stated the opposite.

Demary et al. [4] arrive at a moderate assessment: their study conducted for the Institute of the German Economy (IW) estimates a rise of the gross domestic product by 0.9% that can be derived from AI-usage between 2025 and 2030, so it does not act as a strong growth driver. For the decade starting in 2030, an increase of 1.2% is predicted. Demary et al. see AI as complementary to human work. They also raise the question whether rises in productivity can be accomplished by AI alone or only if AI is flanked by other digitalization technologies like robotics, software, internet access etc.

The saving of processing time is often cited as a reason for productivity gains. Looking at these ambitious expectations, AI seems to be a must-have for companies to stay competitive. However, AI solutions and their integration in a company's way of working often come with considerable costs and sometimes ethical implications. Before making decisions on investment, organizations must be able to assess the expected productivity gains and construct a fact-based calculation to make sure that AI-investments will be amortized and do not cause any uncontrollable risks, especially with regard to reductions in the workforce as a consequence of productivity gains. It seems insufficient to just ask employees about their general personal impression of the extent to which productivity has increased when using (generative) AI, especially when it is unclear whether this can be attributed to the use of AI alone. The research question is: what kind of values can be measured and in which dimensions?

This article compares measurement dimensions and reference values for different use cases and develops a systematic framework for calculating realistic economic effects of AI usage. Instead of calculating each new AI business case from scratch, it might be helpful to have standard categories, benchmarks and a set of indicators that can be measured.

To provide a solid foundation, the concepts of productivity and profitability are clarified and differentiated in Section II. Section III shows the dimensions for measuring AI-induced productivity and profitability gains related to time, cost and quality. In Section IV, some examples and case study projects are presented to illustrate which productivity gains have already been proven and how they have been calculated. Section V describes a Total Cost of Ownership (TCO)-based approach to calculate investments needed to plan, train, implement and run an AI system. Section VI sums up both sides of the equation: cost structure versus profitability to sketch a framework showing how to develop benchmarks in the future. Finally, Section VII draws a conclusion and offers suggestions for future work.

II. Productivity and Profitability

Due to Thommen et al. [5], productivity is defined as the quantitative relationship ratio between output and input of the production process (1):

$$Productivity = \frac{Work\ Outcome}{Input\ Quantitiy\ of\ production\ factors} \quad (1)$$

Since it is impossible to measure productivity for a whole enterprise at once, partial productivities are calculated related to work hours, machine running times or area sizes. For example, an accountant could execute 20 bookings per hour, a punching machine could produce 1.000 parts per hour, or a toy shop could achieve a turnover of 1.000 € per square meter. If the usage of AI is somehow beneficial to the company, these partial productivities can be expected to rise.

This effect can be direct or indirect: An increase in productivity per area means better utilization of limited resources and thus a direct increase in sales. Conceivable areas of application include stationary retail or agricultural production. Conversely more output from a machine or worker per unit of time means - assuming investment or labor costs remain the same (considered here as fixed costs) - that less machine running time or labor is now required for the same result, indirectly reducing costs.

Productivity is an output-oriented concept measured in physical units like pieces or amounts. Since productivity figures can usually also be expressed in monetary units, the concept of profitability (or economic viability) can be used as a substitute for productivity in the planned framework.

Profitability can be defined in different ways. The following equation assumes a direct relationship to productivity via (2):

$$Profitability = \frac{Productivity \times Revenue\ per\ Unit - Total\ Expenditures}{Revenue} * 100\% \quad (2)$$

Alternatively, the concepts of the net profit ratio (after deduction of all taxes) (3)

$$\text{Net Profit Ratio (\%)} = \frac{Net\ Income}{Revenue} \quad (3)$$

or the gross margin ratio (after deduction of all direct costs) (4)

$$\text{Gross Margin Ratio (\%)} = \frac{Gross\ Profit}{Net\ Revenue} \quad (4)$$

can be used.

The central question is: to what extent can the use of AI reliably contribute to the productivity gains predicted by recent studies, and which investments in AI technologies are necessary to leverage this potential? Although there are currently many studies that attempt to quantify the expectations of AI use in this regard, it is difficult to verify whether these expectations will actually materialize. There is a lack of clear assignability and classification of measurement methods. The following section will therefore examine which dimensions and characteristics are suitable for operationalization.

III. Dimensions for Measuring AI-Induced Productivity and Profitability Gains

AI can be classified into different fields based on its purpose, underlying methodologies, and applications. For our framework, we will distinguish between Analytical AI, Generative AI, and Reactive AI.

- Analytical AI focuses on data-driven decision-making, pattern recognition, and predictive analytics. It processes structured and unstructured data, extracts insights, and assists in optimization and forecasting without autonomously generating new creative content. It can be used in the fields of medical diagnosis, fraud detection, predictive maintenance or algorithmic trading as well as for natural language recognition, sentiment analysis, etc.
- Generative AI is designed to create new, synthetic content, such as text, images, music, or videos, by learning patterns from existing data. It uses advanced models like Generative Adversarial Networks (GANs) that allow the creation of videos and Transformer-based architectures like GPT4.x and other Large Language Models for natural language generation.
- Reactive AI operates based on real-time inputs and predefined rules, without memory or learning from past experiences at runtime. It was mainly used for fast-response, rule-based systems like chess-playing systems like "Deep Blue", or older AI-powered, but rule-based chatbots.

Today, especially the methods in Analytical and Generative AI can be used to leverage potentials for productivity - and therefore - profitability gains. There are three dimensions to be improved: time, cost and quality. Table 1 shows the relation between these dimensions and whether Analytical (A) or Generative (G) AI is used. It lists examples for measures that can be used to calculate AI-related profitability increases.

TABLE I. MEASURING DIMENSIONS FOR AI PRODUCTIVITY

Dimension	Context/Scenarios	AI class
Time	Planning time Project planning, Product planning, Logistic optimization (e.g., airports, freight forwarders, harbors, railways)	A+G
	Design time Product design, Service design, Individualization of consumer goods, Developing protein structures for pharmaceutical or chemical applications (e.g., AlphaFold), Developing recipes	A+G
	Production time of physical goods (time needed to produce one piece or unit)	A
	Production time of immaterial artefacts Creation of text, audio, video, e.g., in journalism, marketing, consulting, arts, Creation of program code	G
	Testing time Creation of test cases (e.g., software testing), Automatic test execution and evaluation	A+G
	Delivery time Demand forecasting, Route optimization	A
	Support time Analyze service requests by natural language recognition, Speech-to-Text, Answer customer requests, Analyze customer feedback	G
Cost	Material usage: production factors like raw materials, supplies and energy	A
	Waste, Offcut: raw materials	A
	Required space: inventory optimization	A
Quality	Quality inspection Automatic anomaly detection in production processes, Medical diagnosis (e.g., skin cancer, tumor detection in X-Rays or MRTs, Proofreading, Stylistic improvement of texts, Translation	A+G

With regard to GenAI, it needs to be pointed out that time and cost might tend in a different direction than quality, i.e., gains in the first two dimensions might cause reductions in the third. Consider this example: It is often stated that GenAI helps save a lot of time in producing text and illustrations. Employees working with text, such as journalists or marketers, can produce results in a shorter time or reduce the effort necessary to check translations or edit articles. And this means that one person can create a larger amount of output (i.e., text or graphic elements) in a given time, therefore getting more things done for the same salary. But in this case, productivity gains are more difficult to estimate, since the quality or originality of results is also important for the artefacts. Just speeding things up might lead to counterproductive effects in the long run.

IV. CASE STUDY EXAMPLES FOR SUCCESSFULLY MEASURING PRODUCTIVITY GAINS

The two following tables show some examples for case studies in the fields of Analytical and Generative AI that documented concrete absolute or relative values for productivity gains. In most cases, percentages or absolute values for savings were mentioned, but none of them listed any data on the cost side as described in Section IV. Table 2 lists projects using mainly analytical AI.

TABLE II. CASE STUDIES USING ANALYTICAL AI TO INCREASE PROFITABILITY OR SAVE COSTS.

Company and branch	What was measured?	Scope	Relative or absolute change in productivity / reported savings
Salling Group, Energy consulting [6]	Cost: Energy consumption in supermarket buildings via smart meters or data from energy providers	AI system analyses weather data and energy consumption and optimizes usage of device during closing hours	700 supermarkets were evaluated, savings in the millions are reported
Municipality of Holstebro, Denmark [7]	Cost: Energy consumption in community buildings	AI system analyses weather data and energy consumption and optimizes usage of device during closing hours	Savings: 1 million DKK = ca. 146.000 $
SWMS Systemtechnik Ingenieur-gesellschaft mbH [8]	Cost: Automated production of composite materials using a printing robot arm: usage of 3D printing materials	Reduction of printing errors through AI-supported monitoring: image-based object recognition and segmentation.	Material savings of 1/3 (estimated), Savings in energy for robot and cooling of printed artefacts
Orthopedical insoles [9]	Cost: Material usage in 3D printing instead of insole construction using blanks	AI system calculates ideal form to realize material saving	Material savings: >70% in plastic materials, up to 60% in energy
FRAPORT AG, Aviation [10]	Time: staff are assigned to ground handling based on qualification and availability	AI system IDA simulates and optimizes staff planning	(no data yet, project in beta-status)

Table 3 shows some examples of projects using GenAI. Productivity gains here often mean that standard tasks can be automated, so that the employee gets more time for more difficult tasks.

TABLE III. CASE STUDIES USING GENERATIVE AI TO INCREASE PROFITABILITY OR QUALITY OR SAVE COSTS.

Company & Branch	Scope	What was measured?	Change in productivity / reported savings
heise (IT magazine publisher, online portal provider) [11], [12]	System heiseIO (based on LLM and a process-oriented approach with predefined prompts)	a) Time: Annotation time of 14.000 pictures in a CMS b) Time: Production time of a newsletter	a) 5-15min human-based annotation time saved per picture, total cost of 300 € Daily "Botti" newsletter can be produced 12 minutes faster, saving a total of 1,5 person days per moth
Fieldcode GmbH [13]	System Fieldcode (based on LLM) planning of field service assignments	Time: Ticket diagnosis: analysis of field service requests to solve service problems remotely instead of sending a service technician, optimize "first fix rate" Cost: avoid unnecessary order of spare parts avoid unnecessary travel cost, fuel etc.	Up to 50% of spare parts could be saved, Rise of First fix rate (no exact number given)
Klarna [14]	System Kiki (based on LLM) used for internal knowledge management	Time, Quality: The system answers up to 2.000 questions of employees per day and is used by 85% of all staff	Contracts can be generated in 10 minutes instead of 1 hour Chatbot performs 2,3 million chats with customers (equals work of 700 employees) Estimated profit increase: 40 million $
Boston Consulting Group [15]	General usage of AI	Time, Quality	12% more tasks accomplished, 25% savings in time 40% increase in quality

The two tables show that the case studies can easily be categorized in terms of the dimensions mentioned in Section III. Table 4 shows an overview of all case studies mapped to these dimensions.

TABLE IV. ASSIGNMENT OF CASE STUDIES TO MEASURING DIMENSIONS AND AI CLASS

Case Study	Dimension	AI class
Salling Group	Cost	A
Municipality of Holstebro	Cost	A
SWMS Systemtechnik Ingenieur-gesellschaft mbH	Cost	A
Orthopedical insoles	Cost	A
Fraport	Time	A
Heise	Time	G
Fieldcode GmbH	Time, Cost	G
Klarna	Time, Quality	G
Consulting	Time, Quality	G

The next section discusses how different AI-system investments can be made comparable using a lifecycle

V. COST OF AI-USAGE: A TOTAL COST OF OWNERSHIP-APPROACH FOR AI-SYSTEMS

Before productivity gains can be realized, AI-based systems need to be developed, trained and fine-tuned. To get an overall picture of the total cost of ownership (TCO) of an AI system, the following cost components need to be considered. They can be organized along the life cycle of an AI system, using a TCO-like approach with lifecycle phases and corresponding tasks as follows.

A. System Design and Development

All AI systems need to be modelled and trained. This can either be done using supervised or unsupervised learning, reinforced and/or deep learning. Developing these systems requires a large amount of storage and compute resources like GPUs or other AI-chips. Training data needs to be collected or artificially generated, and the data needs to be cleaned and consolidated. Interfaces to control and monitor the settings are needed and the system may have to be integrated into existing processes. This results in a significant fix-cost block before installing the final system. In the case of prefabricated AI models, this cost block will be covered by later subscription fees.

The cost determinants in this phase are especially the programming time, data engineering time (calculated via salary), on-premises hardware or cloud cost for CPU/GPU time, and energy cost.

B. Customizing

Especially in the case of GenAI, the resulting models need to be finetuned to perform specific tasks or to improve their performance in a particular domain. Guard rails need to be developed to ensure responsible and ethical AI use.

The cost determinants are salary (programmers and domain experts), acquisition of domain-specific data sets, and computing resources.

C. Integration into Controlling

Key Performance Indicators (KPIs) and performance metrics need to be developed in order to monitor the system and to assess its performance. This is a prerequisite to ensure that the AI system meets the desired outcomes

The main cost determinant is the time required to choose and to agree upon KPIs and appropriate metrics with AI engineers, domain experts and executives being involved.

D. Deployment and Documentation

The AI system needs to be deployed within the existing infrastructure, which involves technical setup, integration with systems and platforms already in use, and testing. Documentation facilitates maintenance, troubleshooting and further development.

The cost determinant is the time spent by the technical team.

E. User training

Users need to be initially trained in how to use the AI systems (e.g., required by the EU AI act). The training ensures employees understand AI opportunities, risks, and legal compliance requirements. The curriculum also depends on what tasks the employees are assigned to, e.g., whether they work in the IT department, in a dedicated AI team, human resources etc.

The cost determinants are salary, course fees, course material, travelling and accommodation costs.

F. Operation

Each request to the running system causes a certain amount of costs for inferencing, i.e., producing a solution or an answer. These costs are often covered using subscription fees like user licenses for LLMs on a monthly or per-token basis. For critical systems, human workers need to be kept in the loop to meet ethical requirements.

The cost determinants are subscription fees (fix costs on monthly/annual basis), token consumption (variable cost), salary.

G. User Training Cycle

After certain intervals, these training courses need to be repeated to keep users up-to-date and refresh their knowledge.

The cost determinants are salary, course fees, course material costs, travel and accommodation costs.

H. Risk Management

Installing AI systems in certain processes might also require additional insurance, e.g., to protect against potential damage caused by AI system failures, or monitoring frameworks to assess and mitigate associated risks.

The cost determinants are salary and insurance premiums.

I. Certification for Compliance

Certifications might be required regarding compliance with legal and regulatory standards, which can vary by industry and region (e.g., the AI Act by the European Union). They must be renewed in prescribed intervals. Renewal processes typically involve reassessment and auditing of systems to confirm that they still meet the necessary requirements.

The cost determinants are certification fees on an annual or long-term basis and salaries for the internal and external experts involved in the certification.

This structure can be used to calculate a concrete AI project, resulting in the estimated total costs of the system. It can further be used to calculate the time needed to amortize.

VI. The Integrated Framework for Comparing Costs and Productivity/Profitability Gains

To be able to reliably quantify productivity and profitability gains, the two concepts explained in Sections III and V must now be combined as illustrated in Figure 1. The sum of all profitability increases can be calculated by measuring the difference (Δ) between time, material cost or quality level and multiplying it with the proper computing unit like salary/hour or price/unit. Predicting the benefit of a rise in quality is more difficult to calculate. In a medical environment for example, it could be measured by the follow-up costs of the treatment of a patient who was not correctly diagnosed but would have been using AI-techniques – or by future purchases of a customer who is more satisfied than before.

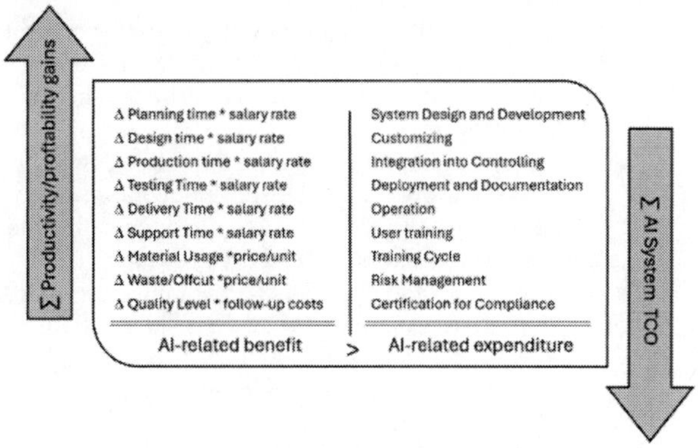

Figure 1. Comparing the benefits of productivity/profitability gains and AI system costs

To calculate a value for an AI-system TCO, more data is needed, for example resulting from past projects and continuous controlling. Companies might search for benchmarks and share experiences. As AI system components become more standardized and included in "software off the shelf", this will become much easier to accomplish.

Finally, the two sums or at least their order of magnitude can be compared arriving at a first judgment whether the benefits outweigh the costs and if so, by what amount. This can prevent companies from running blindly into AI projects that will not be paying off because too many aspects remain unnoticed before the start.

VII. Conclusion and Future Work

Although many companies claim remarkable benefits of AI usage concerning productivity, it is still difficult to find exact numerical proof or compare use cases across branches. Each use case is evaluated on its own, and often only savings, but no cost dimensions are reported. In addition, AI systems are rarely looked at from a TCO-based angle with regard to the whole lifecycle.

Therefore, in this article a framework for measuring and evaluating productivity and profitability gains induced by using analytical or generative AI systems was developed. A volume structure was developed for the beneficial effects, considering time, cost and quality. In addition, AI system cost is structured alongside a TCO approach. Finally, both sides are compared to gain a clearer view on quantitative aspects, which has to be enriched with qualitative aspects like human-AI-cooperation or ethical implications. Integrating these perspectives, the framework can help foster a cautious judgement whether the proclaimed benefits stand on real ground.

Future work should include the following:

- A systematic literature review should be conducted focusing on collecting and categorizing case studies in different industries to gather as much real data as possible. Categorization should include branches, company size, geographical region, type of AI used and governance limitations in force.
- A database with benchmark data should be compiled using the results of the literature review. Data donations from interested companies should be integrated.
- A questionnaire for measuring the single components of the framework should be developed, resulting in a form where companies can enter their specific data to get a first estimation of benefits and cost.
- Institutions like chambers of commerce, industry associations and practical research institutions like universities of applied sciences can help with gathering this data and transferring it into practice.

References

[1] McKinsey & Company, „Auswirkungen von GenAI auf den deutschen Arbeitsmarkt. Eine Chance zur Linderung des Fachkräftemangels". 2023. [Online]. Available from: https://www.mckinsey.de/~/media/mckinsey/locations/europe%20and%20middle%20east/deutschland/news/presse/2023/2023-11-24%20genai%20implikationen%20deutschlands%20arbeitsmarkt/mckinsey_analyse_genai_arbeitsmarkt_deutschland_vf.pdf [retrieved: 05, 2025]

[2] A. Kerkhof, T. Licht, M. Menkhoff, and K. Wohlrabe, „Die Nutzung von Künstlicher Intelligenz in der deutschen Wirtschaft". ifo Institut - Leibniz-Institut für Wirtschaftsforschung an der Universität München, München, 2024. Vol. 77, Iss. 08, pp. 39-43, ifo Schnelldienst, ISSN 0018-974X

[3] A. Hammermann, R. Monsef, and O. Stettes, „Produktiver mit KI?. Wie Unternehmen und Beschäftigte die Produktivitätseffekte einschätzen". IW-Trends, 2024, 51. Jg., Nr. 4, S. 75-94

[4] V. Demary et al., "Gutachten: Wie wird KI die Produktivität in Deutschland verändern? Institut der Deutschen Wirtschaft Köln e.V.", 2025. [Online]. Available from: https://www.iwkoeln.de/fileadmin/user_upload/Studien/Gutachten/PDF/2025/Gutachten_2025-Produktivit%C3%A4t-KI-barrierefrei.pdf [retrieved: 05, 2025]

[5] J.-P. Thommen et al., Allgemeine Betriebswirtschaftslehre (9. Aufl.). Lehrbuch. Springer Gabler, 2020, p.48.

[6] ento.ai (a), "Salling-Gruppe nutzt KI, um Millionen beim Energieverbrauch zu sparen". [Online]. Available from: https://www.ento.ai/de/cases/salling-group-reduces-energy-consumption-by-more-than-eur-2-million [retrieved: 05, 2025]

[7] ento.ai (b), "Holstebro Kommune: Energieeinsparungen dank AI-basiertem System". [Online]. Available from: https://www.ento.ai/de/cases/holstebro-municipality-saves-energy-with-ai-based-system [retrieved: 05, 2025]

[8] Green-AI Hub Mittelstand (a), "KI-basiertes Monitoring von 3D-Druck". [Online]. Available from: https://www.green-ai-hub.de/pilotprojekte/pilotprojekt-swm [retrieved: 05, 2025]

[9] Green-AI Hub Mittelstand (b), „KI-gestützter 3D-Druck orthopädischer Einlagen". [Online]. Available from: https://www.green-ai-hub.de/pilotprojekte/pilotprojekt-herges [retrieved: 05, 2025]

[10] I. Grünewald, "KI optimiert Flugzeugabfertigung am Frankfurter Flughafen. Die Fraport AG führt mit dem "Intelligent Dispatching Agent" (IDA) ein KI-System ein, das die komplexe Koordination der Flugzeugabfertigung erleichtern soll". 28.02.2025. [Online]. Available from: https://www.heise.de/news/KI-Update-Deep-Dive-KI-optimiert-Flugzeugabfertigung-am-Frankfurter-Flughafen-10299459.html [retrieved: 05, 2025]

[11] B. Danneberg, „KI-Prozess in heise I/O automatisiert Metadaten-Generierung". 29.01.2025. [Online]. Available from: https://www.linkedin.com/posts/benjamin-danneberg_ki-digitalisierung-effizienz-activity-7290268305125220352-a9kC?utm_source=share&utm_medium=member_desktop&rcm=ACoAABrr_P4BhHMbau19XKqlGi1IdWjXoaDtZMo [retrieved: 05, 2025]

[12] I. Grünewald, „KI-Update Deep-Dive: KI in der Heise Gruppe". 17.01.2025. [Online]. Available from: https://www.heise.de/news/KI-Update-Deep-Dive-KI-in-der-Heise-Gruppe-10245348.html [retrieved: 05, 2025]

[13] Green-AI Hub Mittelstand (c), „LLM-gestützte Analyse von Tickets im Außendienstmanagement". [Online]. Available from: https://www.green-ai-hub.de/pilotprojekte/pilotprojekt-fieldcode [retrieved: 05, 2025]

[14] R. Maeder, "Wie viel Geld spart Klarna durch Künstliche Intelligenz ein". 04.06.2024. [Online]. Available from: https://www.moneytoday.ch/news/wie-viel-geld-spart-klarna-durch-kuenstliche-inteligenz-ein [sic!] [retrieved: 05, 2025]

[15] F. Dell'Acqua et al., "Navigating the Jagged Technological Frontier: Field Experimental Evidence of the Effects of AI on KnowledgeWorker Productivity and Quality". Working Paper 24-013. 2023. Harvard Business Scool.

The Diversity of Students as a Challenge of AI Adoption in Boosting Efficiency of Study Programmes

An Empirical Study on the Case of a big Austrian University

Larissa Bartok
Center for Teaching and Learning
University of Vienna
Vienna, Austria
e-mail: larissa.bartok@univie.ac.at

René Krempkow
Research and Transfer Unit
IU International University of Applied Sciences
Berlin, Germany
rene.krempkow@iu.org

Abstract - **Artificial Intelligence (AI) is gaining ground in everyday life and administrative data analysis at universities. Therefore, applying machine learning and other methods in modeling academic success at universities, for example, is becoming increasingly important. Our case study from a large Austrian university demonstrates how questions related to academic success, with a focus on diversity indicators, can be investigated at universities using various methods, including AI and administrative data of $N = 2532$ students from Science, Technology, Engineering, and Mathematics disciplines (STEM). This article discusses implications for the impact of applying such models on institutional decision-making at universities regarding academic success. Although it is yet difficult to grasp efficiency within the context of student success, the potential impact of the influence of applying such models, together with possible unwanted effects, is discussed.**

Keywords - Academic analytics; study success; machine learning; diversity indicators

I. INTRODUCTION

Students leave a wealth of data at universities: for example, data provided during admission or examination data. This data can be used by the university for evaluation and quality assurance purposes and processed accordingly to further develop study programs in an evidence-based manner. Well-prepared analyses embedded in processes thus represent, on the one hand, a source of information for decision-makers, and, on the other hand, the interpretation and derivation of measures can improve the quality of offered programs and may help to identify stumbling blocks for study success for certain student groups.

Research on AI-based approaches to student success and on digital study assistance systems using rule-based AI is still manageable [1]. Possible implications of using AI models for university development on academic success are not yet discussed. This gap in research motivates the current study, which presents adaptable models for application across universities to increase the efficiency and quality of study programmes. The efficiency of a study programme within this context refers to the extent to which a programme achieves its intended objectives while optimizing the use of available resources, such as time, funding, and institutional support. It encompasses factors such as the timely completion of degrees (e.g., within the standard duration), high graduation rates, effective resource allocation, alignment with labour market demands, and the overall satisfaction and success of students. According to experience and studies, predictive, AI-based, models seem to be well suited to using empirical data and results of empirical analyses for student success and teaching development, as it also makes it possible to formulate narratives from quantitative results and to involve stakeholders [2][3]. However, it is by no means easy to govern universities (especially in state universities in German-speaking countries). Similarly, this applies to identifying suitable starting points for measures to increase the efficiency and quality of degree programmes, as the reasons for higher or lower academic success can be manifold. They can lie in the characteristics of the students or teachers as well as in the characteristics of the study programmes or the organisation, as we will explain in the following section. Within this article we focus on analyses of the prediction of academic success within the first year of studying and identifying the influence of diversity indicators impacting (or not impacting) academic success based on a selected criterion. Our case study that is making use of data of $N = 2532$ students from Science, Technology, Engineering, and Mathematics programmes at a large public Austrian university. The case originates from a working group composed of university leadership, administrative staff, and study programme directors from STEM disciplines. The objective of this working group was to analyse study programmes with a focus on the entry phase and to identify potential barriers for non-traditional students and students from diverse backgrounds. Therefore, institutional research questions were first defined and answered making use of different analysis approaches, depending on the complexity of the questions.

Our paper is organized as follows. Section II provides a brief theoretical overview of student success and factors influencing student success at Higher Education Institutions (HEIs). Section III demonstrates the methodology of our case study including our institutional research questions. In Section IV our results are described. Our conclusion, discussion and ideas for further investigation close the article.

II. STUDENT SUCCESS AND FACTORS INFLUENCING IT

Student success can be measured in various ways [4][5]. Objective success criteria such as student success rates, passed exams, grades or credit points and graduates within the standard period of study are often used. We evaluate student success in terms of successfully passing the student entrance phase after one year. Since the 2011/2012 academic year, the majority of degree programs in Austria have included a legally mandated introductory and orientation phase during the first semester. This phase comprises initial examinations that must be successfully completed before students are permitted to continue their studies (see UG 2002, §66). When considering the impact diversity indicators have on success, this entrance phase is of relevance, since it is well-known that onboarding of students with diverse backgrounds plays a crucial role for belonging and continuing their studies [6]. Attempts at steering within the framework of the Performance Based Funding (PBF) pursued with the new steering model also try to achieve this using such or similar criteria. In PBF models, in addition to student success rates, the study duration or the proportion of graduates within the standard period of study (plus 2 semesters in some cases) are also used [7] – albeit with only mixed success [10][16][17][18].

When considering the factors that contribute to academic success, it is useful to distinguish between institutional and individual factors [7]. Individual factors are usually included in models at universities to explain and predict study success. Individual factors can be divided into entry conditions (e.g., diversity factors, such as social background, but also previous school education and knowledge or grades in school), context factors (e.g., such as employment or caring responsibilities) and factors of the individual study process (e.g., performance factors, learning behaviour and motivation [7][8]. Although research on the factors influencing academic success varies, all levels significantly impact outcomes. However, performance data (academic or prior school achievements) consistently show the strongest effects in multivariate models.

Empirical analyses in German-speaking universities indicate that student employment significantly affects success [6][10]. Additionally, entry requirements and higher education entrance qualifications, which include diversity factors like age, social, and educational background, also play crucial roles [7][12]. However, a desired steering effect on efficiency and quality can only be achieved if at least all the central influencing factors on the target variable to be steered are recorded [9]. In addition, a change in the central factors must be within the sphere of influence of those responsible at the university. Otherwise, they must be modelled as context factors to be considered, as in performance or quality evaluations, so that corresponding steering attempts can achieve the desired effects [10].

III. METHODOLOGY

In this section we describe our institutional research questions of our case, and the methods used to answer them and to validate the results. Furthermore we describe the sample used.

A. Institutional research questions

The case study we present in the following aims to better understand academic success at the beginning of studies and especially focuses on developing measures specifically designed for STEM programs. Regarding STEM, Austrian universities must increase the number of students and more specifically the number of women in those fields belonging to STEM disciplines. Therefore, the investigation of the influence of diversity indicators on student success is of increasing importance. The transition from school to university, the start of studies and academic performance in the first semester, i.e., arrival at the university, are central to the students' commitment to the university. The target audience are decision-makers at universities and, indirectly, students who are expected to benefit from the measures derived. The following questions are addressed:

1) What is the proportion of students enrolled in a given semester who, after one academic year,...

a) ...have successfully completed all courses suggested?

b) have not taken any courses?

c) have partially completed courses?

2) To what extent can differences be identified between different student groups? Characteristics include: gender, age at entry, university entrance qualification (school type), foreign language, immigrant background and parents' educational background.

3) Which characteristics are most relevant in predicting success in the HEI?

4) What role do interaction effects between combinations of characteristics play?

For investigating questions 1) and 2), common descriptive analysis may be used, whereas question 3) and 4) can only be investigated by using model-based approaches like classical frequentist analysis or AI-based approaches like machine learning models. Within this paper we focus on demonstrating how algorithm-based approaches may help in analysing more complex institutional research questions and therefore help to enhance the efficiency and quality of study programmes.

B. AI Methods modelling student success

We used a variety of Machine-Learning methods to predict student success: A General Linear Model (GLM) with a logistic link function (logistic regression), Random Forests (RF), Boosted Logistic Regression (LogitBoost), Support Vector Machine (SVM) and Gradient Boosting Machine (GBM). Advantages of these models are that they often have more predictive power in comparison to classical frequentist approaches like classical regression analysis.

As questions 1) and 2) are primarily descriptive and serve as preliminary analysis, followed by more advanced, AI-based investigations. To investigate question 3) and 4) we operationalized success by a dichotomous outcome variable (all courses in the entrance phase passed vs. at least one course failed). Logistic regression analysis or a method from the field of machine learning such as random forest can be used to compare the strength of the factors and model interaction effects. Experience has shown that these analyses require more explanation and moderation of interpretation to stakeholders (what do the results mean and what do they not mean) than purely descriptive analyses. That is why we developed graphical visualizations which are easy to interpret. The better interpretation of Odds-Ratio in comparison to importance values led us to report the influence of the variables in terms of odds ratio [13]. All variables related to diversity collected at the university were included in the model as predictors. Which variables should be included depends on the research questions to be answered, theoretical considerations, and the data availability of the respective university. The definition and categorization of the variable values should also be justified by their content. In our case study, we were investigating STEM programs, which is why it is of particular interest to determine whether a science-oriented school type has a positive impact on academic success and, subsequently, whether this positive effect differs between genders. In addition to gender and school type, other variables included in the model were parents' educational background (university vs. no university), foreign language background (yes vs. no), and age.

C. Data

Administrative and exam data of students from eight different study programs (N = 2532) belonging to STEM disciplines at a large Austrian university were used. This analysis was carried out within a working group specifically set up to identify potential adverse conditions for specific student groups and to develop measures to support students.

D. Model Training and Validation Procedure

To evaluate the predictive performance of various classification algorithms, the dataset was first randomly split into a training set (70%) and a validation set (30%), using a non-replacement sampling approach. Cases containing missing values were subsequently removed from both subsets to ensure complete-case analysis. A repeated 10-fold cross-validation procedure with three repetitions was employed to tune and evaluate model performance. For internal resampling during training, 25 resamples were generated based on the outcome variable using stratified sampling. Class probabilities were computed, and all model predictions from resampling iterations were saved to allow for further ensemble and performance analysis.

Model training was performed using the caretList function from the caret Ensemble package [15]. The outcome variable was modeled as a function of all available predictors. Prior to model fitting, features were standardized (i.e., centered and scaled). The following classification algorithms were included in the model list: Logistic regression with a binomial link function (glm), Random forest (rf), LogitBoost (LogitBoost), Support vector machine with linear kernel (SVM) and Gradient boosting machine (GBM). The reasons for selecting these models, in addition to the availability within the respective R package, were a mix of linear and non-linear and simple and complex methods, as well as different ensemble techniques allowing for a comparison of methods with different strengths and assumptions, This ensemble approach allowed for a fair comparison of different learners under the same resampling strategy, enabling both individual model assessment and potential ensemble modelling in subsequent steps.

IV. RESULTS

Research questions 1) and 2) are purely descriptive questions and can be answered without making use of machine learning models. For demonstration reasons, we are inserting a descriptive plot that was used in the communication with stakeholders for each programme separately. Here, we are displaying all programs together.

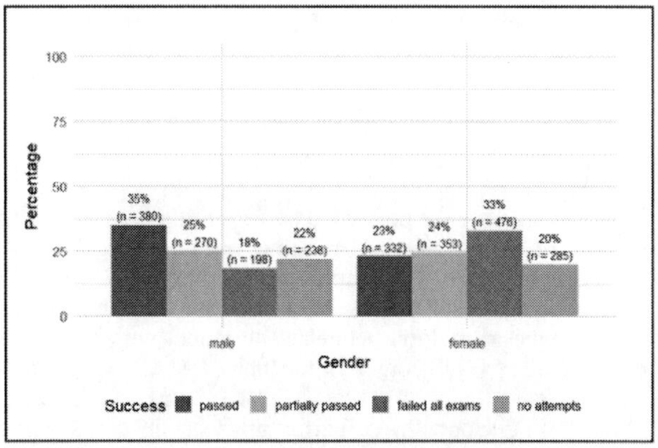

Figure 1. Descriptive differences: Gender

Descriptively speaking, only 35 percent of males and 23 percent of females have passed all entry courses within one year (Figure 1). Students of diverse genders were not represented in the graphic because there were too few observations to include them. Furthermore, it can be demonstrated, that female students more often have negative attempts only, but are attempting exams at the beginning equally often. By looking at the relative differences a gender gap exists in the eight programs analysed together.

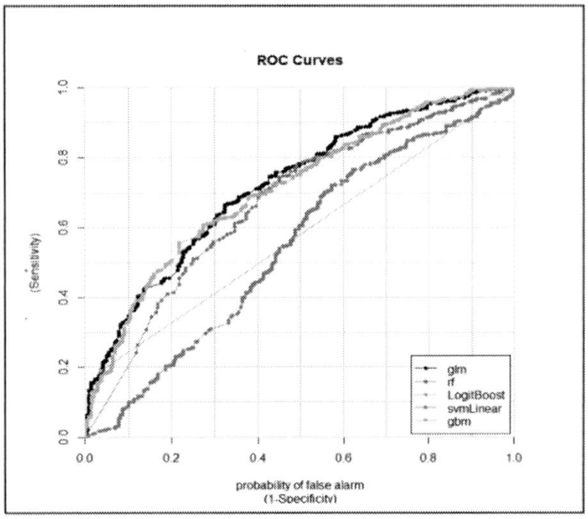

Figure 2. ROC curves

To investigate the predictive power of diversity factors fit indices of the mentioned machine learning models were compared and the ROC-curves were compared (Figure 2: ROC curves). ROC curves are often used to compare the performance of multiple models. The model with the curve closest to the top-left corner (or the highest AUC) is preferred. The visualisation shows that (boosted) logistic regression models (LogitBoost) were performing best in our specific case. A comparison between different models and their fit indices is displayed in Table 1. All the models have a poor to medium fit. The glm with the logistic link function (logistic regression) and the Gradient boosting machine (GBM) fitted best, since their AUC and Kappa values were larger.

TABLE I. MODEL FIT INDICES OF FULL MODELS

Fit of full models	Fit-Indices		
	AUC	*Mean accuracy*	*Mean Kappa*
glm	0.72	0.72	0.14
rf	0.63	0.72	0.03
LogitBoost	0.58	0.70	0.05
SVM	0.55	0.72	0.01
GBM	0.71	0.72	0.14

To investigate the influence of specific diversity indicators the results of the logistic regression (glm) were further analysed: McFadden's R2 of the full model of the logistic regression was 0.11, indicating that the model explains approximately 10.5% of the variance in the outcome compared to the null model.

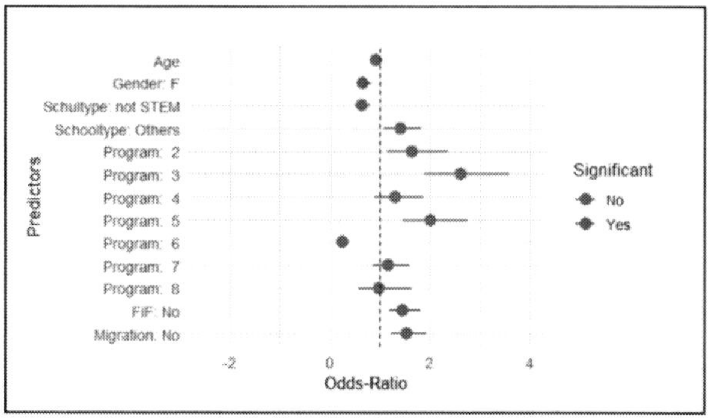

Figure 3. Odds-Ratio Logistic Regression – Full Model

The likelihood-ratio based measure $R^2_{ML}$was 0.118, and the Cragg-Uhler (Nagelkerke) R^2 was 0.169, suggesting modest explanatory power. To answer research question 2) and 3) Odds Ratio of the full model revealed differences between the study programmes on the probability to successfully complete the first courses (Figure 3). These effects were larger than the effects of the diversity indicators. Nevertheless, older students, female students and students attending schools with no science or mathematical background had a lower probability of successfully completing the entrance phase. Students with parents holding a university degree (First in Family: FiF: No) and students with no migration background had better odds to pass all courses. The interaction effect between school type and gender (research question 4) was not significant in the logistic regression model and was therefore not visualized. When modelling a specific study programme (programme 6) only, for this specific programme only age was a significant predictor with a small and positive effect: In this programme older students were having larger probabilities to successfully complete their first year (Figure 4).

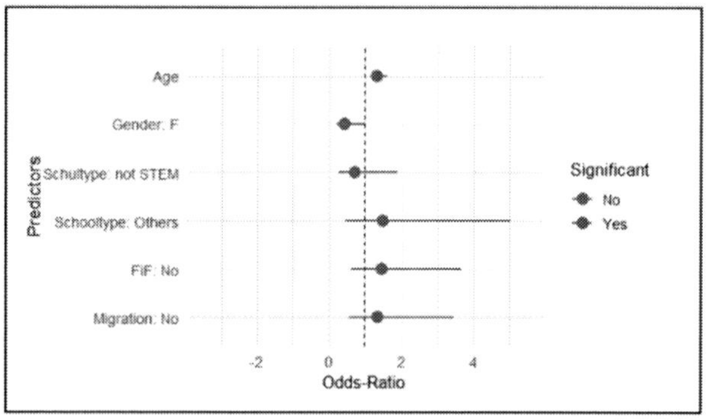

Figure 4. Odds-Ratio Logistic Regression – Full Model programme 6

V. CONCLUSION AND FUTURE WORK

Using the example of passing the first entrance phase, our results show that it is possible to predict study success with AI approaches, especially machine learning. Our models including diversity factors as predictors had a relatively small but measurable impact on student success. On the other hand, models without diversity indicators do have often less explanatory power than models including diversity indicators. This aligns with existing literature that performance-based indicators have strong predictive power but does not mean that the usage of diversity indicators is not relevant for HEIs, because it increases the area under the receiver operating curve and therefore the sensitivity and specificity of the model.

Which diversity indicators impact student success, seem to depend on the study programme and the diversity of the students in the sample, as we assumed based on former analyses [14]. Although data from study programmes belonging to STEM fields were used, findings were different in the respective programmes and diversity indicators were having different impacts on success. This highlights that such an analysis must be carried out individually and consequences and measures must be developed carefully for each individual study programme. AI models can help in analysing and interpreting the data, but which measures are derived are programme and context specific. Furthermore, and especially by comparing the descriptive analysis to the outcomes from models, relevant differences between different student groups exist. If those are not considered, biases by analysing the data and especially when deriving measures to support students or using the analyses for quality insurance processes may result. The analysis of the specific programme (Figure 4) revealed that older students have lower chances to pass the entry phase. A measure derived could be offering a bridging course in which relevant content can be repeated. Another measure that could be derived is the introduction of a mentoring program for older students, which might involve positive discrimination and would need to be carefully considered by experts with knowledge in higher education (research). At this point, the use of AI reaches its limits, and additional human resources are required to derive and implement measures from the results.

Since similar results are now evident in a relatively large number of such analyses, it can be assumed that ineffective forecasts and the measures derived from them to promote student success can only be reliably avoided if diversity indicators are systematically taken into account in AI approaches; and if influencing factors are examined specifically for each study programme. This is therefore a necessary prerequisite for improving the quality and efficiency of study programmes with the help of empirical analyses and AI-supported study success predictions. In addition to predicting student success and dropout, HEIs are also interested in developing study programmes which allow a diverse student body to successfully master their programs. If universities are aiming especially for the entrance phase to let a diverse student body successfully complete, the use of diversity indicators to predict and model study success may be of particularly high relevance. Therefore, investigating the specific effect of these factors, when controlling performance-based indicators is important. This can also help prevent such forecasts from being misused to attract students who are more likely to succeed in their studies from the outset, without the university having to contribute much to this - as is sometimes reported as an unintended effect of student success analyses in other countries [16]. However, a possible prioritisation of study programmes for analyses with limited resources can be derived from the experience that with greater heterogeneity or diversity of students, greater effects of diversity indicators can potentially be expected. Nevertheless, some limitations must be noted here, that are in the same time desiderata for future analyses: Contextual factors, data availability, and the choice of variables play an important role. In the social sciences, it is difficult to find perfectly uncorrelated variables and to create complete models. Therefore, it is important to interpret one's own results with caution and to consider blind spots. Furthermore, predictive performance and the identified importance of the predictors may vary depending on the operationalisation of student success. That is why this study may be repeated with other operationalisations, e.g., ECTS points [13]. In addition, further analyses would be useful to investigate the inner workings of the models, e.g., structural equation modelling (SEM) and hierarchical models; and consideration of other variables known to influence academic success (such psychological constructs as self-concept). Furthermore, the proposed analysis should be extended to further different types of degree programmes and further HEI in order to answer the question of the extent to which the results presented here can be generalised university-, state- or nationwide if necessary. Third, and finally, it would make sense not only to analyse the effects of diversity on academic success, but also to develop a monitoring system for diversity factors to observe them professionally and, if necessary, to prioritise (more or less automatically) degree programmes with significant changes for analysis.

In the longer term, such models could also provide systemic benefits beyond their concrete benefits for individual study programs and universities: They are good examples of linkage possibilities with empirically informed teaching development at universities, which could contribute overall to a culture of stronger evidence orientation in decision-making at universities and thus to an even more systematic promotion of academic success. This can increase not only the quality but also the efficiency of study programmes. Future work therefore should deal with the (more) systematic derivation and development of possible recommendations for action. For example, this could apply to the fact that we have identified a gender difference and have communicated this to the study programme and responsible stakeholder. The following questions arise for the next steps: What decisions can be taken, and under what conditions and contexts? [3] Which departments do the 'translation work' here, which are (only) responsible for the analysis and how does this interact within the university? How can this be organized as a systematic process? AI models can, therefore, help to increase the efficiency and quality of study programmes, but must be applied systematically and indicators should not only be chosen by their predictive power, but also in terms of theory and goals defined by stakeholders. Measures must be derived and implemented by humans with experience in higher education. In addition, such models could not only provide more targeted support for certain student groups if goals and corresponding measures are adequately formulated. Rather, this could also be done for universities that (must) deal with their promotion in a special way due to their profile, their geographical location or their recruitment potential, for example.

ACKNOWLEDGMENT

We would like to thank our colleague Ingrid Purner for creating the opportunity to analyse the data and Robin Gleeson for the useful comments and ideas on our work.

This paper benefited from language refinement assistance provided by ChatGPT (April 2025 version), an AI language model developed by OpenAI. The AI was used solely for language improvement, and the authors reviewed and confirmed the final content.

REFERENCES

[1] M. Lübcke, M., J. Schrumpf, K. Schurz, F. Seyfeli-Özhizalan, T. Thelen, K. Wannemacher, & F. Weber, (eds.)"Mit digitalen Studienassistenzsystemen durchs Studium. Zeitschrift für Hochschulentwicklung", ZFHE, vol. 19, no. 4, pp. 9-13, 2024.

[2] K. R. Isett & Hicks,,. "Pathways From Research Into Public Decision Making: Intermediaries as the Third Community", Perspectives on Public Management and Governance, vol. 3, no. 1, pp. 45-58, 2020.

[3] A. Wegner, R. Krempkow, and C. Thiedig, "From evidence to impact? Practices of evidence use for quality management at German Higher Education Institutions," in *46th Annual EAIR Forum 2024, University College Cork*, Cork (Ireland), Aug. 2024.

[4] S. Falk, J. Kercher, and J. Zimmermann, "Internationale Studierende in Deutschland: Ein Überblick zu Studiensituation, spezifischen Problemlagen & Studienerfolg," *Beiträge zur Hochschulforschung*, vol. 44, no. 2-3, 2022.

[5] R. Krempkow, O. Vettori, and I. Buß, Eds., Studierbarkeit und Studienerfolg, Zeitschrift für Hochschulentwicklung – ZFHE, vol. 17, no. 4, 2021.

[6] V. Tinto, *Leaving College: Rethinking the Causes and Cures of Student Attrition*, 2nd ed. Chicago, IL: University of Chicago Press, 1993.

[7] R. Krempkow, "Determinanten der Studiendauer. individuelle oder institutionelle Faktoren? Sekundärdaten-analyse einer bundesweiten Absolvent(inn)enbefragung," *Zeitschrift für Evaluation*, vol. 19, no. 1, pp. 37–63, 2020.

[8] U. Heublein, J. Ebert, C. Hutzsch, S. Isleib, R. König, J. Richter, and A. Woisch, Zwischen Studienerwartungen und Studienwirklichkeit. Ursachen des Studienabbruchs, beruflicher Verbleib der Studienabbrecherinnen und Studienabbrecher und Entwicklung der Studienabbruchquote an deutschen Hochschulen. Hannover: Deutsches Zentrum für Hochschul- und Wissenschaftsforschung, 2017.

[9] E. Grande, D. Jansen, O. Jarren, A. Rip, U. Schimank, and P. Weingart, Eds., *Neue Governance der Wissenschaft: Reorganisation, Externe Anforderungen, Medialisierung*. Bielefeld: transcript, 2013.

[10] R. Krempkow, "Can Performance-based Funding enhance Diversity of Higher Education Institutions?" in *Diversity and Excellence in Higher Education: Can the Challenges be Reconciled?*, R. Pritchard, M. Klumpp, and U. Teichler, Eds. Amsterdam: Sense, 2015, pp. 231–244.

[11] R. Krempkow and R. Kamm, "Leistungsbewertung unter Berücksichtigung institutioneller Diversität deutscher Hochschulen: Ein Weg zur Förderung von Vielfalt?" in *Diversity und Hochschule. Teilhabebarrieren und Strategien zur Gestaltung von Vielfalt*, U. Klein and D. Heitzmann, Eds. Weinheim: Juventa, 2012, pp. 164–181.

[12] B. Thaler, N. Schubert, A. Kulhanek, N. Haag, and M. Unger, *Prüfungsinaktivität in Bachelor- und Diplomstudien an Universitäten*. Vienna: Institut für Höhere Studien – Institute for Advanced Studies, 2021.

[13] L. Bartok, J. Spörk, R. Gleeson, M. Krakovsky, and K. Ledermüller, "Anwendung statistischer und Machine-Learning-Methoden für Fragestellungen zu Studienerfolg - Erfahrungen in den Projekten ‚Learning Analytics - Studierende im Fokus' und ‚PASSt - Predictive Analytics Services für Studienerfolgsmanagement'," Waxmann Verlag, 2024.

[14] M. Krakovsky, R. Krempkow, L. Bartok, K. Ledermüller, and J. Spörk, "Breaking bias: Measurements, potentials and limitations for modelling study success by performance and diversity factors," *ResearchGate*, Apr. 2024. [Online]. Available: www.researchgate.net/publication/385905974

[15] Z. Deane-Mayer and J. W. Knowles, *caretEnsemble: Ensembles of caret models*, R package version 2.0.1, 2023. [Online]. Available: https://CRAN.R-project.org/package=caretEnsemble

[16] A. Matveeva, "Performance-based funding in higher education: a meta-narrative review and renewed research agenda proposal," *Tertiary Education and Management*, [Online first], 2025. Available: https://doi.org/10.1007/s11233-025-09151-y

[17] J. Castro Galvao, F. Tucker, and P. Attewell, "Bending the Curve: Institutional Factors Associated with Graduation Rates," *Higher Education Policy*, vol. 37, pp. 278–302, 2024.

[18] K. J. Dougherty, S. M. Jones, H. Lahr, R. S. Natow, L. Pheatt, and V. Reddy, "Looking inside the black box of performance funding for higher education: Policy instruments, organizational obstacles, and intended and unintended impacts," *The Russell Sage Foundation Journal of the Social Sciences*, vol. 2, no. 1, pp. 147–173, 2016, doi:10.1353/rus.2016.0007

Implementing a Generative AI Workflow Platform in a Media Company

A Work-in-Progress Case Study of 'heise I/O'

Benjamin Danneberg
CEO Deep Content by heise GmbH
heise group
Leipzig, Germany
e-mail: ben@deep-content.io

Matthias Bastian
CEO Deep Content by heise GmbH
heise group
Frankfurt am Main, Germany
e-mail: matthias@deep-content.io

***Abstract*—This paper presents a case study on the development and implementation of "heise I/O", a proprietary Generative Artificial Intelligence (GenAI) workflow platform within heise group, a major German media company. We outline the strategic approach based on principles of quality, source-based generation, transparency, and human responsibility. Focusing on practical outcomes, we detail initial results and quantifiable impacts across different departments, demonstrating significant resource savings, enhanced content production efficiency, and new operational possibilities. The paper shares key lessons learned from this real-world implementation, highlighting how a structured platform facilitates effective GenAI integration for tangible digital transformation outcomes in a media environment.**

Keywords-Generative AI; Digital Transformation; Media Industry; Organisational Implementation.

I. INTRODUCTION

The transformative potential of generative AI (GenAI) necessitates strategic integration within organisations, particularly for content-intensive businesses like media companies. Recent statistics highlight the adoption of AI technologies in Germany, with only 20% of companies utilising AI according to the Federal Statistical Office [1]. A Cisco study further reveals that merely 6% of German companies consider themselves optimally prepared for AI implementation—a decline from the previous year [2]. This hesitancy stems from various barriers, including knowledge gaps (cited by 71% of companies), legal uncertainties (58%), and data protection concerns (53%) [1].

Recognising both the opportunities and challenges presented by GenAI, the heise group, a leading German media publisher, developed "heise I/O" (Input/Output) [4], a dedicated platform designed to manage and scale GenAI applications effectively and responsibly. This approach addresses a fundamental limitation of generic AI chat interfaces: while tools like ChatGPT offer impressive capabilities, they lack the structure, consistency, and collaborative features required for professional content production environments.

This paper provides a case study on the initial phase of heise I/O's implementation, focusing on the practical results and impacts achieved across different departments. We examine how the platform's structured workflow approach enables teams to leverage LLMs and other AI tools through standardised, reusable prompt processes. By sharing concrete examples and quantifiable outcomes, we aim to contribute practical insights to the growing body of knowledge on organisational AI adoption, particularly in content-intensive industries facing digital transformation challenges.

The remainder of this paper is organised as follows: Section II describes the heise I/O platform, its guiding principles, and implementation approach. Section III presents concrete results and quantifiable impacts across different use cases. Section IV discusses key lessons learned and outlines future development directions. Finally, Section V concludes with implications for digital transformation in media organisations.

II. HEISE I/O: PLATFORM, PRINCIPLES, AND IMPLEMENTATION OVERVIEW

In this section we will discuss the overall platform architecture and our philosophy behind heise I/O:

A. *Platform Architecture and Functionality*

heise I/O functions as a structured workflow engine, enabling teams to leverage Large Language Models (LLMs) and other AI tools through standardised, reusable prompt processes. This controlled approach contrasts with ad-hoc, chat-based AI usage that characterises many early-stage organisational AI implementations.

The platform integrates multiple AI models and capabilities into a unified interface, allowing users to:

- Create, store, and share reusable prompt templates
- Process various input formats (text, audio, images)
- Chain multiple AI operations into coherent workflows
- Maintain version control of prompts and outputs
- Track usage patterns and efficiency metrics

Unlike generic AI chat interfaces, heise I/O is designed specifically for team-based content production, with features enabling collaborative development and quality assurance of AI-assisted workflows. While the platform allows for the creation of new prompt templates and workflows by anyone, typically a core group of trained 'AI ambassadors' or 'power users' initially develops and refines these processes before they are shared more broadly. Standard users primarily utilize existing, tested workflows, though opportunities for proposing new ones exist through collaborative channels.

The heise I/O platform itself provides the environment for modeling these workflows. This involves defining sequences of prompt-based operations, selecting appropriate AI models for each step, and configuring input/output parameters within the platform's interface. Use cases are typically identified through departmental needs analysis and then iteratively translated into these structured prompt chains.

B. *Guiding Principles*

The implementation of heise I/O is guided by four core principles:

1. **Quality and Reliability**: Prompts are designed to consistently deliver outputs that meet professional standards. This requires careful engineering and testing to ensure that the same prompt produces reliably similar quality results across multiple uses.
2. **Source-Based Generation**: AI outputs are grounded in user-provided, trusted sources, rather than relying on the model's internal knowledge or on online research, which can be difficult to control. This approach treats AI as a kind of 'text calculator'—similar to a pocket calculator used in mathematics—that processes specified inputs into desired outputs by following explicit instructions.
3. **Transparency and Control**: All AI processes are documented and visible within the organisation. Instead of individual, unmonitored chat interactions, the platform maintains centralised management of approved prompt processes.
4. **Human Responsibility**: The platform emphasises that humans remain accountable for all final outputs. AI is positioned as a tool that augments rather than replaces human judgment and creativity.

C. *Implementation Approach*

The roll-out of heise I/O began with a three-month testing phase followed by broader deployment across the organisation. Key implementation steps included comprehensive preparation and training activities. The organisation conducted two dedicated "AI Weeks" featuring over 35 training sessions with more than 1000 participants, with the keynote session alone attracting over 250 attendees. These events covered a wide range of AI topics from basic ChatGPT usage to specialised applications of heise I/O, generating significant interest among staff.

Following these initial awareness-building activities, the company developed standardised onboarding workshops to establish a common understanding of AI capabilities and limitations. These workshops focused on practical applications, allowing participants to create their own prompts and explore potential use cases specific to their roles. The training emphasised responsible AI usage and effective prompt engineering techniques that could be learned within a relatively short timeframe.

To sustain momentum, the organisation created initial prompt libraries for common tasks across different departments and appointed "AI ambassadors" within teams to champion adoption and share successful use cases. These ambassadors were tasked with regularly bringing AI topics into team discussions and identifying repetitive production tasks that could benefit from AI assistance. The company also established guidelines for appropriate AI use, including prohibitions against using AI-generated photorealistic images in journalistic contexts to maintain editorial integrity.

This structured approach to implementation allowed the organisation to move beyond experimental, individual AI usage toward systematic integration of GenAI into production workflows. Using AI vision capabilities via API and an optimized workflow in heise I/O, we automatically generated relevant descriptions for 14,000 images at a total cost of only €300. Until today, the company deployed 36 instances of heise I/O, serving over 940 users (including the users from the heise group) with access to more than 250 regularly used prompt processes, demonstrating the scale and depth of the implementation effort.

III. PRACTICAL RESULTS AND QUANTIFIABLE IMPACT

Since its introduction in September 2023, heise I/O has seen rapid adoption at heise group, with over 590 employees now actively using the platform across various departments. Through the automation and optimisation of numerous repetitive tasks, a conservative internal estimate indicates resource savings equivalent to over two full-time person-years within the first year of broad usage [5]. Several concrete cases illustrate the platform's impact:

A. *Automated Newsletter Generation*

For the heise online "Botti" newsletter, delivered twice daily to over 50,000 subscribers via multiple channels, a structured workflow reduced the average creation time from approximately 15 minutes to just 2 minutes per issue. The workflow incorporates:

- Automatic selection and formatting of current news links
- Generation of contextually appropriate introductions and conclusions
- Maintenance of a consistent, unique brand voice through carefully designed prompts

This efficiency gain saves the editorial team over 1.5 workdays per month while maintaining quality and personality in the content. It also illustrates how a process previously handled by a single person can now be distributed across several team members—without any loss in editorial quality.

B. *Podcast Production Efficiency*

The production of the daily "kurz informiert" podcast was significantly streamlined through an integrated AI workflow that includes:

- AI-assisted summarisation of text sources into concise script formats
- Generation of audio narration using a cloned voice of the presenter
- Automated post-processing of audio content

This process efficiency enabled the doubling of daily broadcasts of the full podcast episodes from one to two, directly contributing to an 88% increase in podcast listenership since the beginning of the year, with over 1.4 million listens per month as of today. This highlights AI's role in increasing output frequency and reach without compromising quality.

C. Image Metadata Automation

Generating metadata (alt-text, captions) for large image archives is a time-consuming but necessary task for accessibility and Search Engine Optimization (SEO). Using AI's vision capabilities via an API and a finetuned process via heise I/O, a mass process automatically generated relevant texts for 14,000 images for approximately €300. This task would have required weeks or months of manual work, showcasing AI's scalability and cost-effectiveness for routine content enrichment. The implementation is particularly timely given upcoming accessibility regulations in Germany requiring alt-text for images by mid-2025, demonstrating how AI can help organisations meet compliance requirements efficiently.

D. Content Repurposing

Transforming audio content (like podcast transcripts) into multiple formats (blog posts, show notes, social media teasers) was previously highly manual. With AI workflows in heise I/O:

- Audio files can be automatically transcribed
- Transcripts are processed through customised workflows to extract quotes and create derivative content
- Various output formats are generated simultaneously, maintaining consistent messaging across channels

This process can save up to 4+ hours per podcast, freeing up human resources for more complex, creative tasks and demonstrating the power of chaining AI-assisted steps in a workflow.

E. Marketing and Sales Content

In marketing and sales, heise I/O is used for generating ad copy, email drafts, and product descriptions. For heise regioconcept, implementing AI-assisted text production led to:

- Over €60,000 in saved external costs for content creation
- A 30% increase in order volume within a year
- Improved text quality as rated by both internal reviewers and clients

This illustrates the direct business impact on revenue-generating activities, where AI reduces costs and enables capacity expansion without additional staffing. These results indicate that a structured platform approach, guided by clear principles, enables the successful integration of GenAI into diverse media production workflows, leading to measurable efficiency gains and resource savings.

IV. KEY LESSONS AND FURTHER OUTLOOK

The implementation of heise I/O has yielded several important insights for organisations seeking to integrate GenAI effectively:

A. Platform Structure is Essential

A structured platform approach proves significantly more effective than allowing individual, ad-hoc AI tool usage. This structure provides:

- Quality control through tested, standardised prompt templates
- Knowledge sharing across teams and departments
- Consistency in AI-assisted outputs
- Measurability of impact and efficiency gains

The contrast between chat-based interactions and workflow-based processes is particularly evident in professional content production, where reliability and consistency are paramount. Still, the platform makes use of standard chat support, which is well-suited for background tasks, more creative or individual workflows, brainstorming, and ad hoc assistance.

B. Clear Principles Guide Responsible Implementation

Defining clear principles (source-based generation, human responsibility, transparency) has been vital for establishing trust and ensuring ethical AI application. These principles help address common concerns about AI quality and reliability while providing guardrails for appropriate use.

C. Adoption Requires Ongoing Support and Expectation Management

While initial results are promising, successful user adoption requires:

- Continuous training and support beyond initial onboarding
- Addressing potential resistance by demonstrating tangible benefits
- Managing expectations about AI capabilities and limitations
- Providing time for experimentation and process development

The metacognitive effort [6] required to develop effective AI workflows initially deters some users, but those who invest in this process often discover significant long-term efficiency gains.

D. Future Development Directions

As a work in progress, development continues, focusing on:

- Expanding heise I/O's multimodal capabilities (text-to-video, improved image generation)
- Integrating advanced research tools and improved Retrieval-Augmented Generation (RAG) systems
- Developing "Context on Demand" features that allow readers to explore content at varying levels of depth—based on the same trusted sources used by the editorial team to draft articles.

- Enhancing direct integration with content management and distribution systems

The aim goes beyond simply accelerating the act of "writing things down"—although this shift towards a "direct to draft" approach is a key efficiency gain. More broadly, the goal is to unlock new potential by allowing human experts to focus on higher-value tasks, while AI supports routine content processing. At the same time, it enables improvements in both the quantity and quality of content across departments and among individuals—regardless of their varying levels of AI or digital expertise. In doing so, it actively contributes to shaping the future of digital content creation within the heise group.

V. CONCLUSION AND FUTURE WORK

This case study demonstrates that a structured platform approach to GenAI implementation can yield significant, measurable benefits in media organisations. The heise I/O implementation shows how principles-guided AI integration can enhance productivity while maintaining quality and human oversight in content production.

The results challenge the notion that AI adoption necessarily leads to workforce reduction, instead showing how it can enable capacity expansion, new product development, and higher-value work. This aligns with emerging research suggesting that successful AI implementation often involves augmenting rather than replacing human capabilities [3].

For media organisations specifically, the case highlights how GenAI can address industry-specific challenges, such as content repurposing across channels, metadata generation at scale, and efficient newsletter production—all areas where manual processes have traditionally created bottlenecks.

Future research should examine the long-term sustainability of these efficiency gains and explore how structured AI platforms might evolve to address emerging challenges in content authenticity, personalisation, and cross-modal generation. Additionally, comparative studies across different media organisations could help identify industry-specific best practices for GenAI implementation.

As media continues to digitise, platforms like heise I/O show how AI can be practically integrated into editorial workflows—speeding up routine tasks, improving consistency, and making expert knowledge more scalable, without replacing human judgement or creativity.

ACKNOWLEDGMENT

We would like to thank all employees of the heise group for their willingness to be brave and try new things.

REFERENCES

[1] Statistisches Bundesamt, "Usage of AI in German Businesses", Press Release, Nov 2024. [Online]. Available: https://www.destatis.de/DE/Presse/Pressemitteilungen/2024/11/PD24_444_52911.html [retrieved: Apr, 2025]

[2] Cisco, "AI Readiness in Germany decreases slightly", Cisco News Blog, Dec 2024. [Online]. Available: https://news-blogs.cisco.com/emea/de/2024/12/02/cisco-studie-ki-readiness-in-deutschland-sinkt-leicht/ [retrieved: Apr, 2025]

[3] Microsoft and Civey, "AI Usage in German Enterprises" Market Research Report, Apr 2024. [Online]. Available: https://news.microsoft.com/de-de/microsoft-umfrage-ki-foerdert-die-produktivitaet-und-verbessert-das-zeitmanagement-in-deutschen-unternehmen/ [retrieved: Apr, 2025]

[4] heise I/O, Software, May 2025, [Online]. https://heise-io.de/

[5] KI PRO, Deep Dive "Generative AI's Real Impact: Cases & Results from the heise group", Dec 2024. [Online]. Available: https://pro.heise.de/ki/

[6] L. Tankelevitch et al., "The metacognitive demands and opportunities of generative AI", In Proceedings of the 2024 CHI Conference on Human Factors in Computing Systems, May 2024, pp. 1-24

Are AI Tools Helping The Students Too Much?

Radiah Rivu
IU International University of Applied Sciences
Munich, Germany
e-mail: sheikh-radiah-rahim.rivu@iu.org

***Abstract*—With recent advances in the development and usage of Artificial Intelligence (AI), we experienced a surge among the student body to take advantage of its many benefits. Despite the advantages, with AI taking over the major part of the work, we often face the dilemma of having students unwilling to engage cognitively in the learning process. This is especially true for works such as seminars, projects, and theses. In this idea paper, we present an expert interview conducted among six university professors to explore how AI adoption has led to negative student productivity outcomes. Based on this, we explore the question, "Are AI tools helping the students too much?" and provide a list of suggestions to quantify learning productivity and performance when using AI tools.**

Keywords-AI, Framework, Education

I. INTRODUCTION

In recent years, various technologies have gained popularity such as virtual reality [1], augmented reality [2] and Artificial Intelligence (AI). Among these mentioned, the popularity of AI technologies has pierced into our daily lives and we now knowingly or unknowingly embraced AI adoption in all sectors of our lives [3]. One such is the education sector, where both teachers and students use AI tools to assist in their work [4]. Although we have not fully grasped the magnanimous extent to which AI will change our lives, we acknowledge that AI is changing the world and will continue to do so. This forces us to ask, are all metrics associated with AI for good? Or do we also need to consider performance paradoxes: situations where AI adoption can lead to neutral or negative productivity outcomes? This idea paper explores the performance paradox in the education sector. We investigate how often students and teachers use AI tools for assistance and attempt to answer the question Are AI tools helping the students too much?

We present a qualitative interview with six experts (university professors) to understand their perspective. Their experiences tell us that the scenario of teaching and learning is constantly changing with AI tools, and we need to reform our metrics to use AI adoption effectively. Currently, in many cases, AI tools are a hindrance to critical thinking and creative development of students. We present the need for a refined framework to quantify learning productivity and performance using AI tools.

In section II, we present a brief literature review on AI tools and its impact on the education sector. Section III presents the methodology used to design and conduct our expert interview. The results are presented and discussed in section IV. We end our work in section V with the conclusion and future work.

II. RELATED WORK

AI is now having an impact everywhere, from machines, robots, and cars to mobile voice assistance and many more applications. This technology is influencing the future of every industry and changing the lives of all humans. With its numerous positives, there are also severe dangers ahead of us.

Ng et al. [5] present a review article showcasing how AI literacy has evolved from 2000 to 2020. Zhu et al. [6] introduce a research framework for smart education. The authors argue that there are numerous benefits to adapting to the latest technologies, such as AI, to assist a smart learning environment. Smart education empowers students, educators, and administrators in many ways [7].

Basha acknowledges the balance between positives and negatives in the education sector [8]. The author offers suggestions such as greater parental control over students to ensure proper and ethical usage of AI. However, as mentioned, there needs to be a deeper understanding of AI usage to uplift student performance and ensure that AI is not a hindrance to learning.

In this literature review, we find that industry and academic professionals all agree that AI is here to stay, and it comes with many positives. But we must also assess the dangers associated with it and work to mitigate them. One such context is the education sector, where students are becoming highly dependent on AI tools to complete their coursework, and we now contribute to this area with a framework to reduce the drawbacks.

III. METHODOLOGY

We now present our qualitative interview to understand how AI adoption in learning affects student productivity. The interview was conducted with six university professors aged between 35-65 years. We consider the participants to be experts in their fields with varying years of professional experience (5-15 years). The interview focused on questions targeted at understanding the current use of AI tools among students, how this is affecting students' performance, and whether there is a need to reform the usage of AI in learning and education.

The interviews were conducted online and with voluntary participation. Interviews and discussions revolved primarily around the following questions:

1. Do you witness your students using AI tools for assignments or projects?
2. Are there negative sides to using AI, if so, what are they?
3. Should there be metrics to evaluate the effectiveness of

using AI by students?
4. What kind of framework do you propose to restrict the use of AI?
5. In what area are students most affected and what can we propose to mitigate it?

IV. Results & Discussion

All professors unanimously agree that all students use AI tools to varying degrees and it negatively impacts their abilities. There is no denying that there are numerous benefits to using AI tools, for example, any auto-correction tools are now widely used by students to check for spelling and grammar mistakes, and even suggest better formation of sentences. These are frequently used by students to write their project reports or other assignments. But we believe these affect students and using AI tools to a large extent would negatively impact their learning skills and their ability to independently perform any assignment. According to the experts, these tools always limit creativity and make students dependent on external sources. One professor (expert P4) mentioned that students now are so dependent on AI tools to generate assignments, reports, and papers that they are unable to understand the concepts, and they pass a course at only a superficial level. Blind trust in such technology can also result in a loss of analytical and critical thinking. Ubiquitous technologies are designed and intended for people for use in their daily lives, and the education sector is no exception.

All professors discussed the use case scenario where students are doing their master's or bachelor's level thesis writing. A majority of the students turn in their reports where AI is doing the writing, as a result, different theses from different students look the same, read the same, using the same vocabulary. While we acknowledge that AI tools are here to stay and will assist the students, we believe there is an urgent need to understand both the positive and negative impacts on students. This will help teachers understand the students better and allow teachers to evaluate students and teach them concepts better, because the eventual goal is for the students to learn the concepts and apply them independently.

The discussion around a possible framework opened up various aspects that needs to be looked into. P1 says, "I would not say to restrict AI usage but rather open it to a certain limit. At the end of the day, it is a tool that could benefit them". Similar to this, expert P2 also agrees that AI tools should not be restricted, but we need to understand how students should be using them so that it is not used in a counterproductive manner. Based on our interviews, we believe there is a need to impose a ethical AI usage framework and ensure that the students are still able to complete the tasks themselves. We suggest the following steps as a first draft to a framework

1. Make it compulsory for students to perform certain sections of the work without assistance.
2. Record sections of the activities.
3. Classify different aspects of coursework and limit the usage of AI tools in restricted sections.
4. Implementation of oral evaluations of students instead of only written coursework.

V. Conclusion and Future Work

In this idea paper, we presented an open-ended interview with six university professors and discussed how positively or negatively AI tools impact the students. One limitation of our study is that it was only with a limited number of experts. As part of future work, we aim to have a higher sample population to represent our target community better. In addition, we would also like to understand the students' perspective on how AI makes an impact on their learning curve.

Our discussions indicate that all students do use AI tools for assistance, and more often than not, this leads to students losing their creativity or critical analysis skills. AI tools are beneficial in many contexts, but we need to limit their capabilities for the betterment of the students. But this may also entail a higher workload for the teachers. There is a need to establish a framework to measure effectiveness, critical analysis, creativity, and writing assessment, and a scale to ensure that AI tools are being used ethically, and the extent to which AI tools can be used for assistance. For future works, we plan to conduct a survey among students to better understand the use of AI for their university assignments to refine our proposed framework.

References

[1] R. Radiah *et al.*, "Remote vr studies: A framework for running virtual reality studies remotely via participant-owned hmds", *ACM Trans. Comput.-Hum. Interact.*, vol. 28, no. 6, Nov. 2021, ISSN: 1073-0516. DOI: 10.1145/3472617.

[2] G. A. Murillo Gutierrez, R. Jin, J. P. I. Ramirez Paredes, and U. H. Hernandez Belmonte, "A framework for collaborative augmented reality applications", in *Companion Proceedings of the ACM SIGGRAPH Symposium on Interactive 3D Graphics and Games*, ser. I3D Companion '25, Association for Computing Machinery, 2025, ISBN: 9798400718335. DOI: 10.1145/3722564.3728390.

[3] R. Lee, *Artificial Intelligence in Daily Life*. Jan. 2020, ISBN: 978-981-15-7694-2. DOI: 10.1007/978-981-15-7695-9.

[4] Q. Chang, X. Pan, N. Manikandan, and S. Ramesh, "Artificial intelligence technologies for teaching and learning in higher education", *International Journal of Reliability, Quality and Safety Engineering*, vol. 29, no. 05, p. 2 240 006, 2022.

[5] D. T. K. Ng *et al.*, "A review of ai teaching and learning from 2000 to 2020", *Education and Information Technologies*, vol. 28, no. 7, pp. 8445–8501, 2023.

[6] Z.-T. Zhu, M.-H. Yu, and P. Riezebos, "A research framework of smart education", *Smart learning environments*, vol. 3, pp. 1–17, 2016.

[7] H. Singh and S. J. Miah, "Smart education literature: A theoretical analysis", *Education and Information Technologies*, vol. 25, no. 4, pp. 3299–3328, 2020.

[8] J. Y. Basha, "The negative impacts of ai tools on students in academic and real-life performance", *International Journal Of Social Sciences And Commerce1*, vol. 3, pp. 1–16, 2024.

Learn how Digital Transformation Could Diffuse into Organisations

Impact of Motivation and Innovation on Digital Competences and Learning

Sandra Starke
Banku Augstskola School of Business and Finance
Riga, Latvia
sandra.starke@ba.lv

Iveta Ludviga
Riseba University
Riga, Latvia
Iveta.ludviga@riseba.lv

Abstract—**Digital transformation reshapes workplaces, requiring individuals to develop digital competencies. This study examines how self-determined motivation and innovation adoption influence digital competence and sustained learning. Based on the theories of Self-determination (SDT) and Diffusion of Innovation (DOI), we analysed survey data from 152 participants via PLS-SEM modelling. The findings show that innovation adoption significantly drives digital competence, while motivation alone has a limited direct effect. However, digital competence mediates the relationship between motivation, innovation adoption and learning. These insights highlight continuous learning as a core capability for digital transformation. Organisations should prioritise upskilling, and policymakers should foster frameworks supporting innovation adoption. Future research should explore additional factors influencing digital adaptation.**

Keywords- ***Digital transformation; digital competences; learning; innovation adoption; self-determination; knowledge management.***

I. Introduction

Digital transformation reshapes workplaces, jobs, and tasks [1], requiring employees to develop digital competencies to adapt to evolving job demands. Governments expect that new technologies and digital offerings will benefit companies and citizens. Therefore, the current restrained acceptance of digital technologies needs to be investigated. Research indicates that the benefits can only be achieved when individuals are ready to adopt it [2]. Factors, like motivation, self-efficacy, innovation adoption, leadership support and organisational learning, are highlighted as critical enablers in previous literature [3]. Deci & Ryan's Self-Determination Theory emphasises the role of autonomy, competence, and relatedness in fostering intrinsic motivation [4]. Meanwhile, Rogers' Diffusion of Innovation Theory focuses on the attributes influencing how innovations spread among individuals [5]. By combining Self-Determination Theory and Diffusion of Innovation Theory, we link the motivation to engage with the perception and adoption of innovations, as previous studies show that motivation affects adoption. However, the whole pathway (including competence and learning outcomes) is still not sufficiently explored. New competence profiles have been developed and adapted to the changed work requirements. Hartmann, et al. [6] identified and categorised so-called "future skills", which are defined as competencies to solve challenges in an uncertain and changing environment. However, there is still insufficient knowledge about new competencies for "learning 4.0" in workplaces [7]. Existing research on digital transformation often investigates individual motivation and innovation adoption independently and lacks integrated models showing how they affect digital competence and learning. There is a lack of empirical evidence better to understand digital learning triggers and scalable competency development. To fill the existing knowledge gap on prerequisites of individual digital competencies, we combine the research streams of innovation adoption and motivation with studies investigating education and learning, developing "future" competencies for transformation [8]. These new insights will contribute to digital transformation by empirically testing how motivation and innovation adoption contribute to digital competence and learning using an integrated framework, as the rapid pace of technological change makes this interplay more urgent. The rest of this paper is organised as follows. Section II describes the theoretical background and the derived hypothesis. Section III describes the methodology. Section IV displays the results; Section V addresses the ongoing scientific discussion. Section VI concludes with the contributions of this paper and the future research agenda.

II. Theoretical background and Hypothesis Development

Since there is no common definition of digital transformation, this paper adopts the summarizing postulated by Vial [9] and defines digital transformation as "a process aiming to improve services, processes, or treatments by triggering significant changes through combinations of information (documentations, data), computing (AI), communication (networking, virtual treatments), and connectivity technologies (interoperability)". To succeed in digital transformation and sustain this never-ending process of learning, organisations need to develop dynamic capabilities. Dynamic capabilities are defined as the "...firm's ability to integrate, build, and reconfigure internal and external competences to address rapidly changing environments" [10]. Developing digital competencies, knowledge management, and deployment is a new challenge [11]. Learning and knowledge are the dynamic capabilities for continuous innovation to enable digital transformation [12]. We assume sustained learning in this context as a new essential dynamic capability and digital competencies, therefore, as the first building block to be developed for this desired outcome. This paper investigates the relationship between motivation, innovation adoption, and digital competencies & learning on an individual level.

A. Dependent variable: Learning

Current literature displays learning as a basic factor in performing in digital environments through knowledge and competence. However, there is no common concept of learning in digital transformation. Crossan et al. [13] highlight the complexity and different viewpoints on individual, group, and organisational levels, as well as cognitive and behavioural factors. Learning enables individuals and organisations to perform and innovate under rapidly changing conditions. Fiol et al. [14] define organisational learning as "...the process of improving actions through better knowledge and understanding". Argyris et al. highlight individuals' needs and the effect on their well-being and motivation to improve learning [15]. This adaptability and continuous learning must be established to perform in changing environments under uncertain conditions [16]. Previous research implies the positive influence of organisational learning as a contextual factor on innovation adaptation and digital competencies [17]. Individual learning, in contrast, is an intrinsic factor that is assumed to have a reinforcing effect on the presumed positive influence of self-determined motivation on digital competencies. This paper measured and tested learning on organisational and individual levels to better understand the mechanisms impacting the targeted transformation process [18].

B. Independent variable: Self-determined motivation

Self-determination theory was developed to understand intrinsic motivation and why people do things out of interest for their own sake. Deci et al. postulated that all employees have basic needs for autonomy, competence and relatedness; their satisfaction and motivation cause this effect [4]. Applying this theory to digitally transformed workplaces, it explains motivation as a basic mechanism for employees to withstand changing situations. Interacting with the environment and adapting leads to learning over time [19]. Based on this, we assume that employees are more motivated to acquire digital competencies when their basic needs are satisfied by empowering, strengthening, and connecting them [20].

Hypothesis 1 (H1): An individual's self-determined motivation has a positive effect on digital competences in the context of digital transformation.

C. Independent variable: Innovation adaption

Diffusion of Innovation theory (DOI) as social science theory explains the spreading of innovation over time as a process [5], individuals and their perceptions of technology and processes are decisive. According to DOI, the stages of adoption depend on five perceived attributes (relative advantage, compatibility, complexity, trialability and observability).

DOI was developed to describe the stages of how an innovation spreads over time, diffusing as a process. These aspects are antecedents to categorising users and their tendency to adopt innovation. The categorised groups (innovators, early adopters, early majority, late majority and laggards) are important to differentiate for organisations to develop strategies on how these personalities can be targeted [21]. We assume that the perceived attributes of innovation are relevant antecedents for the willingness of individuals to acquire digital competencies to work with new technologies and digital processes.

Hypothesis 2 (H2): Individual innovation adoption positively affects digital competencies in the context of digital transformation.

D. Mediating variable: Digital competence

Knowledge and competence affect employees´ confidence in digital technology [22]. As digital competencies enable employees to participate actively in a digitalised environment [23], organisations need to identify their employees' existing and required competencies and develop solutions to transform their human capital, adapting to changing technologies [24].

There are recommendations and initiatives from the European Union that emphasize the scope and importance of key competencies for all citizens in the private sphere, in the labour market and for the economy. In their council recommendations, the EU suggests their member states foster these key competencies, defined as "a combination of knowledge, skills and attitudes" for lifelong learning [25]. Based on this, the European Commission developed a digital competence framework for citizens (DigComp), including the competence areas of communication, networking, digital literacy, security and content development [26] with knowledge, skills and attitudes illustrating each competence.

This research paper wants to shed light on the antecedents to transform human capital on the individual level. Therefore, it focuses on digital competencies by adopting the DigComp framework. We assume digital competencies are fundamental for learning in digital transformation.

Hypothesis 3 (H3): Digital competencies mediate the effect of motivation and innovation adoption on learning.

According to this theoretical framework, we developed and quantitatively tested the constructed model as displayed in Figure 1.

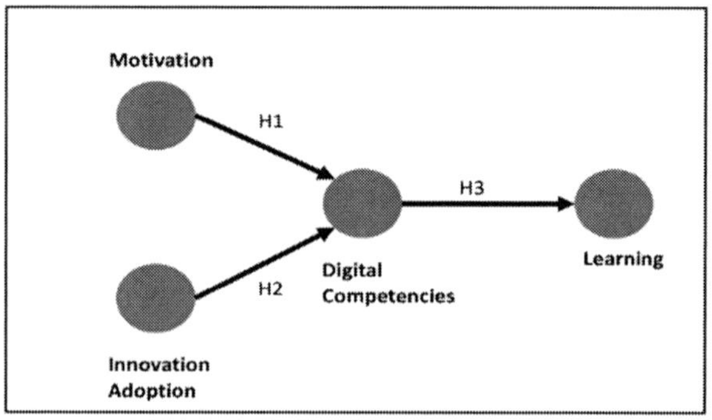

Figure 1. Constructed model

III. METHODOLOGY

Five variables were defined based on existing research and theories, and a conceptual model was developed. A questionnaire was designed to test this model, asking for personal and organisational information in addition to items and measurements applied in previous studies [27] . The hypothesis and measures were tested using a questionnaire on LinkedIn and Prolific platforms. Those platforms allow directly access working professionals across industries in digitally impacted roles, offering controlled diversity and reducing selection bias. Since different scales were used to avoid common method bias (5-point Likert scale for digital competencies, 7-point Likert scale for other items), the statistical analysis in the software Smart PLS were calculated with standardized data.

Variables

Items to measure organisational learning are adopted by Arranz et al. [28], measuring knowledge resources as the main input for innovation. Items for individual learning were adapted from Lee et al. [29], measuring students' behavioural and cognitive learning factors. These items adequately measure the desired outcome, as organisational and individual learning result from individual behaviours and their ability to explore, detect, and solve problems, and the organisation's ability to change established routines and perform in new digital environments [30].

The independent variables are based on established scales. Self-determination motivation items were developed based on the Basic Needs Scale [4], which was adopted in previous studies [31]. This scale measures the dimensions of autonomy, competence and relatedness. To measure innovation adoption, the items were developed based on Roger´s Diffusion of Innovation theory [5], which was widely applied in this research field to test innovation adoption [32].

The items in the survey measure the five perceived attributes of relative advantage, complexity, compatibility, trialability, and observability, which are accepted in research as technological antecedents for innovation adoption on the individual level [33]. The possible mediator, digital competence, is composed of the level and importance of the dimensions, since the European Commission emphasises both [34]. Items measuring the level of competencies are based on the competence areas developed by the DigComp framework, in combination with attitudes towards learning as an appropriate measurement in the human-centred approach [35]. In addition, the importance of digital competencies is measured based on the O*net program [36], which aims to investigate and provide information about the competencies in the labour market that impact the U.S. economy. This database and its measures are established and widely applied to investigate the needs of organisations and employees [37].

Survey Design

The questionnaire comprised 52 questions in English and was translated into German (can be provided with a separate Appendix). It was distributed as a survey in both languages via "LinkedIn" to reach an appropriate sample of employees with basic digital capabilities and extended with participants completing the questionnaire in English by a collector using the online platform Survey Monkey. Participants were asked to pass on the survey link by sharing it on social networks or directly. This purposive sampling is a commonly used approach in research [38]. The survey was also placed via the platform "Prolific" to expand the range of responses. Prolific is a marketplace for online survey research, which is applied in other research on digital transformation in healthcare [39]. The tools SmartPLS 4 and Jamovi were used to analyse the gathered data.

IV. RESULTS

The survey received responses from 152 participants: 126 in English and 26 in German. Fifty-two per cent of the respondents are female, 47 per cent are male, and 1 per cent are diverse. Most participants are employees (25%) or seniors / experts (27%); 23 per cent hold management positions. Forty per cent are aged 41 and above, while the majority of participants (47%) are aged between 25 and 40. To analyse the data, the software Jamovi and Smart-PLS was used. First, the variance was tested with principal component analysis in Jamovi. The resulting 25% variance is below the threshold of 50%, indicating that the item characteristics differ [40]. Based on this result, common method bias is not prevalent in this study. PLS-SEM is an appropriate tool for multivariate analysis and is widely used in business research [41]. Since all items are based on constructs applied in other contexts, Exploratory Factor Analysis and Confirmatory Factor Analysis were performed in Jamovi as a first step in constructing the model.

Outer Model results

Confirmatory factor analysis was applied in Jamovi based on the created subdimensions to investigate the model fit (Table 1).

RSMEA < .05 indicates a good, < .08 a reasonable and over 0.1 a poor model fit, chi-square represents the difference between the expected and observed data (chi-square 0 = expected and actual data are equal), a lower chi-square represents a good model fit. The results are presented in Table 1, the chi-square test indicates no exact fit, RSMEA indicates a reasonable model fit.

Cronbach´s alpha for all variables is > 0.7, for convergent validity, average variance extracted (AVE) should be > 50%, which is also reached, so internal consistency and item reliability are given [42]. The results are displayed in Table 2.

TABLE I. CONFIRMATORY FACTOR ANALYSIS

Fit measure	**Test for exact fit**		
RMSEA	X^2	*df*	*p*
0.0782	1700	881	<.001

a. Indicators analysed in Jamovi
b.

TABLE II. OUTER MODEL INDICATORS

Variables	Outer Model Indicators			
	Cronbach ´s alpha	*Average variance extracted (AVE)*	*Composite reliability (rho_a)*	*Composite reliability (rho_a)*
Motivation	0.800	0.458	0.811	0.854
Innovation Adoption	0.870	0.404	0.887	0.894
Digital Competence	0.900	0.420	0.907	0.915
Learning	0.788	0.476	0.820	0.842

c. Indicators analysed in Jamovi

TABLE III. INNER MODEL RESULTS

Construct	Construct			
	Digital Competence		*Learning*	
	Path co-efficient	*P-Value*	*Path co-efficient*	*P-Value*
R^2	**0.534**		**0.515**	
Motivation	0.156	0.088		
Innovation	0.601	0.000		
Digital Competence			0.781	0.000

d. Indicators analysed in Jamovi

Inner Model results

R2 measures the extent to which the dependent variable is predicted by the independent variables, with values above 0.75 described as substantial, 0.5 as moderate, and 0.25 as weak [41]. The inner model results are displayed in Table 2.

The moderating variable digital competencies can be predicted to be 53% by both independent variables: motivation and innovation adoption. The constructed model demonstrates good predictive power for the outcome variable learning (51%). The path coefficient of 0.601 supports the hypothesised relationship between innovation adoption and digital competencies (H2) and is statistically significant with a p-value of 0.000. The relationship between motivation and digital competencies (H1) is weaker (0.156) and not statistically significant (p-value of 0.088). The hypothesised positive effect, moderated by digital competencies on learning (H3), is also supported (path coefficient of 0.718 / p-value of 0.000).

V. DISCUSSION

Digital transformation massively impacts the labour market. Previous research focuses on the benefits of increasing the efficiency of processes and cost-containment measures, emphasising potential barriers to successful implementation [39]. Dynamic capabilities theory is widely used as a theoretical framework for digital transformation. However, building advantages and withstanding in rapidly changing digital environments requires individual participation. Knowledge, skills and competencies are often mentioned synonymously in recent papers [43]without a clear definition or distinction. Competence and learning are emphasised as inevitable digital transformation prerequisites, but concrete concepts and measurements are rare.

In this study, we aimed to provide clear definitions, examine the assumed effects of motivation and innovation adoption on individual-level digital competencies, and investigate the impact of organisational learning and the significance of digital competencies as contextual factors. The developed measures are internally consistent and reliable, as demonstrated by the analysis of the outer model.

The inner model analysis highlights the assumed relationship between motivation, innovation adoption, digital competencies, and learning. The results align with other studies. Talwar et al. [44] display the importance of engaging and motivating all stakeholders since digitalisation strategies may fail due to reluctance to adopt innovation. Companies need to reconfigure and encourage employees to be innovative [45].

The insignificant relationship between self-determined motivation and digital competence contradicts our assumption that intrinsic motivation is a key driver for learning and skill acquisition. Other factors, such as external requirements for using technology, are more relevant to developing digital skills than one's own motivation. External triggers, like mandatory use and exposure to technology might override internal drivers. Motivation types should be investigated more deeply to explore interactions with contextual enablers, such as training availability or technological pressure.

The variable of digital competence significantly impacts learning. Overall, the developed construct provides evidence for the hypothesised mechanisms. According to the Exploratory Factor Analysis results and the rejected relationship between motivation and the development of digital competencies, a need for deeper investigation into these relationships and improvement of the constructs arises. These results are a building block for further in-depth research, reworking the questionnaire to enhance comprehensibility. Future studies could explore the potential moderation of factors like age or ease of use on the willingness to adopt new technology.

VI. CONCLUSION

Digital transformation disrupts workplaces, and employees must be prepared to use digital technology confidently and be open to innovation. We investigated the effects and relationships of motivation, innovation adoption, digital competencies, and learning as relevant factors in digital transformation and showed that digital competencies are gaining more importance in legislation to enable citizens to participate in the change. For organisations, it is indispensable to adopt and transfer these efforts. Transforming their current human capital towards new knowledge and mindsets with sustained learning is the most relevant dynamic capability in digital transformation.

The study makes several contributions. First, it enhances knowledge by testing the Self-Determination Theory in digital work environments. Contrary to theoretical assumptions, the findings indicate that motivation alone is insufficient to foster the development of digital competence. External factors, such as organisational requirements and environmental conditions, appear to be more influential. Second, the study extends the Diffusion of Innovation Theory by introducing digital competencies as a mediating variable, emphasising that competence acquisition is critical for successful digital transformation. Third, it proposes that sustained learning should be regarded as a dynamic capability; organisations must navigate digital transformation effectively as a significant aspect of organisational adaptability. This finding expands dynamic capabilities theory by recognising learning as an ongoing capability that enables organisations to integrate, build, and reconfigure their competencies in response to evolving digital environments.

It has practical implications and advises managers on integrating employees and designing training methods, allowing for independent content development along with straightforward access and testing options.

This study has its limitations. Since the aim was to test the developed measures and the construct, it was placed on social media for convenient access. The sample size of 152 does not allow generalisation of results, but it is suitable for obtaining feedback and improving the questionnaire. The result might be biased due to the author's social network, which mainly comprises individuals working in educational contexts or healthcare. Further research should investigate the learning factor as a new concept, develop adequate measurements, and raise the question of whether digital competence is an outcome of deliberate learning or functional adaptation.

REFERENCES

[1] D. Howcroft and P. Taylor, "'Plus ca change, plus la meme chose?'-researching and theorising the 'new' new technologies," *New Technol Work Employ*, vol. 29, no. 1, pp. 1–8, Mar. 2014, doi: 10.1111/ntwe.12026.

[2] T. Dirsehan and C. Can, "Examination of trust and sustainability concerns in autonomous vehicle adoption," *Technol Soc*, vol. 63, p. 101361, Nov. 2020, doi: 10.1016/j.techsoc.2020.101361.

[3] Venkatesh, Morris, Davis, and Davis, "User Acceptance of Information Technology: Toward a Unified View," *MIS Quarterly*, vol. 27, no. 3, p. 425, 2003, doi: 10.2307/30036540.

[4] E. L. Deci and R. M. Ryan, *Intrinsic Motivation and Self-Determination in Human Behavior*. Boston, MA: Springer US, 1985. doi: 10.1007/978-1-4899-2271-7.

[5] E. M. Rogers, *Diffusion of Innovations*. New York: Free Press, 1962.

[6] J. Hartmann, M. Heckner, and U. Plach, "Future Skills bei Studierenden - Messung und Einflussfaktoren ," *Die Neue Hochschule*, pp. 24–27, Jun. 2023, doi: https://doi.org/10.5281/zenodo.10057167.

[7] S. Carretero, R. Vuorikari, and Y. Punie, "The Digital Competence Framework for Citizens," 2017.

[8] U.-D. Ehlers, *Future Skills*. Wiesbaden: Springer Fachmedien Wiesbaden, 2020. doi: 10.1007/978-3-658-29297-3.

[9] G. Vial, "Understanding digital transformation: A review and a research agenda," *The Journal of Strategic Information Systems*, vol. 28, no. 2, pp. 118–144, Jun. 2019, doi: 10.1016/j.jsis.2019.01.003.

[10] D. J. Teece, G. Pisano, and A. Shuen, "Dynamic capabilities and strategic management," *Strategic Management Journal*, vol. 18, no. 7, pp. 509–533, Aug. 1997, doi: 10.1002/(SICI)1097-0266(199708)18:7<509::AID-SMJ882>3.0.CO;2-Z.

[11] K. S. R. Warner and M. Wäger, "Building dynamic capabilities for digital transformation: An ongoing process of strategic renewal," *Long Range Plann*, vol. 52, no. 3, pp. 326–349, Jun. 2019, doi: 10.1016/j.lrp.2018.12.001.

[12] D. Ellström, J. Holtström, E. Berg, and C. Josefsson, "Dynamic capabilities for digital transformation," *Journal of Strategy and Management*, vol. 15, no. 2, pp. 272–286, 2022, doi: 10.1108/JSMA-04-2021-0089.

[13] M. M. Crossan, H. W. Lane, R. E. White, and L. Djurfeldt, "Organizational Learning: Dimensions for a Theory," *The International Journal of Organizational Analysis*, vol. 3, no. 4, pp. 337–360, Apr. 1995, doi: 10.1108/eb028835.

[14] C. M. Fiol and M. A. Lyles, "Organizational Learning," *Academy of Management Review*, vol. 10, no. 4, pp. 803–813, Oct. 1985, doi: 10.5465/amr.1985.4279103.

[15] R. T. Golembiewski, "Organizational Leaming: A Theory of Action Perspective," *J Appl Behav Sci*, vol. 15, no. 4, pp. 542–548, Oct. 1979, doi: 10.1177/002188637901500410.

[16] W. H. Starbuck, A. Greve, and B. L. T. Hedberg, "Responding to Crises," *Journal of Business Administration*, pp. 111–137, 1978, [Online]. Available: http://ssrn.com/abstract=2708264

[17] S. Ivaldi, G. Scaratti, and E. Fregnan, "Dwelling within the fourth industrial revolution: organizational learning for new competences, processes and work cultures," *Journal of Workplace Learning*, vol. 34, no. 1, pp. 1–26, 2022, doi: 10.1108/JWL-07-2020-0127.

[18] C. Ivory, F. Sherratt, R. Casey, and K. Watson, "Getting caught between discourse(s): hybrid choices in technology use at work," *New Technol Work Employ*, vol. 35, no. 1, pp. 80–96, Mar. 2020, doi: 10.1111/ntwe.12152.

[19] Z. Wang and A. Panaccio, "A Longitudinal Investigation of the Changes in Work Motivation and Employees' Psychological Health," *Adm Sci*, vol. 12, no. 4, p. 193, Dec. 2022, doi: 10.3390/admsci12040193.

[20] W. Schaufeli, "Engaging Leadership: How to Promote Work Engagement?," *Front Psychol*, vol. 12, Oct. 2021, doi: 10.3389/fpsyg.2021.754556.

[21] L. Robinson, "A summary of diffusion of innovations," 2009.

[22] A. Ullrich, M. Reißig, S. Niehoff, and G. Beier, "Employee involvement and participation in digital transformation: a combined analysis of literature and practitioners' expertise," *Journal of Organizational Change Management*, vol. 36, no. 8, pp. 29–48, May 2023, doi: 10.1108/JOCM-10-2022-0302.

[23] U.-D. Ehlers, "Future Skills-The Key to Changing Higher Education," Project Next Skills. [Online]. Available: www.NextSkills.org

[24] M. Augier and D. J. Teece, "Understanding complex organization: the role of know-how, internal structure, and human behavior in the evolution of capabilities," *Industrial and Corporate Change*, vol. 15, no. 2, pp. 395–416, 2006.

[25] Council of the European Union, "Council Recommendation of 22 May 2018 on key competences for lifelong learning.," May 2018.

[26] European Commission, J. R. Centre, R. Vuorikari, S. Kluzer, and Y. Punie, *DigComp 2.2, The Digital Competence framework for citizens – With new examples of knowledge, skills and attitudes*. Publications Office of the European Union, 2022. doi: doi/10.2760/115376.

[27] D. B. Audretsch and M. Belitski, "Knowledge complexity and firm performance: evidence from the European SMEs," *Journal of Knowledge Management*, vol. 25, no. 4, pp. 693–713, May 2021, doi: 10.1108/JKM-03-2020-0178.

[28] N. Arranz, M. F. Arroyabe, J. Li, and J. C. F. de Arroyabe, "An integrated model of organisational innovation and firm performance: Generation, persistence and complementarity," *J Bus Res*, vol. 105, pp. 270–282, Dec. 2019, doi: 10.1016/j.jbusres.2019.08.018.

[29] J. Lee, H.-D. Song, and A. Hong, "Exploring Factors, and Indicators for Measuring Students' Sustainable Engagement in e-Learning," *Sustainability*, vol. 11, no. 4, p. 985, Feb. 2019, doi: 10.3390/su11040985.

[30] O. Dörner and S. Rundel, "Organizational Learning and Digital Transformation: A Theoretical Framework," in *Digital Transformation of Learning Organizations*, Cham: Springer International Publishing, 2021, pp. 61–75. doi: 10.1007/978-3-030-55878-9_4.

[31] C. Meske and I. Junglas, "Investigating the elicitation of employees' support towards digital workplace transformation," *Behaviour & Information Technology*, vol. 40, no. 11, pp. 1120–1136, Aug. 2021, doi: 10.1080/0144929X.2020.1742382.

[32] R. Raman, S. B, V. G, H. Vachharajani, and P. Nedungadi, "Adoption of online proctored examinations by university students during COVID-19: Innovation diffusion study," *Educ Inf Technol (Dordr)*, vol. 26, no. 6, pp. 7339–7358, Nov. 2021, doi: 10.1007/s10639-021-10581-5.

[33] A. Othman, A. Al Mutawaa, A. Al Tamimi, and M. Al Mansouri, "Assessing the Readiness of Government and Semi-Government Institutions in Qatar for Inclusive and Sustainable ICT Accessibility: Introducing the MARSAD Tool," *Sustainability (Switzerland)*, vol. 15, no. 4, 2023, doi: 10.3390/su15043853.

[34] V. Bikse, I. Lusena-Ezera, P. Rivza, and B. Rivza, "The Development of Digital Transformation and Relevant Competencies for Employees in the Context of the Impact of the COVID-19 Pandemic in Latvia," *Sustainability*, vol. 13, no. 16, p. 9233, Aug. 2021, doi: 10.3390/su13169233.

[35] D. Biggins, D. Holley, G. Evangelinos, and M. Zezulkova, "Digital Competence and Capability Frameworks in the Context of Learning, Self-Development and HE Pedagogy," 2017, pp. 46–53. doi: 10.1007/978-3-319-49625-2_6.

[36] E. and T. A. National Center for O*NET Development by the U.S. Department of Labor, "O*Net Resource Center." Accessed: Dec. 17, 2023. [Online]. Available: https://www.onetcenter.org/overview.html

[37] L. Roemer, P. Lewis, and J. Rounds, "The German O*NET Interest Profiler Short Form," *Psychological Test Adaptation and Development*, vol. 4, no. 1, pp. 156–167, Jul. 2023, doi: 10.1027/2698-1866/a000048.

[38] I. Mergel, N. Edelmann, and N. Haug, "Defining digital transformation: Results from expert interviews," *Gov Inf Q*, vol. 36, no. 4, p. 101385, Oct. 2019, doi: 10.1016/j.giq.2019.06.002.

[39] S. Iyanna, P. Kaur, P. Ractham, S. Talwar, and A. K. M. Najmul Islam, "Digital transformation of healthcare sector. What is impeding adoption and continued usage of technology-driven innovations by end-users?," *J Bus Res*, vol. 153, pp. 150–161, 2022, doi: 10.1016/j.jbusres.2022.08.007.

[40] D. Navarro and D. Foxcroft, *Learning statistics with jamovi: a tutorial for psychology students and other beginners*, vol. Version 0.70. 2019. Accessed: Jan. 14, 2024. [Online]. Available: http://www.learnstatswithjamovi.com

[41] J. F. Hair, C. M. Ringle, and M. Sarstedt, "PLS-SEM: Indeed a Silver Bullet," *Journal of Marketing Theory and Practice*, vol. 19, no. 2, pp. 139–152, Apr. 2011, doi: 10.2753/MTP1069-6679190202.

[42] A. Alojairi, N. Akhtar, H. M. Ali, and A. F. Basiouni, "Assessing Canadian business IT capabilities for online selling adoption: A Net-Enabled Business Innovation Cycle (NEBIC) perspective," *Sustainability (Switzerland)*, vol. 11, no. 13, 2019, doi: 10.3390/su11133662.

[43] C. Troise, M. Tani, D. Matricano, and E. Ferrara, "Guest editorial: Digital transformation, strategic management and entrepreneurial process: dynamics, challenges and opportunities," *Journal of Strategy and Management*, vol. 15, no. 3, pp. 329–334, Jul. 2022, doi: 10.1108/JSMA-08-2022-363.

[44] S. Talwar, M. Talwar, P. Kaur, and A. Dhir, "Consumers' resistance to digital innovations: A systematic review and framework development," *Australasian Marketing Journal*, vol. 28, no. 4, pp. 286–299, Nov. 2020, doi: 10.1016/j.ausmj.2020.06.014.

[45] D. Nylén and J. Holmström, "Digital innovation strategy: A framework for diagnosing and improving digital product and service innovation," *Bus Horiz*, vol. 58, no. 1, pp. 57–67, Jan. 2015, doi: 10.1016/j.bushor.2014.09.001.

Enhancing Patient Care: Machine Learning's Role in Reducing Wait Times for Medical Procedures

Mohamad El-Hajj , Liam Collins , Jackson Steed
Department of Computer Science MacEwan University
Edmonton, Alberta, Canada
elhajjm@macewan.ca, collinsl25@mymacewan.ca, steedj3@mymacewan.ca

***Abstract*—The healthcare system faces a critical challenge with extended wait times for medical procedures, significantly impacting both patients and healthcare professionals. While increasing funding and hiring more doctors may seem like effective solutions, these approaches are often impractical due to various constraints. This research examines the factors driving medical procedure wait times in Canada, specifically in British Columbia, Nova Scotia, and Quebec, highlighting the urgent need to address delays caused by resource limitations. By leveraging machine learning techniques—including random forest methods, k-means clustering, and linear regression—alongside statistical models such as bar graphs, correlation matrices, and z-score normalization, the study, conducted in both Python and R Studio, identifies key contributors to these delays. Based on the findings, a strategic approach to physician hiring is proposed, emphasizing the optimization of seniority levels. Specifically, the study recommends capping the hiring of entry-level doctors at 18% and senior-level doctors at 5%, while increasing the absolute population of entry-level physicians by 27% and reducing the physician-to-100,000 population ratio by 2%, which could lead to a 15% reduction in wait times. By addressing the complexities of medical procedure delays, this research aims to enhance the efficiency and fairness of surgical care delivery.**

***Index Terms*—Canadian medical system; clustering; medical wait times; decision trees; medical care analysis**

I. Introduction

The duration patients wait for surgical procedures is a key measure for assessing the effectiveness and availability of healthcare systems. In Canada, there is often more demand for timely surgeries than resources available, resulting in extended wait times that can substantially impact patient well-being and public health in general. It is crucial for policymakers, healthcare professionals, and patients to comprehend the factors that lead to these wait times.

Despite concerted efforts to enhance operational efficiency within the healthcare sector, significant disparities in wait times for surgical procedures continue to exist among various provinces and territories in Canada. These variations stem from a complex interplay of factors such as differences in healthcare infrastructure, the distribution of medical personnel, patient demographics, and the allocation of resources. Rectifying these discrepancies necessitates thoroughly examining the root causes and adopting tailored interventions to streamline the provision of surgical services.

The main goal of this research project is to examine the waiting periods for a range of surgical procedures in diverse Canadian provinces, including **British Columbia**, **Nova Scotia**, and **Quebec**. The aim was to pinpoint the primary elements impacting these wait times using an extensive dataset encompassing patient characteristics, surgery types, and healthcare resource metrics. This analysis sought to reveal important patterns and fluctuations that can provide valuable insights for policymakers and contribute to enhancements in surgical wait times on a national scale.

This research seeks to answer several critical questions:

1) What are the average **wait times** for different types of surgeries across the 3 Canadian provinces, and what practices contribute to these differences?
2) How do factors such as the ratio of **medical professionals** to the population, healthcare infrastructure, and patient demographics influence surgical wait times?
3) What is the ratio of **seniority levels** for physicians that achieve the lowest wait times?

Machine learning tools—including the random forest method, k-means clustering, and linear regression—were employed alongside statistical models such as bar graphs, correlation matrices, and z-score normalization. Data analysis and insight extraction were conducted in Python and R Studio. The findings will highlight the current state of surgical wait times across Canadian provinces and provide actionable recommendations for healthcare policymakers and administrators who aim to reduce wait times and enhance patient care.

The paper contains an overview of existing literature on surgical wait times, detailed descriptions of the datasets used and methodology, presenting the findings, and discussing their implications for healthcare policy and practice. This comprehensive analysis aims to contribute to ongoing efforts to enhance the efficiency and equity of surgical care in Canada.

The remainder of this paper is organized as follows: the next section discusses Related Work and the Methods employed. This is followed by the Data section, which addresses the relevance of the data. In the Analysis section, we present the preliminary findings from the data. The Discussion section reviews these findings. Finally, we conclude with the Conclusion and Future Work sections.

II. Related work | Methods

Marshall et al. [1] conducted a unique study that focused on the increase in long wait times for physicians and the impact these wait times have on healthcare workers. The researchers analyzed surveys sent to Nova Scotia physicians in which physicians were asked about the challenges experienced due to these long wait times and whether they had any suggestions for improving the wait times. This study saw that 22% of the responses mentioned that they had to work outside their expertise because of the long wait times, resulting in longer treatment times and potentially lower quality treatments. The participants suggested that more trained physicians are needed to reduce Canada's long wait times issue, highlighting the importance of changes to the way physicians are hired in Canada.

Expanding on this issue Liddy et al. [2] analyzed wait times from primary care clinics across Canada, focusing on the wait times between referral and appointment. The study took wait time information from 22 primary care clinics across seven provinces. They were able to conclude the median national wait time of 78 days. They also found that Saskatchewan and British Columbia maintained the shortest waits while New Brunswick and Quebec had the longest. Reinforcing the disparities in healthcare access across Canada and the need for region specific changes.

Similar issues were found Cole et al. [3] focused on urological surgery patients to try and identify bottlenecks and find factors for identifying wait times. The researchers looked at 322 charts of patients undergoing surgery and studied certain data points to find predictors for wait times. Through this data, the researchers determined an average wait time of 75 days. Their analysis also showed that 47% of the wait time is accounted for in the time from referral to decision. The study strongly emphasized this factor because, generally, this period is not recorded or considered when looking at wait time reduction policies. Emphasizing the inefficiencies within the referral process and how it should be considered when looking to improve wait times.

Taking a broader approach, Naiker et al. [4] examined articles from significant health databases in search of patterns or similarities between the articles to find a more effective means of combating long wait times in Australia. The 152 articles that were investigated showed three significant factors contributing to wait times: resource alignment, operational efficiency, and process improvement. This research suggests that focusing on these three areas would result in the most considerable improvement in wait times.

Jaakkimainen et al. [5] researched the wait times from referral to appointment with a physician. The study focused on data from the Electronic Medical Record Administrative Data Link Database and included wait times and the personal characteristics of each patient, such as age and socioeconomic status. According to the study, patients' personal characteristics have no relationship with wait times. They were able to find the median wait times for both medical and surgical specialists and concluded that their findings showed much longer wait times than those presented by governmental sources. According to the researchers, this discrepancy is most likely due to the exclusion of waiting after a referral for an appointment.

Finally, Stanfinski et al. [6] thoroughly investigated the methods that positively improve wait times from decision to treatment. The study examined interviews, studies, and documents from 17 countries to identify consistent factors for improving wait times. Multiple reviewers properly vetted the records, with duplicates and non-eligible records removed. The analysis revealed eight approaches that displayed strong evidence for positive wait time improvement, with the strongest approach being targeted funding.

This research focuses primarily on the impact of the seniority level of physicians on wait times, with additional analysis of population ratios, cases, and physicians. These factors are often not considered when studying medical wait times, so little research has been conducted on these relationships. As a result, this analysis provides a unique insight into the factors that potentially impact medical wait times.

III. Data

This section looks into the data that was used for this analysis. It covers how the original datasets were cleaned and manipulated to create the final datasets. Finally, it covers the overall structure of the cleaned datasets.

A. Original Datasets

Two datasets were used for this analysis of surgical wait times across Canada. The first evaluated surgical wait times from 2008 to 2022 across British Columbia, Quebec, and Nova Scotia are based on comprehensive data from provincial health databases and hospital records. Data was taken from Canada Expenditure Data (1975-2023) [7], Canada Physician Data and Population (1971-2022) [8], and Canada Priority Procedure Wait Time Data (2008-2023) [9]. Additionally, detailed reports on BC Surgical Wait Times (2009-2023) [10], along with practitioner services and expenditures by local health authorities and specialties [11], provide an in-depth understanding of healthcare resources and expenditures impacting surgical wait times.

The second data set used more recent data, Canada's expenditure data (1975-2024) [12], Canada's physician data and population (1971-2023) [13], and wait times priority procedures in Canada (2013-2023) [14]. This second data set evaluated wait times across all provinces, with added expenditure columns for each province. This allowed for further evaluation of the factors affecting surgical wait times across Canada.

B. Data Structure

In this analysis, 17 dimensions were utilized, each playing a crucial role in shaping the findings and conclusions, as shown in Table I. These dimensions encompass key factors such as physician seniority and wait times for essential surgeries across the three provinces.

For the second data set, 24 dimensions were used and evaluated. This data set is similar to the original, with a few new notable columns. The population ratio is the number of physicians over 100,000 in each province. Various types of spending include drug, public health, administration, other institutions, and professional and additional health spending, seen in Table II.

TABLE I: DESCRIPTION OF VARIABLES USED IN DATASET 1

Code	Definition
Year	Fiscal year of data recording (2008-2022).
Province	Province where data was recorded (British Columbia, Quebec, Nova Scotia).
Health Region	Specific regions within each province.
Surgery Type	Types of surgeries recorded.
Wait Times (50th Percentile)	Median wait times for surgeries.
Wait Times (90th Percentile)	90th percentile wait times for surgeries.
Number of Cases	Total number of cases for each surgery type.
Number of Physicians	Total number of physicians for each surgery type.
New Graduates (0-5 years)	Number of physicians with 0-5 years of experience.
Graduates (6-20 years)	Number of physicians with 6-20 years of experience.
Graduates (21-35 years)	Number of physicians with 21-35 years of experience.
Graduates (>36 years)	Number of physicians with more than 36 years of experience.
Population	Total population served in each health region.
Total Expenditure	Total spending on all specialist categories from the Surgery Type column across the three provinces for different fiscal years.
Hospital Expenditure	Total spending on all specialists by health region in the three provinces for different fiscal years.
Physician Expenditure	Total spending on physicians in all specialist categories across the three provinces for different fiscal years.

TABLE II: DESCRIPTION OF VARIABLES USED IN DATASET 2

Code	Definition
Province	Province the data was recorded.
Health Region	Specific region within each province.
Year	Fiscal year of data recording (2008-2023).
Surgery Type	The type of surgery recorded.
Wait Times (50th Percentile)	Median wait times for surgeries.
Wait Times (90th Percentile)	90th percentile wait time for surgeries.
Number of Cases	Total number of cases for each type of surgery.
Specialty	Specialty of Physicians.
Number of Physicians	Total number of Physicians for each type of surgery.
New Graduates (0-5 years)	Number of graduates with 0-5 years of experience.
Graduates (6-20 years)	Number of graduates with 6-20 years of experience.
Graduates (21-35 years)	Number of graduates with 21-35 years of experience.
Graduates (>36 years)	Number of graduates with more than 36 years of experience.
Population	Population within each province of that year.
Population Ratio	The ratio of physicians to the 100,000 population within each province.
Hospital Spending	Yearly hospital spending within each province.
Other Institution Spending	Yearly spending on other institutions within each province.
Physician Spending	Yearly spending on physicians within each province.
Other Professionals	Yearly spending on other healthcare-related professionals.
Drug Spending	Yearly spending on drugs within each province.
Public Health Spending	Yearly public health spending within each province.
Administration Spending	Yearly administration spending within each province.
Other Health Spending	Yearly spending outside of other spending columns.
Total Spending	Yearly total spending within each province.

C. Data Cleaning and Integration

Initial examinations of the dataset involved identifying missing values, resolving inconsistencies, and correcting formatting errors that obscured the integrity of the information. Once each dataset was cleaned, they were linked to their respective dataset. This involved merging records from diverse datasets using shared identifiers, such as year, province, health region, and type of surgery. This resulted in the two datasets necessary for the analysis.

D. Creation of Final Dataset

Two new columns were created using binning.

1) **Graduates**: Physicians were categorized according to their experience level.
2) **Wait Time**: The waiting times were sorted into two groups: the 50th percentile and the 90th percentile. The 50th percentile is the average wait time for all the data that 50% of the data fit into. The 90th percentile represents the average wait time below which 90% of the data points fall to better analyze the outliers.

E. Binning Process:

Wait times were grouped into different categories based on their frequency. Each category represented a particular range of wait times, improving analysis of the frequency of different wait times in different areas.

Categorizing graduates based on their experience levels using binning highlighted the impact of experience on surgical wait times. Each category represented a cohort of graduates with a five-year range of experience, enabling examination into how these varying levels of experience affect the attainment of shorter surgical wait times.

F. Final Dataset Description

The first dataset comprises records of over 10,000 surgical procedures performed in three Canadian provinces. The second dataset contained over 6,000 records of wait times across all provinces and health regions. These are a comprehensive collection of crucial information, including the year of the surgery, the province where it was carried out, the specific type of surgery, and the corresponding wait times. Initial analysis extracted summary statistics illustrating the distribution of key variables and the disparities observed across various regions.

IV. Analysis and Methodology

This section discusses the methodologies used to evaluate each research question outlined in the Introduction.

A. Question 1. Wait times across provinces

All surgical procedures were compared during the examination rather than focused on specific operations. Bar graphs were used to present the average wait times in the 90th percentile for all surgeries across the three provinces, as shown in Figure 1. This figure shows that Quebec has the highest average wait times, followed by Nova Scotia and British Columbia.

In the second dataset, another bar graph was used to visualize the mean wait time between the provinces depicted in Figure 2. The study focused on British Columbia, Quebec, and Nova Scotia to gain more accurate insight. This graph shows that Nova Scotia has the highest average wait times of the 90th percentile. Quebec is the second highest, and British Columbia has the lowest, similar to Figure 1. A correlation matrix was constructed on all features to better understand the relationships within the data visualized in Figure 3. This data set only compared the average wait times between the three provinces.

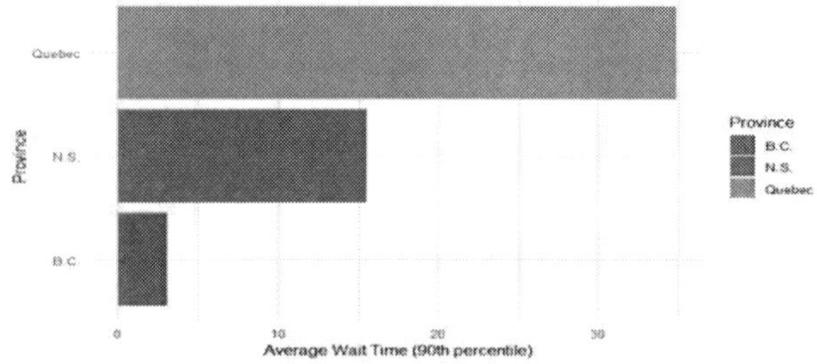

Fig. 1. Average Wait Time by Province Across All Surgery Types Dataset 1

B. Question 2. The effect of external factors

The Random Forest method was used as a regression tool to determine the factors most influential when predicting waiting times for all surgeries. The random forest method creates multiple decision trees and uses the average of the results to make the final decision tree. This is a more robust tool than decision trees because it is less likely to overfit the data [15]. An essential step in this analysis was determining the five regions with the longest and shortest wait time. This was

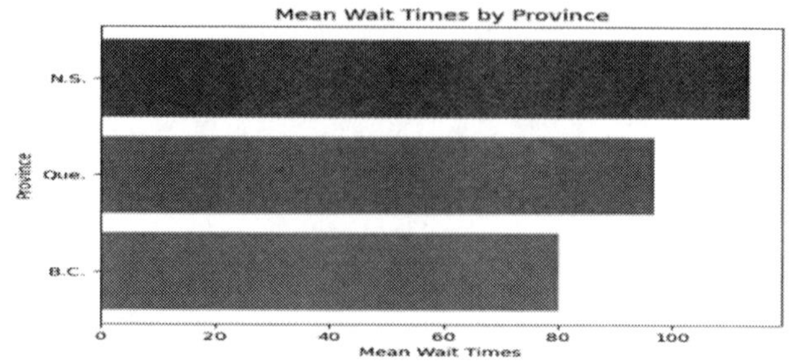

Fig. 2. Average Wait Time by Province Across All Surgery Types Dataset 2.

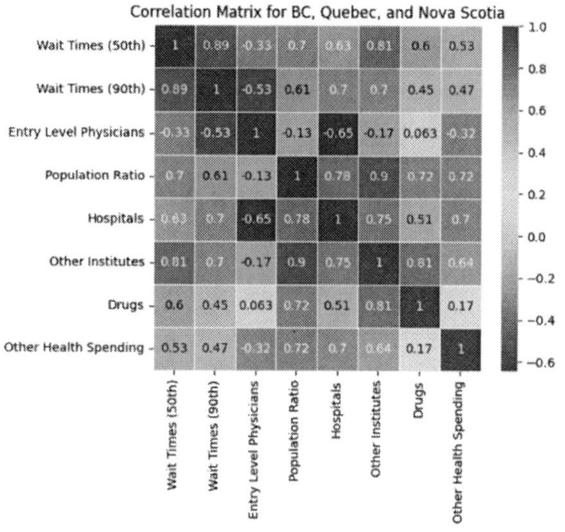

Fig. 3. Surgical Wait Time Correlation Matrix for BC, Quebec, and Nova Scotia Abbreviated for Formatting

done to narrow the focus on the regions of significance. Data from those key regions was used for the rest of the analysis.

Key factors analyzed included population, number of cases, number of physicians, and how many of each type of Doctor was employed in that region. Before running the algorithm, data was split into training and testing data with a 0.7 ratio for training data and a random seed. Feature importance was determined using importance scores for each feature. To predict wait times based on the features present in the dataset.

In the second dataset, z-score normalization was used on the data given by:

$$Z = \frac{X - \mu}{\sigma} \quad (1)$$

where:

- Z: The Z-score, which represents the number of standard deviations a value X is from the mean.
- X: The value for which the Z-score is being calculated.
- μ: The mean of the dataset.
- σ: The standard deviation of the dataset.

This equation is used to bound the values in each column between -1 and 1. This prevents scale from affecting future predictions. To predict values of wait times in the 50th percentile, Linear regression with backward elimination was used. The three provinces were analyzed to predict wait time data for the 50th percentile. Linear regression is a statistical analysis tool used to predict the value of the dependent variable. Backward elimination is a variable selection procedure that considers all independent variables and removes each variable that does not meet the criterion for elimination. The criterion for elimination in this analysis was having a p-value more significant than the 5% threshold. Z-score normalization is where the original value has the mean subtracted from it and then divided by the standard deviation to put it between 1 and -1 so that all values will have equal scaling [16]. After creating a model, the predicted changes to reduce the wait times using minimizing calculations and inverse transforms were performed.

C. Question 3. Seniority level of physicians

The analysis conducted for question 2 found that the wait time for medical services was significantly influenced by the ratio of the experience level of doctors to the total number of doctors in each region. For example, the ratio of entry-level doctors to the total number of doctors in an area was particularly influential. K-means clustering was employed to visually represent the dataset's variations to better understand these differences. K-means clustering allows the grouping of the data so that data points within each group are more similar than data points in other groups. This process involves the initial random placement of cluster centers, followed by the random assignment of each data point to a specific cluster. Subsequently, the algorithm iterates to minimize the distance between the data points and the cluster centers by reassigning points and adjusting the center positions [17].

After analyzing the importance scores using the random forest method, it was identified that the abundance of each doctor category in the area was the most crucial factor, as depicted in Figure 4. Subsequently, clustering was conducted based on the proportion of different types of doctors (e.g., entry-level, intermediate-level, mid-level, and senior level) relative to wait times for all surgical procedures. Establishing the decision boundary and cluster centers aimed to determine the optimal number of each type of doctor required to minimize wait times in different health regions.

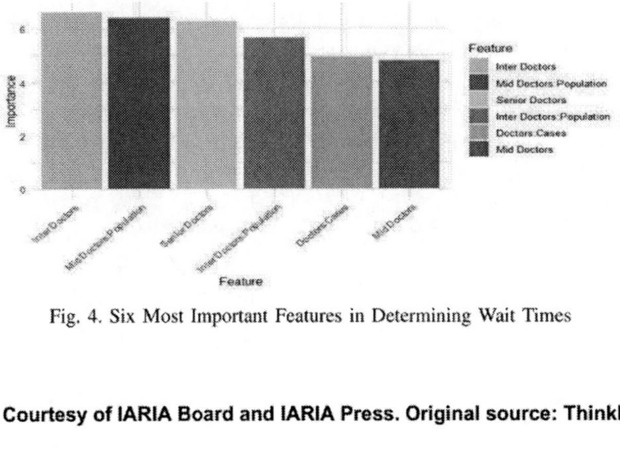

Fig. 4. Six Most Important Features in Determining Wait Times

Similarly, in the second dataset, the ratio and experience of physicians were an influential factor when predicting wait times of the 50th percentile. Specifically, entry-level and senior physicians were the most influential factors when predicting wait time. The physician-to-population ratio was also found to be a very important factor.

The coefficient values were taken to calculate the percentage change of the independent variables, found in Table III. The normalized values of the average value were calculated in each column of the independent variables using 1. The minimize function in the Scipy library was used to determine the changes necessary to find a specific value from the linear regression equation. The target value was determined as 75 days because of the average wait time in Sweden for hip surgeries since it has a very low average wait time with a similar system to Canada [18]. The results gave normalized values of the independent variables necessary to reach this number, which was converted using 1. Equation 1 was adjusted to revert the data back to its original scale.

These results found the percentage change based on the original means of the new values. Showing that the linear regression equation could be used to predict necessary changes to lower wait times.

V. Discussion | Evalution

This section will analyze and discuss the results for each research question using advanced analytical tools and methodologies. Each question is addressed separately in the following sections..

A. Question 1. Wait times across provinces

This initial analysis from Figure 1 suggests that the shortest wait times may predominantly originate from B.C. This prompts further exploration into what unique factors in B.C. may differentiate it from the other provinces. The results from the second dataset appeared to confound these findings as well.

The findings from the correlation matrix created from the second dataset in Figure 3, show results with negative correlations of -0.33 and -0.53 for entry-level physicians with wait times of the 50th and 90th percentile, respectively. The physician population ratio has a high positive correlation of 0.7, with hospitals at 0.63, other institutions at 0.81, drugs at 0.6, and other health spending at 0.53. This provides evidence that the ratio of physicians to population and these areas of spending have strong relationships with wait times in both the 50th and 90th percentiles. These findings indicate potential predicting factors of wait times. Overall, the second dataset positively correlated with the overall physician population ratio, spending on hospitals, drugs, other institutions, and other health spending. With negative correlations with entry-level physicians. These findings show that certain age groups could have an effect on lowering wait times across provinces, while spending in certain areas may not lower wait times.

B. Question 2. Effect of external factors

After comprehensively analyzing the chosen features and their impact on wait times, the random forest method was

TABLE III. LINEAR REGRESSION RESULTS

Dependent Variable:	Wait Times (50th Percentile)					
R-squared:	0.756					
Adjusted R-squared:	0.738					
F-statistic:	42.36					
Prob (F-statistic):	1.25e-12					
	coef	**std err**	**t**	**P>|t|**	**[0.025**	**0.975]**
Constant	96.6855	2.751	35.149	0.000	91.130	102.241
New Graduates (0-5 years)	-32.9924	4.909	-6.720	0.000	-42.907	-23.078
Graduates (>36 years)	29.2295	4.887	5.982	0.000	19.361	39.098
Physician-Population Ratio	23.0773	2.776	8.314	0.000	17.471	28.683

used for prediction. This method proved to be effective and relatively accurate in forecasting wait times. The performance metrics evaluated included Mean Absolute Error (MAE), Mean Squared Error (MSE), and R-squared value (RSQ). MAE represents the average difference between the predicted and actual wait times. MSE is similar to MAE but squares the differences, giving more weight to larger disparities. RSQ serves as a measure of how well the regression line can predict the actual data values [19]

TABLE IV. PERFORMANCE METRICS OF RANDOM FOREST REGRESSION CLASSIFIER

Metric	Combined (C)	Shortest (S)	Longest (L)
Wait Time (WT)	12.76	3.16	49.47
MAE	4.23	2.24	17.88
MSE	47.77	16.54	413.26
RSQ	0.87	-0.10	0.25

The analysis was initially conducted separately for the five regions with the shortest wait times, the five regions with the longest wait times, and the combined dataset for the shortest and longest wait time regions. The results are in Table IV.

We analyzed the wait times in the combined dataset and obtained the following results:

The average wait time for the combined dataset was 12.76 days. The average for the shortest wait times was 3.16 days; it was 49.47 days for the longest. The MAE values were low across all columns, indicating minimal error in the predictions.

The MSE for the combined data was 47.77, which is relatively high compared to the mean value. For the shortest wait times, the MSE was 16.54, suggesting good accuracy. However, the MSE was significantly high for the most extended wait times at 413.26, indicating substantial error for the most significant values.

The RSQ value for the combined dataset was 0.87, meaning the predictions accounted for 87% of the variance. For the shortest wait times, the RSQ value was -0.1, indicating a poor fit. For the longest wait times, the RSQ value was 0.25, showing that the model explained 25% of the variance but did not represent the data well.

After analyzing the data, it was found that the combined dataset produced the most accurate results and the highest RSQ. As a result, it was decided to concentrate on the combined model and dataset for further analysis. The MAE value was favorable, representing a low percentage of the average wait time for the combined dataset (33%). This indicates that the error is acceptable and the model's predictions are reliable.

While the MSE is relative to the values in the dataset, the calculations revealed that it is only 27% of the squared average wait time. This suggests there may be some more significant errors, but overall, the model's performance is satisfactory. Furthermore, the high RSQ value demonstrates that the regression model effectively captures underlying patterns in the data and serves as a strong predictor of wait times.

During the study, it was crucial to thoroughly evaluate this method. The data derived from this method played a critical role in the third part of the analysis. Fine-tuning was performed to enhance the precision of this method and guarantee the utilization of the most precise information.

It was found that linear regression produced the best results for the second dataset. After normalization on the dataset, a regression equation was run using backward elimination to produce the results in Table III With an RSQ of 0.756 and an adjusted RSQ of 0.738, this model accounts for 74% of the variance in the dependent variable in the dataset, with the independent variables suggesting this model is a good fit. The model is statistically significant with a high F-statistic of 42.36 and a low p-value of 1.25 e-12. This data shows that this model is significant, and the findings are relevant.

C. Question 3. Seniority levels of physicians

In this analysis, the random forest model was used to determine the importance scores for each variable when predicting wait times. The results showed that there were four distinct features within the dataset. Specifically, the seniority level ratio among physicians employed in the healthcare region was a significant factor. Among these four features related to the ratio of doctor types to the total number of doctors, the top 7 features were observed, ranked by importance, and included the ratios of various doctor types. Interestingly, the intermediate and mid-level doctor ratios were essential in predicting wait times.

To expand on the analysis, k-means clustering was conducted on the ratio of doctors within each experience level. The clustering was performed on entry-level, intermediate-level, mid-level, and senior-level doctors and wait times. The resulting clusters are visually represented in figures 5a, 5b, 5c, and 5d.

The clustering analysis grouped healthcare regions into long and short wait time clusters based on physician ratios, with centroids calculated to determine the optimal proportion of doctors at each experience level. Figure 6 visualizes these

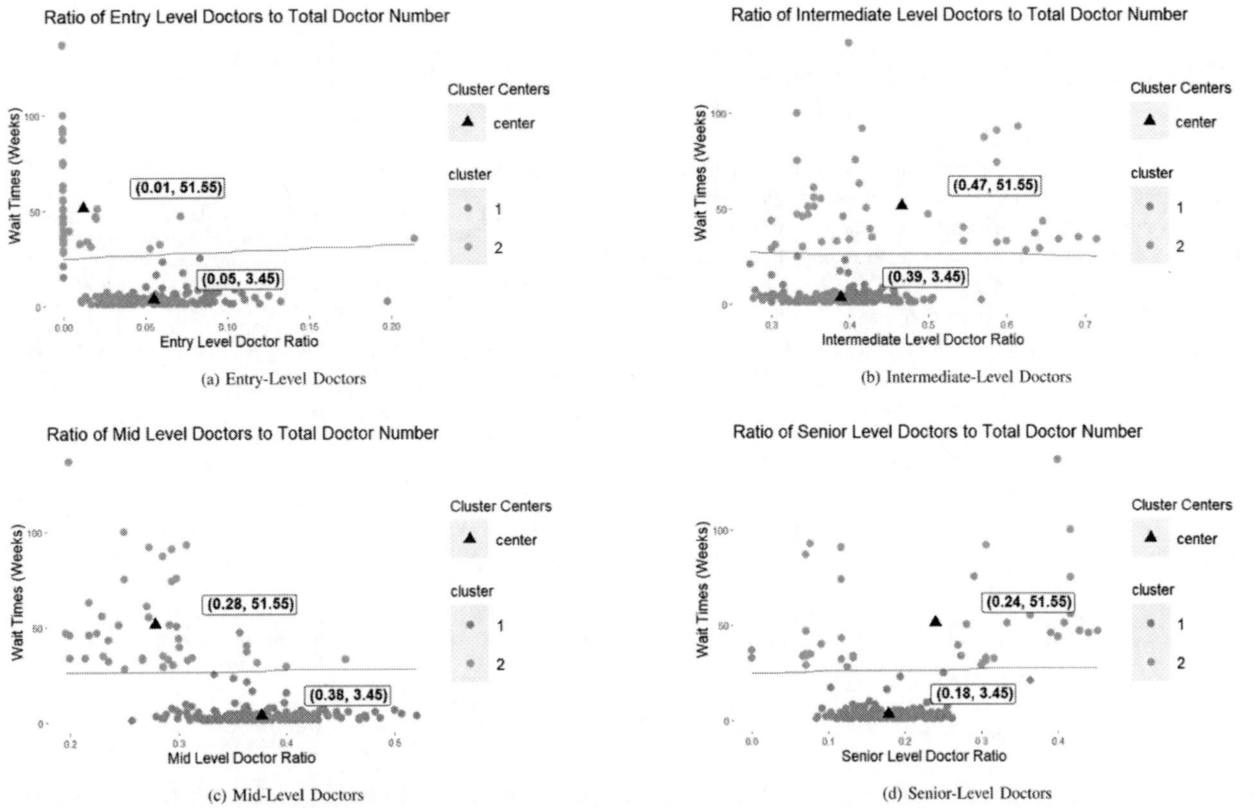

(a) Entry-Level Doctors

(b) Intermediate-Level Doctors

(c) Mid-Level Doctors

(d) Senior-Level Doctors

Fig. 5. K-Means Clustering of Doctors and Wait Times Across Different Levels.

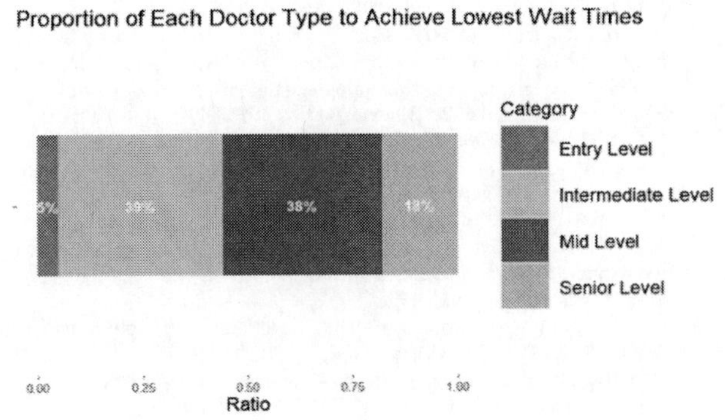

Fig. 6. K-means clustering of senior level doctors and wait times.

proportions within the short wait time cluster, highlighting the importance of recruiting doctors in strategic ratios rather than simply increasing overall numbers.

This insight supports the concept of a "magic ratio", where healthcare regions with shorter wait times maintain a specific balance of physician experience levels. Adhering to this ratio is expected to reduce wait times, while deviations significantly increase delays for critical procedures. To optimize workforce planning, healthcare facilities should limit the combined hiring of entry-level and senior-level doctors to 25% of total staff capacity, ensuring a balanced distribution that enhances accessibility and efficiency

Using the model created by the second dataset in Table III, it can be seen that three columns are the most significant in predicting wait times in the 50th percentile. Entry-level graduates have a negative correlation coefficient of -32, senior physicians have a positive correlation coefficient of 29, and the physician-population ratio is 23. This information shows that as the number of entry-level graduates increases, the wait times decrease within the provinces. While the senior physicians and physician-population ratio increases, the wait times across the provinces also increase. From this, an increase in entry-level graduates with a freeze on senior-level physicians could help reduce the physician-population ratio and thus decrease the wait times across the provinces. The next step in the analysis was to evaluate the optimal percentage change in the independent variables to reach optimal wait times. Using the median wait time of hip surgeries in Sweden gathered from the OECD [18] of 75 days, this was used as a target to determine the percentage change needed to reach this value. After minimizing the model with the constraint that senior-level doctors cannot be lowered, the inverse transform of the results is performed, and the percentage change is calculated. It was found that for entry-level graduates, a 27.22% increase and a -2.7% decrease in the physician-population ratio would reduce the predicted wait times to the target 75 days. Upon examination, it is essential to consider the factors contributing to this phenomenon. This analysis suggests that physicians just starting their careers or nearing the end of their professional journey may exhibit decreased efficiency in patient care. However, the abundance of new physicians could help reduce wait times due to external factors such as their ability to develop new skills to accommodate new issues within the healthcare system. It is reasonable to expect new doctors to be less efficient, as they are still in the learning phase and refining their skills. On the other hand, doctors with 35 or more years of experience would have developed the expertise and protocols necessary to care for many patients efficiently. While they may outperform new doctors, they do not appear as effective as mid-career and seasoned doctors. This indicates that these more experienced doctors may be operating at a reduced level due to additional factors. With continued worries about a straining healthcare system, maintaining a manageable physician-population ratio may be critical to prevent further issues arising from the ever-increasing wait times for surgeries across the provinces.

It is crucial to emphasize the significance of hiring experienced doctors with less than 35 years of experience since graduation. Most of the workforce should comprise middle- and intermediate-age groups to ensure patients receive timely and efficient care.

VI. Conclusion and Future Work

This paper focuses on the factors influencing wait times for medical procedures in Canada, specifically analyzing data from British Columbia, Nova Scotia, and Quebec over several years. The research identified a significant link between wait times and the seniority levels of physicians. To address this, the paper suggests strategic hiring practices in healthcare facilities: limit entry-level doctors to 18% and senior-level doctors to 5%. Additionally, increasing the number of entry-level physicians by 27% and reducing the physician-to-100,000 population ratio by 2% could potentially decrease wait times by 15%. The study aims to improve the efficiency and fairness of surgical care in Canada by thoroughly examining wait times and their contributing factors.

This research provides a limited look at the relationship between physicians' seniority, physician-population ratios, and wait times for medical procedures, based on a small sample from three provinces. To better understand how physician seniority affects wait times, the study should include data from more provinces and territories across Canada. More specific details on surgeries and their wait times are necessary. By expanding the data, we can analyze wait times for specific procedures and identify ways to reduce delays, particularly for high-priority or high-volume cases. Linking types of surgeries to relevant physicians can highlight areas in Canadian healthcare that need improvement. Additionally, applying advanced machine learning and statistical methods can enhance the findings and lead to stronger conclusions.

References

[1] E. G. Marshall, L. Miller, and L. R. Moritz, "Challenges and impacts from wait times for specialist care identified by primary care providers: Results from the maap study cross-sectional survey," *Healthcare Management Forum*, vol. 36, no. 5, pp. 340–346, 2023, pMID: 37415463. [Online]. Available: https://doi.org/10.1177/08404704231182671

[2] C. Liddy, I. Moroz, E. Affleck, E. Boulay, S. Cook, L. Crowe, N. Drimer, L. Ireland, P. Jarrett, S. MacDonald, D. McLellan, A. Mihan, N. Miraftab, V. Nabelsi, C. Russell, A. Singer, and E. Keely, "How long are Canadians waiting to access specialty care? retrospective study from a primary care perspective," *Canadian family physician Medecin de famille canadien*, vol. 66, pp. 434–444, 06 2020.

[3] E. Cole, W. Hopman, and J. Kawakami, "High resolution analysis of wait times and factors affecting surgical expediency," *Canadian Urological Association journal = Journal de l'Association des urologues du Canada*, vol. 5, no. 1, pp. 13–17, 2011.

[4] U. Naiker, G. FitzGerald, J. M. Dulhunty, and M. Rosemann, "Time to wait: a systematic review of strategies that affect out-patient waiting times," *Australian health review : a publication of the Australian Hospital Association*, vol. 42 3, pp. 286–293, 2017. [Online]. Available: https://api.semanticscholar.org/CorpusID:25968727

[5] L. Jaakkimainen, K. Tu, J. Barnsley, E. Salkeld, H. Lu, and R. Glazier, "Waiting to see the specialist: Patient and provider characteristics of wait times from primary to specialty care," *BMC family practice*, vol. 15, p. 16, 01 2014.

[6] T. Stafinski, F. Nagase, M. Brindle, J. White, A. Young, S. Beesoon, S. Cleary, and D. Menon, "Reducing wait times to surgery—an international review," *Journal of Hospital Management and Health Policy*, vol. 6, 01 2021.

[7] Canadian Institute for Health Information, "National health expenditure trends, 2023: Data tables – series d1," 2023, Ottawa, ON: CIHI. [Online]. Available: https://www.cihi.ca/sites/default/files/document/nhex-series-d1-2023-data-tables-en.xlsx

[8] C. I. for Health Information, "Supply, distribution and migration of physicians in Canada, 2022 — historical data," 2023, Ottawa, ON: CIHI.

[9] ——, "Wait times for priority procedures in Canada – data tables," 2024, Ottawa, ON: CIHI. [Online]. Available: https://www.cihi.ca/sites/default/files/document/wait-times-priority-procedures-in-canada-2024-data-tables-en.xlsx

[10] G. of Canada, "2009 2023 annual surgical wait times," 2013, health Sector Information Analysis and Reporting. [Online]. Available: https://catalogue.data.gov.bc.ca/dataset/7c1bf2a8-96bb-4ad5-888d-a90672eb306e/resource/6cd508eb-7e31-4c86-b070-dc698131fa9a/download/2022 2023-annual-surgical-wait-times.xlsx

[11] ——, "BC health practitioners services and expenditures by specialty," 2011, integrated Analytics, Primary Care, Acute Care & Workforce.

[12] C. I. for Health Information, "National health expenditure trends, 2024: Data tables - series d1," 2024, [Data set]. [Online]. Available: https://www.cihi.ca/sites/default/files/document/nhex-series-d1-2024-data-tables-en.xlsx

[13] ——, "Supply, distribution and migration of physicians in Canada, 1971-2023 [data set]," 2024. [Online]. Available: https://www.cihi.ca/sites/default/files/document/supply-distribution-migration-physicians-in-canada-1971-2023-data-tables-en.xlsx

[14] ——, "Wait times priority procedures in Canada 2024," 2024. [Online]. Available: https://www.cihi.ca/en/explore-wait-times-for-priority-procedures-across-canada

[15] I. et al, "What is a decision tree?" 2024. [Online]. Available: https://www.ibm.com/topics/decision-trees

[16] IBM, "Modified z score," February 29 2024. [Online]. Available: https://www.ibm.com/docs/en/cognos-analytics/11.1.0?topic=terms-modified-z-score

[17] ——, "What is k-means clustering?" 2024. [Online]. Available: https://www.ibm.com/topics/k-means-clustering

[18] OECD, *Waiting Times for Health Services: Next in Line*. Paris: OECD Publishing, 2020. [Online]. Available: https://doi.org/10.1787/242e3c8c-en

[19] IBM, "Forecasting statistical details," 2024. [Online]. Available: https://www.ibm.com/docs/en/cognos-analytics/11.1.0?topic=forecasting-statistical-details

Exploring the Influence of Technology Exposure on Computer Science Self-Concept

A study among young adults in Germany

Claudia Hess, Sibylle Kunz, Cornelia Heinisch and Adrienne Steffen
IT & Engineering / Management
IU International University of Applied Sciences
Erfurt, Germany
e-mail: claudia.hess@iu.org; sibylle.kunz@iu.org; cornelia.heinisch@iu.org; adrienne.steffen@iu.org

Abstract— **Given the high demand for qualified computer scientists, understanding young adults' career decisions in this field is crucial to ensuring an adequate talent supply. Despite the high demand, women remain underrepresented. This paper examines one particular influencing factor: technology exposure. Based on quantitative data from over 800 young people in Germany, it analyzes how the availability of information and communication technology affects young adults' perception of their skills, abilities, and competence in the field of computer science. Special emphasis is placed on gender differences within this context of digitization adoption.**

Keywords-technology exposure; impact of ICT usage; young adults; computer science self-concept.

I. INTRODUCTION

In recent decades, there has been a high demand for well-trained specialists in the field of Information and Communication Technology (ICT), and industry has complained about a shortage of skilled workers. Although advances in Artificial Intelligence (AI) raise questions about the extent to which ICT jobs will be impacted by automation and whether there will still be a need for ICT professionals, recent studies [1] predict a continued strong demand for ICT professionals, as well as specialists skilled in working efficiently with ICT and AI systems. The required extensive re- and upskilling will only be successful if people are interested in Computer Science (CS). A large gender gap can be seen here. Despite the importance of ICT roles, women continue to be significantly underrepresented. In 2023, only 19.4% of ICT specialists in the EU were women, compared to 80.6% men [2]. This gender disparity poses several problems, including the loss of diverse perspectives that are vital for innovation and a reduced talent pool that makes it more challenging for companies to fill critical roles.

In light of these challenges, it is important to explore the factors that influence young men's and women's decisions regarding a career in CS. A critical driving factor is a person's perception and beliefs about their abilities, skills, and competence in this field. Past experiences, feedback, the immediate environment, and comparison with others influence this self-concept. One particular factor is exposure to technology, which is the focus of this paper. While many studies, particularly within school contexts, examine how ICT availability and use affect students' confidence and competence in using technology or its impact on math and science achievement, this study takes it a step further. It investigates whether exposure to technology can inspire interest in CS by making young people more comfortable with the basic concepts and applications of technology. To this end, data from a study on more than 800 young adults conducted in Germany in 2024 is analyzed. Understanding these dynamics will help educators, policymakers, and industry leaders encourage a diverse range of young people, especially women, to pursue careers in CS.

This paper is structured as follows. Section II presents the theoretical background on technology exposure and its effects. Section III explains the methodology used in the presented study, introduces the sample as well as limitations. Then, Section IV presents the data analysis. Section V includes the discussion of the findings. Finally, Section VI concludes the paper and outlines areas for future research.

II. THEORETICAL BACKGROUND

A. Technology Exposure of Young Adults

Exploring the aspect of technology exposure requires understanding that it encompasses a wide array of experiences and opportunities through which individuals interact with information and communication technologies. Salanova and Llorens extracted in their literature review different indicators connected with technology exposure, especially "the amount of time using technology, times used before feeling comfortable, frequency of technology use, participation in technology training, use of technology at work and at home, personal computer ownership, computer usage frequency and computer usage level" [3]. Apart from the term "technology exposure", the terms "technology experience" and "technology use" are also commonly used [3], as well as "ICT use" [4]. The impact of young adults' exposure to technology has been particularly studied. Figure 1 shows the four different perspectives taken:

1) Availability and use of ICT devices at home: Access to digital devices, such as computers, tablets, smartphones, game consoles and even VR glasses at home allows young people to explore technology on their own. The presence of ICT devices can encourage experimentation and the development of digital literacy from an early age [5]. In addition to availability, the type of usage can be differentiated according to whether it is used for leisure, such as social media or gaming, or for schoolwork [4].

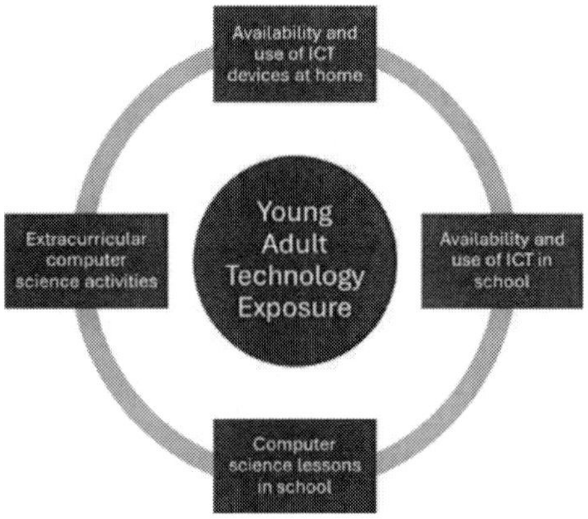

Figure 1. Technology exposure of young adults, Source: own depiction.

2) Availability and use of ICT in school: In many countries, and especially since COVID-19, ICT has become available in schools. Students of all ages are learning basic ICT skills, such as creating presentations, using spreadsheets or ten-finger typing. Sometimes, technology is integrated into different subjects, which helps students recognize the relevance of ICT across diverse fields. The extent to which ICT is used as a tool for learning—such as engaging in interactive learning experiences via websites and mobile apps—can have a significant impact on students' familiarity with technology [6].

3) Computer science lessons in school: In recent years, many countries have introduced in-school offerings of CS education, though lesson frequency and depth often vary [7]. In Germany, the annual "computer science monitor" published by the German Informatics Society reveals significant differences between federal states, ranging from minimal voluntary classes to compulsory CS lessons for all school types [8]. Formal CS education, which includes hands-on experiences, such as programming or robotics, can foster students' interest in the field [9]. Such lessons provide foundational knowledge and boost students' confidence in pursuing studies or careers in the field.

4) Extracurricular computer science activities: Participation in technology-related extracurricular activities, such as coding clubs, robotics teams, or competitions allows students to explore technology in creative and applied ways [9]. Students may also be exposed to online tech communities where people discuss technology trends, share projects, and exchange knowledge. These interactions not only provide informal learning opportunities, but also help build a sense of belonging to the broader tech community.

B. Impacts of Young Adult Technology Exposure

The effects of technology exposure on young adults have been analyzed from different perspectives.

1) Impact on students' performance in science and math: In the last fifteen years, many studies have used the data from OECD's Programme for International Student Assessment (PISA), which evaluates how well 15-year-olds can apply their knowledge and skills in reading, mathematics and science to real-world tasks. In particular, the effects of ICT use in classrooms for teaching and learning purposes as well as ICT availability at home on students' performance in math and science were analyzed for various countries [4][10]. None of these studies specifically examined the impact on CS achievement, as CS was traditionally not in the focus of PISA.

The review of a large number of studies in [4] shows mixed results on how ICT availability, use, and engagement affect students' math and science scores. To provide clarity, they compared the results of the four PISA surveys from 2009, 2012, 2015 and 2018. They found no meaningful positive link between math or science performance and ICT use, whether that use occurred in or out of school, and whether it was tied to specific academic subjects or not [4]. Similarly, [11] examined the relationship, noting mixed effects of ICT availability on academic achievement, with a negative direct effect for males, neutral for females, and positive indirect effects via ICT mastery and autonomy—topics explored further in the next paragraph.

2) Impact on digital literacy: Exposure to ICT also influences comfort and competence with ICT. Starting in 2025, PISA will include a new assessment, the "Learning in the Digital World" test, which will evaluate how well students can use computational tools to engage in an iterative process of building knowledge and tackling real-world problems [12]. Pre-tests indicate that students who regularly use ICT across various subjects tend to perform better [6]. Moreover, students who feel confident in their ICT skills and show interest in ICT perform at higher levels. Further studies investigate more specific aspects of students' ability to use ICT tools effectively. For instance, [13] examines how the usage of educational technology affects students' internet self-efficacy. While these studies focus on digital literacy, CS self-concept is about how confident students feel when it comes to engaging with CS tasks.

3) Impact on career decisions in STEM: Research has examined whether and how technology exposure increases the sense of familiarity, confidence and interest in pursuing STEM subjects and, consequently, influences an informed career decision regarding STEM. Among the different perspectives of technology exposure, these empirical studies often focus on STEM school lessons or STEM programs. An example is the impact analysis of a program for students about robotics design and production in the USA, which increased participants' career choice in STEM [14]. While many studies have examined the effects of various variables on young adults' STEM career choices (e.g., interest, self-efficacy, influence by family) [18], less attention has been given to the role of ICT availability and use at home or during leisure time in career choice specifically in CS.

C. Ability Self-Concept

The expectancy-value theory by Eccles and Wiegfield [15] posits that a person's motivation to engage in a particular task is determined on the one hand by their expectation of success in that task, and on the other hand, on the value they place on it. It helps explain motivational factors that translate into behavioral outcomes, such as selecting a particular study program or career path [16]. The ability self-concept refers to a person's perception of their own competence in a particular domain, e.g., to perform tasks or succeed in activities. An example that is extensively studied is the self-concept of math ability, or short math self-concept. It is influenced by previous experiences regarding math, feedback from significant others, such as parents, teachers, and peers, the immediate social environment, and social comparisons, e.g., to classmates in math tasks [16].

1) Computer Science Self-Concept

Just as with math self-concept, the idea of self-concept can be applied to CS, referring to the question "How do I assess my own skills in CS?". While some studies address the self-concept of computer ability [16], these usually focus on general computer usage skills, such as using software, or internet navigation. In contrast, CS self-concept is concerned with perceiving CS as an academic and professional field, including for instance programming, understanding algorithms, or problem-solving. It reflects confidence in handling tasks central to the field, such as coding or designing computational solutions. Unlike math and science self-concept, the CS self-concept seems not well covered.

2) Gender differences in STEM-related self-concepts

Past research often revealed gender differences in STEM-related self-concepts, being already apparent at school. Typically, boys express greater confidence in their success and skills in areas traditionally considered male-dominated, such as mathematics, physical sciences, and sports [16]. Conversely, girls tend to have a higher self-concept of their verbal abilities compared to boys.

III. METHODOLOGY

A. Study Design

The data analyzed in this paper come from a German-wide study on young adults' CS career choices. Ethical clearance was obtained from the ethics committee of the authors' institution. In June 2024, an online survey was conducted with a reputable market research organization using their market panel of young adults in all German federal states. This form of collaboration was chosen because regulations on whether and how students can be contacted via schools differ among Germany's federal states. The study was funded by the authors' higher education institution.

The online questionnaire contained closed and open-ended questions, taking a total of about 15 minutes to complete. It asked for the determinants of students' career decisions and their perceptions of CS as a viable professional path. One set of questions was about technology exposure.

B. Sample Composition

The survey targeted 15- to 20-year-olds who are deciding on a career or have recently done so. As the aim of the study is to analyze the factors influencing career choice, it was crucial that participants were in this decision phase, hence excluding those outside this age group. Those under 15 often have not yet chosen a profession, while those over 20 usually have. A total of 822 respondents participated in the survey. The sample comprised 315 (38.3%) young men, 506 (61.6%) young women, and one person who identified as non-binary (0.1%). Table I summarizes the sample characteristics.

TABLE I. SAMPLE CHARACTERISTICS

Age	Results			
	Female N (%)	*Male N (%)*	*Non-binary N (%)*	*Total N (%)*
15	37 (7.3%)	44 (14.0%)	0	81 (9.9%)
16	60 (11.9%)	53 (16.8%)	0	113 (13.8%)
17	84 (16.6 %)	58 (18.4%)	0	142 (17.3%)
18	133 (26.3%)	75 (23.8%)	0	208 (25.3%)
19	99 (19.6%)	37 (11.7%)	1 (100%)	136 (16.6%)
20	93 (18.4%)	48 (15.2%)	0	141 (17.2%)
Total	**506 (100%)**	**315 (100%)**	**1 (100%)**	**822**

C. Research Questions

The studies in Section II analyzed technology exposure effects on various aspects but, to our knowledge, did not examine its impact on CS self-concept. Building on the Expectancy-Value Theory, we hypothesize that as students become more familiar with ICT, they will develop a greater appreciation for the underlying principles of these technologies, thereby increasing their interest and belief of success in promising and well-paid technical careers. Analyzing a particular subset of the study should help fill this research gap by examining whether technology exposure at home has a positive impact on young adults' CS self-concept. Special emphasis is placed on gender differences, as studies in STEM often report significant gender disparities.

D. Limitations

There are some limitations based on the study design and the data obtained. Although the participants were drawn from all federal states, the data are not fully representative of all German students and should not be generalized. Regarding the respondents' age, the young men were slightly younger than the young women. The data set contains only one non-binary person, who was excluded from all gender-specific analyses as no meaningful statistical conclusions can be drawn from a single participant. Moreover, the assessment of technology exposure has certain limitations, notably that it did not quantify the frequency of use of each device in terms of hours per week, nor did it assess the purpose of use like it was done for instance by [10].

IV. Data Analysis

A. Young Adults' Technology Exposure at Home

The survey asked about the use of ICT devices at home, especially a computer/laptop or tablet, the constant availability of Internet access, and the availability of a game console or Virtual Reality (VR) glasses. A 5-point Likert scale was used [1-strongly disagree to 5-strongly agree].

1) Overview

Table II shows the extent of technology exposure of the young adults surveyed. The vast majority of the young adults, 83.4% (sum of the top-2 boxes "agree" and "strongly agree"), have consistent internet access, underscoring prevalence of connectivity. Only 7.2% report limited internet access, indicating a minority facing potential barriers to ICT.

About two-thirds, 66.3% (top-2 boxes), regularly use a computer or laptop at home, indicating widespread access. A small percentage, 13.9% (top-2 boxes), do not engage in regular use, which may reflect either a lack of necessity or access. Tablets are also common (61.5%, top-2 boxes). A higher percentage (19.9%) report not using tablets regularly compared to computers/laptops (13.9%). Game consoles are popular, with 66.1% reporting access and 17.8% without. VR glasses have the least exposure, with only 19.6% reporting access and 67.2% lacking or not using them at home. These low figures reflect either the novelty, cost barrier, or niche market status of VR technology compared to more established devices like computers and tablets.

2) Gender Differences

The next step was analyzing gender differences. Figure 2 shows the technology availability and accessibility reported by young women and men for all five statements. Using an independent samples t-test, statistically significant gender differences could be identified.

Regarding the regular use of a computer or laptop, young men have a higher mean score (M_m=4.04, SD_m=1.108) compared to young women (M_f=3.75, SD_f=1.164). The difference is statistically significant (t(691)=-3.164, p<.001) with a small effect size (Cohen's d= -0.256), suggesting a slight gender preference towards computers among males. The opposite is the case for tablets, which are used more by young women (Mf=3.79, SDf=1.204) than young men (Mm=3.46, SDm=1.369). This difference is also statistically significant (t(602)=-3.518, p<.001) with a small effect size (Cohen's d= -0.260).

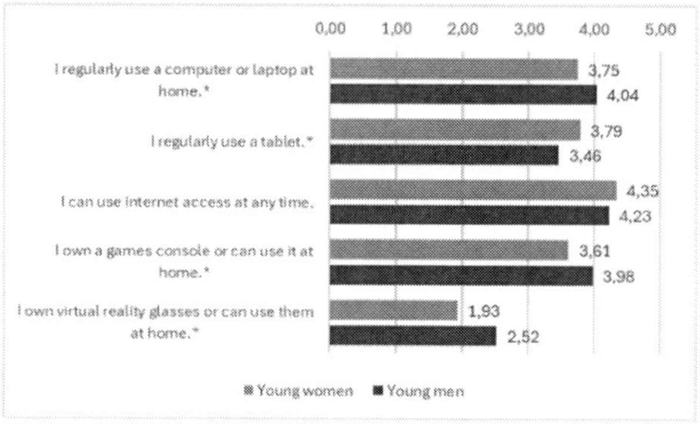

t-test, N female: 506, N male: 315, *, p < .001

Figure 2. Gender Differences in Technology Exposure.

Young men (M_m=3.98, SD_m=1.182) reported higher values with regard to the ownership and use of games consoles than young women (M_f=3.61, SD_f=1.311). This difference is statistically significant (t(717)=-4.219, p<.001) with a small effect size (Cohen's d=-0.296), indicating a more noticeable gender disparity.

With respect to the ownership or use of VR glasses, young men have a substantially higher mean (M_m=2.52, SD_m=1.408) compared to young women (M_f=1.93, SD_f=1.191), indicating greater access or usage among males. This disparity is statistically significant (t(584)=-6.175, p<.001) with a medium effect size (Cohen's d= -0.461).

Regarding the availability of internet access, there is no statistically significant difference between the genders (M_f=4.35 / M_m=4.23, SD_f=0.915 / SD_m=1.078).

B. Young Adults' Computer Science Self-Concept

To assess CS self-concept, an established scale based on the expectancy-value theory was used, adapting items from [17] originally measuring expectations of math success. For instance, the item "I am talented at math" was changed to "I am talented at computer science". While this approach uses an established scale, it carries the risk that essential CS-specific attitudes or experiences may be overlooked, potentially leading to an incomplete or less valid assessment of CS self-concept. The same 5-point Likert scale as for technology exposure was used.

TABLE II. RESULTS ON TECHNOLOGY EXPOSURE

Technology exposure at home	Answers: Total number = 822 (100%)				
	Strongly disagree N (%)	*Disagree N (%)*	*Neutral N (%)*	*Agree N (%)*	*Strongly agree N (%)*
I regularly use a computer or laptop at home.	35 (4.3%)	79 (9.6%)	163 (19.8%)	236 (28.7%)	309 (37.6%)
I regularly use a tablet.	70 (8.5%)	94 (11.4%)	153 (18.6%)	229 (27.9%)	276 (33.6%)
I can use internet access at any time.	18 (2.2%)	41 (5.0%)	77 (9.4%)	223 (27.1%)	463 (56.3%)
I own a games console or can use it at home.	74 (9.0%)	72 (8.8%)	133 (16.2%)	245 (29.8%)	298 (36.3%)
I own virtual reality glasses or can use them at home.	362 (44.0%)	191 (23.2%)	108 (13.1%)	98 (11.9%)	63 (7.7%)

For the independent samples t-test, these items are aggregated for each participant to a single score "CS self-concept". The average CS self-concept in the sample was M=2.96 (SD=0.950). The results show some caution in self-assessing one's competence, with many values falling in the moderate range. Comparing genders, young men have a higher average CS self-concept (M_m=3.35, SD=0.891) than young women (M_f=2.72, SD=0.906). The difference is statistically significant (t(819)=-9.735, p<.001) with a medium to large effect size (Cohen's d = 0.699).

C. *Impact of Technology Exposure On CS Self-Concept*

Having analyzed technology exposure and CS self-concept separately, the relationship between these two concepts is explored. Like the CS self-concept, the overall technology exposure scale score for each participant is calculated based on the mean score of the above presented five items measuring various aspects of technology exposure.

1) *Correlation*

First, it is explored whether there is a positive correlation between technology exposure and CS self-concept. The hypothesis is: The higher a young adult's overall exposure to technology, the higher their CS self-concept. Pearson's Correlation Coefficient was calculated. According to [18], there was a moderate to strong positive correlation between technology exposure and CS self-concept, $r(820)=.403$, $p<.001$. Looking only at young men, a strong positive correlation can be seen with $r_m(313)=.542$, $p<.001$, while there is a moderate positive correlation ($r_f(504)=.292$, $p<.001$) for young women.

2) *Regression Analysis: Technology Exposure as Predictor of Computer Science Self-Concept*

The next step was to examine whether technology exposure predicts the CS self-concept. Overall, the regression analysis showed a moderate effect with $R^2 = .163, F(1,820) = 159.297, p < .001$. For young women, the analysis indicated a small effect, with $R^2 = .084, F(1,504) = 47.134, p < .001$. Conversely, for young men, a strong effect was observed, with $R^2 = .294, F(1,313) = 130.110, p < .001$. These results suggest that technology exposure has varying predictive power on the CS self-concept based on gender. For young women, the small effect size highlights that technology exposure is a minor predictor of their CS self-concept. In contrast, it is a substantial predictor for young men. Approximately 30% of their CS self-concept is explained by technology exposure. This means that there are other factors that explain the remaining 70%, which could be factors, such as school experiences, family background, or friends.

V. Discussion and Implications

The data indicates gender differences in technology exposure at home, with males generally reporting higher usage of computers/laptops, game consoles, and VR technology, while females reported higher usage of tablets. The differences, though statistically significant, mostly indicate small effect sizes except for game consoles and VR, which show moderate gender-specific preferences. These results are in line with a German-wide study on the media equipment and media usage of teenagers (12-19 years) in 2024 [19]. In terms of owning devices, boys are more likely to own fixed and portable game consoles and computers compared to girls. In contrast, girls tend to own smartphones, tablets, and e-book readers more frequently than boys [19, pp. 7–8]. The study did not ask for the ownership or usage of VR glasses.

Bitkom e.V. analyzed the usage of consumer technology in Germany in 2024 [20], differentiating between age groups but not gender. In the group of 16 to 29-year-olds, 43% have already used VR glasses. Nearly half of this age group thinks VR glasses will become standard household equipment in the future. In the study presented here, about 20% of young adults reported the availability of a VR glass at home. This discrepancy between usage and availability suggests that while many young adults may have tried VR glasses, possibly at exhibition centers, in museums or event arenas, fewer of them have made the transition to owning this technology. This might be due to factors, such as cost, perceived need or little knowledge of possible applications.

The analysis in Section IV showed an overall moderate effect of technology exposure on young adults' CS self-concept. Placing this effect in the context of device availability suggests that widespread access to ICT devices can nurture general comfort with ICT. While this baseline familiarity may build initial confidence, more advanced experiences – like using a computer for programming or a VR setting for simulations – may contribute more significantly than passive use for entertainment. This underscores the importance of school lessons that provide creative, hands-on, project-based CS learning opportunities and integrate CS concepts across subjects (e.g., use and discuss generative AI in art). Partnerships with industry can further reinforce exposure to real-world applications of CS. Additionally, other factors contribute significantly to an individual's CS self-concept, highlighting the complexity of self-concept formation, where experiences like school interactions, family support, peer influence, role models and personal interest play a crucial role, too [16][17]. Linking CS education in schools with the family and ICT usage at home—such as involving parents in collaborative digital projects including for instance programming or simulations in VR environments—could strengthen students' perception of CS as valuable and accessible.

The analysis shows a gender disparity in the predictive power of technology exposure, suggesting young women need additional initiatives to address other influential factors. With statistically significant lower levels of exposure to computers, notebooks, and game consoles for young women, there is a clear need for targeted efforts to bridge this gap. Enhancing access to technology is essential, but equally important is addressing broader motivational and confidence-related barriers. Comprehensive strategies that foster inclusive learning environments, provide relatable role models, and actively challenge stereotypes can encourage young women to develop a stronger CS self-concept.

VI. Conclusion and Future Work

The study examined the relationship between technology exposure and CS self-concept among young adults, with a particular focus on gender disparities. The findings suggest that while technology exposure plays a role in shaping CS self-concept, it is not the sole factor, especially in the case of young women. It is recommended to complement this quantitative analysis in future research with a qualitative analysis. The sample contains open questions about critical incidents regarding CS. A first screening has revealed that some incidents describe successfully using ICT, installing software, or solving hardware issues, and highlight how overcoming technical problems can foster a sense of pride and motivate further exploration of CS. Moreover, age-specific differences, e.g. under and over eighteen, could be explored. If the quantitative survey is to be repeated, the questions regarding technology exposure should be refined. A further topic not yet considered is to examine the impact on economically disadvantaged youth who might have less access to more expensive ICT devices. By addressing these areas, future work can inform strategies that create a diverse and inclusive CS workforce.

Acknowledgment

The authors gratefully acknowledge the support of their institution, which funded this research as part of a research incubator initiative.

References

[1] AI-Enabled ICT Workforce Consortium, "The Transformational Opportunity of AI on ICT Jobs," 2024. [Online]. Available from: https://www.cisco.com/c/dam/m/ai-enabled-ict-workforce-consortium/report.pdf, retrieved: 05, 2025

[2] eurostat, "ICT specialists in employment." [Online]. Available from: https://ec.europa.eu/eurostat/statistics-explained/index.php?title=ICT_specialists_in_employment, retrieved: 05, 2025

[3] M. Salanova and S. LLorens, "Exposure to Information and Communication Technology and its Relationship to Work Engagement," *Cienc. Trab.*, vol. 11, pp. 55-62, no. 32, 2009.

[4] M. Courtney, M. Karakus, Z. Ersozlu, and K. Nurumov, "The influence of ICT use and related attitudes on students' math and science performance: multilevel analyses of the last decade's PISA surveys," *Large-Scale Assess. Educ.*, vol. 10, no. 8, pp. 1-26, Aug 2022, doi: 10.1186/s40536-022-00128-6.

[5] J. Hu and J. Hu, "The influence of age at first regular digital device access on digital reading performance: the mediating effect of cognitive flexibility," *Humanit. Soc. Sci. Commun.*, vol. 11, no. 1, pp. 1–18, Jun. 2024, doi: 10.1057/s41599-024-03292-y.

[6] OECD, "Technology use at school and students' learning outcomes: exploring the relationship with new data from Germany," *OECD Education Spotlights*, vol. 17, 2022. [Online]. Available from: https://www.oecd.org/content/dam/oecd/en/publications/reports/2024/12/technology-use-at-school-and-students-learning-outcomes_4c4f92e6/422db044-en.pdf, retrieved: 05, 2025

[7] M. Oda, Y. Noborimoto, and T. Horita, "International Trends in K-12 Computer Science Curricula through Comparative Analysis: Implications for the Primary Curricula," *Int. J. Comput. Sci. Educ. Sch.*, vol. 4, no. 4, pp. 1–25, Apr. 2021.

[8] German Informatics Society (GI), "2024/25 - informatik monitor." Available from: https://informatik-monitor.de/2024-25, retrieved: 05, 2025

[9] C. Chen, J. Rothwell, and P. Maynard-Zhang, "In-school and/or out-of-school computer science learning influence on CS career interests, mediated by having role-models," *Comput. Sci. Educ.*, vol. 34, no. 4, pp. 753–777, Oct. 2024, doi: 10.1080/08993408.2023.2290435.

[10] X. Hu, Y. Gong, C. Lai, and F. K. S. Leung, "The relationship between ICT and student literacy in mathematics, reading, and science across 44 countries: A multilevel analysis," *Comput. Educ.*, vol. 125, pp. 1–13, Oct. 2018, doi: 10.1016/j.compedu.2018.05.021.

[11] S. Li, X. Liu, J. Tripp, and Y. Yang, "From ICT availability to student science achievement: mediation effects of ICT psychological need satisfactions and interest across genders," *Res. Sci. Technol. Educ.*, vol. 40, no. 4, pp. 529–548, Oct. 2022, doi: 10.1080/02635143.2020.1830269.

[12] OECD (Organisation for Economic Co-operation and Development), "PISA 2025 Learning in the Digital World Framework (Second Draft)," 2023. Available from: https://www.oecd.org/en/topics/sub-issues/learning-in-the-digital-world/pisa-2025-learning-in-the-digital-world.html, retrieved: 05, 2025

[13] X. Chen, "The role of the exposure of education technology on learners' internet self-efficacy," *Trans. Soc. Sci. Educ. Humanit. Res.*, vol. 5, pp. 606–617, Apr. 2024, doi: 10.62051/ccwnzw48.

[14] S. R. Yoel and Y. J. Dori, "FIRST High-School Students and FIRST Graduates: STEM Exposure and Career Choices," *IEEE Trans. Educ.*, vol. 65, no. 2, pp. 167–176, May 2022, doi: 10.1109/TE.2021.3104268.

[15] J. S. Eccles and A. Wigfield, "In the Mind of the Actor: The Structure of Adolescents' Achievement Task Values and Expectancy-Related Beliefs," *Pers. Soc. Psychol. Bull.*, vol. 21, no. 3, pp. 215–225, Mar. 1995, doi: 10.1177/0146167295213003.

[16] M. Sáinz and J. Eccles, "Self-concept of computer and math ability: Gender implications across time and within ICT studies," *J. Vocat. Behav.*, vol. 80, no. 2, pp. 486–499, Apr. 2012, doi: 10.1016/j.jvb.2011.08.005.

[17] S. González-Pérez, R. Mateos de Cabo, and M. Sáinz, "Girls in STEM: Is It a Female Role-Model Thing?," *Front. Psychol.*, vol. 11, pp. 1–21, Sep. 2020, doi: 10.3389/fpsyg.2020.02204.

[18] J. Cohen, *Statistical Power Analysis for the Behavioral Sciences*, 2nd ed. 1988.

[19] S. Feierabend, T. Rathgeb, Y. Gerigk, and S. Glöckler, "JIM-Studie 2024 - Jugend Information Medien," Medienpädagogischer Forschungsverbund Südwest (mpfs), 2024. [Online]. Available from: https://mpfs.de/app/uploads/2024/11/JIM_2024_PDF_barrierearm.pdf, retrieved: 05, 2025

[20] Bitkom e.V., "Die Zukunft der Consumer Technology – 2024," 2024. [Online]. Available from: https://www.bitkom.org/sites/main/files/2024-09/bitkom-studie-zukunft-der-consumer-technology-2024.pdf, retrieved: 05, 2025

A Framework for Digital Business Processes

Florian Allwein
Department for IT and Technology,
IU International University of Applied Sciences
Berlin, Germany
e-mail: florian.allwein@iu.org

Abstract—**As society and businesses are changing due to digital transformation, traditional, analogue business processes need to be rethought and re-built. While information Systems research aims to support decision-makers in organizations with theoretically founded insights to support digitalization in practice, it sometimes lacks conceptual clarity, making it harder to apply its recommendations. This is especially true regarding terminology: There are no generally agreed-on definitions for central terms like "information" and "data", which would be helpful for organizations aiming to digitalize previously analog processes. This paper presents a framework covering digital processes in general. It shows how facts of the world are turned into digital data, then into information, which serves as the basis for decision-making. By defining digital data as digital representations of signs in the physical world and information as views of specific digital data, enriched by relevant context, it hopes to contribute to a clearer understanding of these terms. The framework is derived from an analysis of two sample processes, a) using a smartwatch to track movement and b) predictive maintenance in railway infrastructure using smartphones. It should be useful to research digitalization processes in other areas as well. Moreover, practitioners should find it helpful for discussions of digitalization projects.**

Keywords-framework; digital transformation; digitalization; data; information.

I. INTRODUCTION

Technological progress in areas like sensor technology, artificial intelligence or machine learning are driving digital transformation and creating opportunities to collect and analyze data at unprecedented scale [1]. As society and businesses are changing as well, digital transformation continues to be an area of the highest relevance as companies and organizations of all sizes are struggling to move their services and business models online, reconceptualizing what they do in the process. Moving business processes from the physical world (sometimes called the analog paradigm) to the digital world (the digital paradigm) may be challenging, but also offers an opportunity to rethink these business processes and the underlying business models, opening up potential for innovation along the way.

Existing research on digital transformation, however, often shows an astonishing lack of conceptual clarity: The key terms of "data" and "information" are not clearly defined, and definitions are sometimes contradictory or overlapping. This can be illustrated in the established research field of Information Systems (IS), which broadly looks at the interaction between organizations, information systems and the people using them [2].

Yet for a successful digital transformation to occur, it is important to have a clear conceptual framework outlining what happens in digitalization and, not least, unambiguous definitions of the main terms. As will be shown in Section II, there are currently no clear definitions of the terms "information" and "data" in research in the Information Systems field, which also limits our understanding of the processes involved in digitalization. Consequently, this paper will address the research questions: (1) "How can data and information be conceptualized, and (2) what happens to data and information in the process of digitalization?"

This conceptual paper presents a framework for digitalization, which was initially developed in a prior case study [1]. Section II will establish the theoretical background and discuss related works in the literature on IS and related fields. It outlines a framework conceptualizing the digitalization of business processes. Section III will briefly present the methodology of this paper. Findings will be presented in Section IV, which applies the framework to the case of predictive maintenance using smartphones in railway infrastructure. In Section V, the research questions are addressed and recommendations for practitioners planning digitalization projects are given. Section VI summarizes contributions to theory and practice and outlines possible future research directions.

II. THEORETICAL BACKGROUND

This section discusses fundamental terms. It follows Verhoef et al.'s [3] distinction between digitization, digitalization and digital transformation. Existing definitions of the terms "data" and "information" are then discussed and a framework is proposed to describe how facts of the world are turned into digital data, then into information, in the process of digitalization.

A. Digitalization, Digital Transformation

This paper draws on a broad theoretical background, mainly in the IS literature. For the key terms of digitalization and digital transformation, the definitions of Verhoef et al. [3] are used. They refer to three phases of digital transformation:

1. "Digitization is the encoding of analog information into a digital format (i.e., into zeros and ones) such

that computers can store, process, and transmit such information" (p. 891).

While essential, this purely technical process of encoding is not particularly exciting for organizations. The value of digital information (or data?), however, is seen in the following stages:

2. Digitalization "describes how IT or digital technologies can be used to alter existing business processes" (p. 891) and
3. Digital transformation is defined as "a change in how a firm employs digital technologies, to develop a new digital business model that helps to create and appropriate more value for the firm" (p. 889).

This helps to illustrate the relevance of digital transformation: "Digital transformation affects the whole company and its ways of doing business (…) and goes beyond digitalization – the changing of simple organizational processes and tasks" (p. 889). Thus, having digital data available is necessary to enable organizations to reconsider their business processes and business models. Both represent considerable opportunities to increase efficiency or identify new revenue streams [4].

B. *Data, information*

From these definitions, it becomes clear that data and information play a crucial role in digital transformation, as they constitute the key phenomena of relevance in digital systems. The first eminent publication on information was by Shannon [5], which is seen as the start of the field of information theory and has influenced fields from computer science to statistics and economics. However, as a communication engineer, Shannon was concerned with the efficient transmission of information, not with its meaning, so his theory does little to resolve the conceptual issues around digital transformation.

Unfortunately, the IS literature does not use the terms "data" and "information" with sufficient precision. McKinney and Yoos [6] show that, following the token view (the most common one according to their research), "information" is actually seen as synonymous with "data". Likewise, the definitions by Verhoef et al. [3] discussed above only refer to "information", not "data", hence a clearer distinction is needed.

Looking at the business management literature, there are more straightforward definitions. According to Laudon & Laudon [7], "data" are defined as "streams of raw facts" (p. 609) and "information" as "data that have been shaped into a form that is meaningful and useful to human beings" (p. 612). This is helpful for a clearer understanding: Data have something to do with raw facts, while information is primarily useful for human users. It also aligns well with the etymology of data as "that which is given". Previous attempts to equate data to facts of the world [8], however, have not been successful. To avoid confusion, this paper will refer to "digital data" throughout.

Starting from facts, in fact, should still be relevant to understand processes of digital transformation, as their purpose ultimately is to find out about events in the physical world, and potentially to affect them. Krcmar [9] discusses a hierarchical view of codes, data, information and knowledge: Syntax turns codes into data; context adds meaning to data, thus creating information. This is a useful view as it clearly distinguishes between the four different concepts.

Certainly, at this point, we can claim that there are enough differences between data and information to warrant using different terms.

C. *A framework for digital business processes*

Based on the literature discussed above, a general framework describing digital processes (e.g., business processes) was developed [1]. The framework describes how facts of the physical world are eventually converted into digital data, which is presented as information in order to influence decisions. For illustration purposes, the framework is used to discuss the simple everyday case of using a smartwatch to track a user's movements. The framework is shown in Figure 1. Specifically, the process runs as follows:

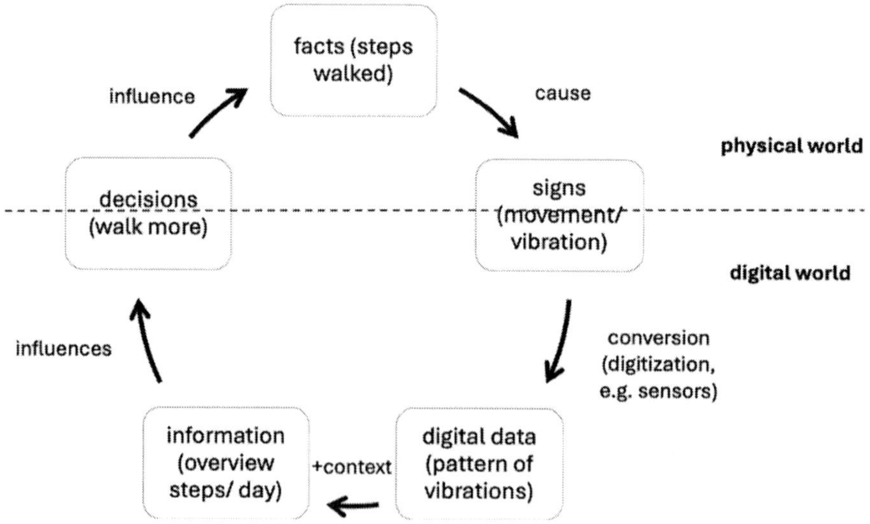

Figure 1. Framework for digital business processes

- As mentioned, the framework shows how facts in the physical world are eventually turned into digital data (in the digital world). The dotted line represents the boundary between the physical and the digital world. Signs and decisions can both be located either in the digital or the physical world.
- The framework starts at the top, with the **facts of the world** relevant for the process in question. In this example, this is the number of steps taken by the person who wears the smartwatch.
- The **facts of the world** cause **signs** that can be measured – in this case, specific patterns of movement in the smartwatch. Signs can be either physical (as in this case) or digital (when looking at digital processes – see below).
- If necessary, the **signs** are then digitized. In this case, this is done by the motion sensor in the smartwatch, so the signs are turned into **digital data** corresponding to the specific pattern of vibrations that indicates a step has been taken.
- These raw **digital data** are not useful in themselves, but can be presented in a way that is, i.e., turned into **information**. This could be done by adding context to the data or by formatting them in a way that is meaningful to its users.
- In the end, the smartwatch will give a piece of **information**, e.g., the number of steps taken on this particular day, ideally compared to a target value that was defined before.
- This is presented in a way that supports **decision-making**. In this case, the user may decide to walk some more in order to reach their daily step target.
- Obviously, and crucially, this process also affects the original **facts** (number of steps), as the purpose of information systems is usually not just to measure effects in the real world, but also to change them.

The framework outlined will be discussed in the following sections, with a focus on how it can be applied to different contexts.

III. METHODOLOGY

The research design and methodology in this paper is relatively straightforward. The paper set out to answer the research questions: (1) "How can data and information be conceptualized, and (2) what happens to them in process of digitalization?". This section will briefly outline how this is done.

The proposed framework is based on prior studies as well as a review of the literature on Digital Transformation. It is presented for the first time in English. The case study focuses on using smartphones for predictive maintenance in railway infrastructure. It is based on a case study in German [1], which analyzed the literature on the topic, discussing some previous research. The relevant key papers are listed in Table 1.

TABLE I. KEY PAPERS

Paper	Content	Findings
Nunez et al. [10]	Reporting on projects for cost effective maintenance in railways	Axle box acceleration measurements and smartphones both useful in coordination with other signals like GPS
Falamarzi et al. [11]	Review of various sensor technologies for inspecting railway infrastructure	Smartphones as cost-effective probe to collect acceleration data, gyroscope and GPS data, mostly for measuring ride comfort
Rodriguez et al. [12]	Review of earlier projects; methodology for measuring ride comfort	Possible to measure track performance and ride comfort using smartphones
Stübinger & Stavrianidis [13]	Reporting on a project by Siemens Mobility with Swiss Rail (SBB)	Project used smartphones to successfully measure some maintenance aspects, in conjunction with existing backend systems

The focus of the current, conceptual paper is on developing this framework and discussing ways it might be useful in other areas of research.

IV. CASE STUDY FINDINGS

A. *Predictive Maintenance*

The framework presented above can also be used to discuss cases of predictive maintenance, where collecting and analyzing facts about the world in the form of digital data is also a key aspect. Mobley [14] describes the basic approach:

"The common premise of predictive maintenance is that regular monitoring of the actual mechanical condition, operating efficiency, and other indicators of the operating condition of machine-trains and process systems will provide the data required to ensure the maximum interval between repairs and minimize the number and cost of unscheduled outages created by machine-train failures" (p. 4).

Consequently, transferring the framework to the realm of predictive maintenance shows it can be used to discuss processes of digitalization in this area as well. In this case,

- the starting point of the process is again **facts of the world**, i.e., the "actual mechanical condition" of a machine.
- These cause **signs** in the physical world, i.e., the "indicators of the operating condition", e.g., movement or vibration.
- These are then converted into **digital data**, e.g., by sensors.
- These **digital data** (i.e., "the data required") can be enriched with an appropriate context and used as **information** to support **decisions** (i.e., "ensure the maximum interval between repairs").

- The **decisions** that are made in this way in turn affect the original **facts** (i.e., "minimize the number and cost of unscheduled outages created by machine-train failures").

In predictive maintenance, it is not the facts of the world being digitized, but certain signs in the physical world indicating them. Specifically, it is not the mechanical condition of the railway track itself, but the measurable signs indicating this condition, e.g., slight variations in the movement or vibration patterns of the train. These are turned into digital data and, by contrasting this with previous data, a context is established that can yield information about the track's condition (specifically whether it is damaged). This can inform decisions (e.g., adapting the maintenance intervals for the track), which again influence the initial facts (the track's condition).

B. *Example: Maintenance of railway infrastructure using smartphones*

The capture of facts of the world and their processing as digital data for predictive maintenance can be illustrated by the case of railway operators using commercially available smartphones to detect damage to railway infrastructure [1]. To this end, there have been various experiments with apps that are installed on smartphones, which are positioned at various points on a train and continuously provide data on the condition of the tracks via, e.g., the smartphone's acceleration or gyro sensors. As such data can ideally be collected every time a train is running, changes over time can be identified and used to infer possible maintenance requirements.

Initial results are promising. Nunez et al. [10] and Rodriguez et al. [12] evaluate the previous use of various sensor technologies In railways, finding that smartphones are useful for some aspects of predictive maintenance. This is supported by Falamarzi et al.'s review of the literature on various technologies for the maintenance of railway lines [11]: "The combination of different sensors has made smartphones a cost-effective probe which can be used to collect acceleration data, gyroscope and GPS data in railway vehicles, mostly for measuring ride comfort" (p. 6). At the same time, the authors qualify that the use of these technologies is still in at an early stage.

Stübinger & Stavrianidis [13] present an app developed by Siemens Mobility, which supports the monitoring of rails in daily use. This is traditionally done with special track measuring trains, which, however, cannot be used on a daily basis. In this example, three smartphones were placed in a regular train for a day and collected data, which were also combined with other external data:

"The smartphone app enables the recording and use of all relevant data from the smartphone sensors (e.g., Global Navigation Satellite Systems sensor (GNSS), accelerometers and gyroscope) during regular train operation. The optimum use of a smartphone for detecting faults in the infrastructure also requires the combination of additional external and freely available information with the sensor data. For example, the track monitoring smartphone app uses the OpenStreetMap map material that is integrated through a special interface" (p. 10).

A traditional measuring train was used for comparison. The quality of the data was found to be similar: "Valid use of the data can be established based on the good qualitative comparability of the smartphone data with that of the accelerometers in the train vehicle body" (p. 12). The app is integrated into existing measurement and monitoring solutions for trains and rails [15]. Thus, the way the underlying system works is similar to the process shown in our framework: digital data is collected from sensors and external sources, processed and made available for analysis.

The case study has shown that protective maintenance is fundamentally about converting facts of the world into digital data and using this as information to support decision-making. Consequently, it can be described in the terms of the framework presented in this paper.

V. Discussion

A. *Addressing the Research Questions*

The framework has been introduced and discussed with reference to the two cases discussed, wearing a smartwatch as well as predictive maintenance in railway infrastructure using smartphones. This section will draw on these cases in order to address the research questions, then develop some recommendations for applying the framework in other contexts.

1) *RQ1: How can data and information be conceptualized?*

The problem discussed at the beginning of this paper was the lack of conceptual clarity around the terms "data" and "information". Using the proposed framework, we can now propose alternative definitions:

Data, or specifically **digital data**, can be defined as digital representations of signs in the physical world, which in turn represent facts of the physical world. In our examples, the facts are the variables of interest in the physical word that are monitored and consequently modified. In order to do this, some measurable signs representing these facts need to be identified. If these signs are not digital, a way to digitize them has to be found.

Information, on the other hand, is defined as views of specific digital data, enriched by relevant context, that serve to support specific decisions either by humans or automated systems. The challenge is to identify the relevant digital data and any context necessary and to present them in a way that best supports the necessary decisions.

2) *RQ2: What happens to data and information in the process of digitalization?*

In the process of digitalization, relevant facts of the world are identified. Next, measurable signs relating to these facts are identified. These signs are then digitalized, i.e., converted into digital data if needed. The digital data is then enhanced with context and presented in a way that is useful for supporting decisions, i.e., it is turned into information. This information is then presented in a way that can support decisions, either by humans or automated systems.

It is worth pointing out that, as digital transformation progresses, such processes are becoming more pervasive. Specifically, the on-going digital transformation of many organizations makes it possible to obtain considerably more digital data, as more sensors and new data sources become available. This can be seen both in the fact that individuals carry more digital devices (and sensors) like smartphones or smartwatches, but also in automobiles, which have become digital devices in their own right in recent years [16]. Moreover, with technologies like noSQL databases and cloud computing, information can now be stored in almost any quantity and analyzed in real time.

B. *Recommendations*

The framework and associated definitions can thus support efforts at digitalization, especially around digitizing processes of supporting decisions based on facts of the world. This should be relevant for most business processes. Some specific recommendations for starting and designing such processes can be suggested.

1) *Identify relevant signs*

Obviously, information systems are always based on facts of the world. Being aware of this can help focus on facts and guide discussions about which facts are relevant for a specific business decision. The next step would then be to consider how these facts manifest in measurable signs that can be used for decision-making and, if necessary, think of ways to digitize them.

One example would be the number of customers in a specific timeframe, either in online or physical stores. In online stores, visitors leave information that can be tracked and analyzed, including how they arrived at the store website (e.g., from a search engine, a newsletter,…), how they navigate through the site, what purchases they made (if any), from which page (URL) they exited the store etc. Using the proposed framework, these would all be seen as signs in the digital world.

Similar signs exist for customers visiting physical stores in the real world. Here, data collected from cash desks can reveal insights about the number of customers throughout the day, revenues etc. If the store is using loyalty programs, these insights can also be tied to specific customers, revealing more insights about their behavior [17]. Some stores have come up with ways to analyze customer footfall while preserving privacy, e.g., by installing cameras to count customers entering the store, while only taking pictures of their feet [18].

2) *Consider UX and interaction design*

In order to be useful, digital data must be brought into a form that can support decisions. Thus, it must be presented in a way that supports these decisions and enhanced by any necessary context. This turns data into information.

For supporting the decision-making process, it is important to present exactly the right bits of information, and do this in a way that best supports decision-making. Insights from the field of User Experience research (UX) and interaction design [19] can be particularly helpful here. Thus, the next recommendation is to carefully think through the processes involved, the exact bits of information needed, and the best ways to present them. It can be especially relevant to consider external information that can be used in the process. As we have seen, the Siemens system for predictive maintenance in railway infrastructure [13] also uses geolocation data, weather data etc.

3) *Evaluate automatization options*

Once the useful signs, data and information have been identified, processes should be discussed with a view on automating them as far as possible. This can be illustrated by the case of using smartwatches for tracking activities: Some apps are able to automatically recognize typical signs (in this case, movement patterns, e.g., signaling that the user is running) and automatically trigger the desired reaction, e.g., recording the exercise activity, in this case the run, from the moment the pattern started.

Likewise, decisions should be automated, as, for example, is the norm in industrial production processes. Significant innovation can be expected in the area of business process automation in the near future as tools like Robotic Process Automation (RPA) or AI based tools like Microsoft Copilot are being used more broadly, and also in smaller organizations.

C. *Theoretical contributions*

The theoretical contributions of this paper consist in the definitions of digital data and information given above, as well as the framework for digitizing (business) processes, which should be useful for future research.

D. *Practical contributions*

The framework also represents an important practical contribution, as it is hoped that it will help practitioners plan projects of digitalization, identify useful facts of the world and ways they can be digitized.

VI. Conclusion and Future Work

As small and large organizations everywhere continue to search for ways to digitally transform their existing business, a clear understanding of the processes involved is beneficial.

It is hoped that this research, and the framework presented, can contribute towards addressing the problems outlined at the beginning of this paper: The lack of clear definitions of the terms "information" and "data" as well as the limited understanding of the processes involved in digitalization caused by this ambiguity.

It is also hoped that the framework can support digitalization initiatives by putting a focus on relevant facts of the world and ways they can be digitized. Consequently, practitioners are especially encouraged to use the framework to structure discussions of digitalization projects.

This research, however, comes with clear limitations. The framework is still in an early stage of its development and will benefit from further testing on real-life examples. Future research should focus on critical discussions of the framework, as well as evaluating its explanatory powers in other areas of digitalization. It would be particularly helpful to have future case studies applying the framework in different contexts of digitalization.

REFERENCES

[1] F. Allwein, "Wie kann die Digitale Transformation voraussagende Instandhaltung unterstützen?" [How can Digital Transformation support Predictive Maintenance?] in Predictive Maintenance: Innovationen, Anwendungen und Herausforderungen in der industriellen Praxis [Predictive Maintenance: Innovations, Applications and Challenges in Industrial Practice], M. Eifler, M. Nawito, and M. Venschott, Eds., Springer Gabler, 2025, in press.

[2] A. S. Lee, "Retrospect and prospect: Information Systems research in the last and next 25 years," Journal of Information Technology, vol. 25, no. 4, pp. 336–348, Dec. 2010, doi: 10.1057/jit.2010.24.

[3] P. C. Verhoef et al., "Digital transformation: A multidisciplinary reflection and research agenda," Journal of Business Research, vol. 122, pp. 889–901, Jan. 2021, doi: 10.1016/j.jbusres.2019.09.022.

[4] A. Osterwalder and Y. Pigneur, Business Model Generation: A Handbook for Visionaries, Game Changers, and Challengers. John Wiley & Sons, 2010.

[5] C. E. Shannon, "A Mathematical Theory of Communication," Bell System Technical Journal, vol. 27, no. 3, pp. 379–423, Jul. 1948, doi: 10.1002/j.1538-7305.1948.tb01338.x.

[6] E. H. McKinney and C. J. Yoos, "Information about information: a taxonomy of views," MIS Quarterly, vol. 34, no. 2, pp. 329–344, Jun. 2010.

[7] K. C. Laudon and J. P. Laudon, Management Information Systems: Managing the Digital Firm. Harlow, Essex: Pearson Education, 2014.

[8] F. Allwein, "Research Commentary: Data as Facts of the World," IS Channel, vol. 11, pp. 21–23, 2016.

[9] H. Krcmar, Informationsmanagement [Information Management]. Berlin, Heidelberg: Springer Berlin Heidelberg, 2015. doi: 10.1007/978-3-662-45863-1.

[10] A. Nunez et al., "Smart technology solutions for the NeTIRail-INFRA case study lines: Axle box acceleration and ultra-low cost smartphones," Proceedings of the 7th Transportation Research Arena 2018, 2018, Accessed: May 19, 2025. [Online]. Available: https://repository.tudelft.nl/islandora/object/uuid%3A501de6b4-38a4-43fd-9e92-dd82ee464748

[11] A. Falamarzi, S. Moridpour, and M. Nazem, "A Review on Existing Sensors and Devices for Inspecting Railway Infrastructure," jkukm, vol. 31, no. 1, pp. 1–10, Apr. 2019, doi: 10.17576/jkukm-2019-31(1)-01

[12] A. Rodriguez, R. Sañudo, M. Miranda, A. Gómez, and J. Benavente, "Smartphones and tablets applications in railways, ride comfort and track quality. Transition zones analysis," Measurement, vol. 182, p. 109644, Jun. 2021, doi: 10.1016/j.measurement.2021.109644.

[13] L. Stübinger and K. Stavrianidis, "Track monitoring smartphone app," ETR - Eisenbahntechnische Rundschau, pp. 10–13, Sep. 2022.

[14] R. K. Mobley, An Introduction to Predictive Maintenance. Elsevier, 2002.

[15] Siemens Mobility, "Measurement and monitoring for rail systems", Siemens Mobility Global. Accessed: May 19, 2025. [Online]. Available: https://www.mobility.siemens.com/global/en/portfolio/digital-solutions-software/digital-services/measurement-monitoring.html

[16] A. Lyyra, K. Koskinen, C. Sørensen, and T. Marion, "Tethered Architectures in Cyber-Physical System Development: The Case of Tesla's Autopilot System," Jul. 10, 2023, Rochester, NY: 4515061. doi: 10.2139/ssrn.4515061.

[17] C. Duhigg, Power of Habit: Why We Do What We Do in Life and Business, Random House Trade Paperback Edition. New York: Random House Trade Paperbacks, 2014.

[18] Affine, "In-Store Traffic Analytics: Retail Sensing with Intelligent Object Detection," Medium. Accessed: May 19, 2025. [Online]. Available: https://affine.medium.com/in-store-traffic-analytics-retail-sensing-with-intelligent-object-detection-51f7aea13a1a

[19] J. Preece, H. Sharp, and Y. Rogers, Interaction Design: Beyond Human-Computer Interaction. John Wiley & Sons, 2015.

Digital Transformation in the UK Government

A Research Programme

Brian Gannon
Fachgruppe IT und Technik
IU Internationale Hochschule
Germany
email: brian.gannon@iu.org

Abstract— **This ongoing research programme tells the story of the successful digital transformation initiative conducted by the UK government between 2010 and 2019. Spearheaded by the Government Digital Services (GDS) unit, a part of the UK Cabinet Office, the 'Digital by Default' programme redefined the way information technology (IT) solutions could be developed in the public sector and showed that it is possible for digital technology to streamline and improve online delivery of government services for citizens. The research documents the trajectory of the initiative from its beginning in 2010 to the establishment of a mature GDS in 2019, addressing such themes as the political and social imperatives that led to GDS; the role of key individuals in the project and the challenges of introducing radical technology-driven change into central government. Based on data collected from the main participants in the transformation programme, it identifies the enabling factors, the transformation initiatives, and the successes and failures experienced along the way. This paper outlines the context of the overall research programme and highlights emerging themes. These include identification of success factors, such as the necessity of obtaining senior political sponsorship at every stage, the dependence on people and skills to make the change happen, and the huge effort required to change culture and mindset in sometimes labyrinthine, stolid and vast government departments. It also provides a perspective on some of the challenges faced, and failed expectations of the programme. Although much of the data was collected in 2018, it is acknowledged that change of this scale takes time. Accordingly, a follow-up round of data gathering and analysis is planned in 2026 to assess the lasting effects of this transformation.**

Keywords: digital transformation; government; UK Government Digital Services.

I. Introduction

In recent years, digital technology has become pervasive, easy to use and affordable. Almost all aspects of modern life have been transformed by the availability of online services, and for many people, digital technology (the 'digital channel') is the preferred and increasingly the only way to use business services. In many industries, companies use digital channels to provide services not only because it is what customers want, but also because it is less expensive, easier to use and easier to change.

Use of digital technology to provide public services is not widespread. In the UK, for the most part, government services are provided to citizens using non-digital means such as mail, meetings and telephone calls. Moreover, the UK government has had a mixed track record of getting value for its sizeable IT investment over the past 30 years and has a poor reputation for procuring and deploying technology effectively [9]. Writing in 2004, Sir John Bourn, the head of the National Audit Office noted that: "The history of failure of major IT-enabled projects has been characterised by overspends, delays, poor performance and abandonment of projects at major cost." [18]. In 2011, his successor Sir Amyas Morse, speaking about the £12 billion National Health Service (NHS) National Programme for IT (NPfIT), said: "This is yet another example of a department fundamentally underestimating the scale and complexity of a major IT-enabled change programme." [19]. The UK is not alone in struggling with public IT projects. Many of the developed economies have suffered expensive project failures, such as the troubled implementation of HealthCare.gov ('Obamacare') in the US [12] and the problems experienced with implementing the Queensland Health Payroll System in Australia [4].

The structure of this paper is as follows. In Section 2, the origin and outcome of the GDS digital by default programme is summarised. Section 3 describes the context and methodology of the research, and Section 4 sets out preliminary conclusions and emerging themes. The paper concludes by setting out the planned stages of further research in Section 5.

II. A Successful Public Sector Transformation

Public sector projects are not doomed to failure. More enterprising administrations have seen in the online world and associated development technologies an opportunity to remodel the way in which government services are provided to citizens. An exemplar is the former Soviet Republic of Estonia, which has developed one of the world's foremost digital democracies underpinned by a robust, ubiquitous digital infrastructure, and capable of providing all government services to the citizen via online channels [13].

Another striking success has been the digital transformation effected in the UK. In 2010, a general election brought to power a government formed by a coalition of the Liberal Democrat and Conservative parties. On taking office, this government set up an organisation called the Efficiency and Reform Group (ERG) with the aims of saving money, transforming the way public services are delivered, improving user experience and supporting UK growth. A letter from Martha Lane Fox, the government's Digital Champion, had earlier urged a radical redesign of how government services should be provided to citizens [15]. Ostensibly in response to a request to review direct.gov, the UK government's online presence, the letter addressed a much wider question: how could the UK government use the Internet both to communicate and interact better with citizens and to deliver significant efficiency savings?

Ms. Lane Fox's recommendation was summarised in the subtitle to her report – 'Revolution, not Evolution'. Francis Maude, the government minister responsible for efficiency and reform, agreed to adopt all her recommendations. In 2011 he recruited Mike Bracken to lead a new government agency named Government Digital Services (GDS), which had an objective of making public services simpler and better by using digital technology. GDS set about building common digital platforms; changing the way government procures IT services; consolidating government online services and making them easy to access and use; and streamlining high-volume transaction services.

Within two years GDS and Bracken had changed the mindset about the UK government's capability to effect change using technology. It implemented the award-winning gov.uk portal, a simple, effective gateway for citizens to find information about public services. It identified 25 services across government for end-to-end service redesign ('exemplars') to show how new approaches could make it easier for citizens to access services online and help remove unnecessary costs and to prove that central government departments could design and provide services efficiently through digital channels. Through the exemplars, GDS sought to change the perception of government as wasteful and slow in technology matters, and to position the UK government as a leader in digital transformation. In parallel, GDS re-designed government procurement to accommodate small and medium sized companies, opening competition to a wide range of innovative and flexible firms; and it championed the use of open-source technologies and agile development approaches, resulting in less dependency on large software vendors, quicker deployment and lower cost. This stimulated growth in the digital technology sector across the UK, predominantly for small to medium enterprises, and generated significant annual savings for the taxpayer [7].

In short, GDS showed that it is possible to provide easy to use, cost-effective online public services designed around the citizen's needs. Although in recent years, it has been criticised for failing to redefine its role as it has grown, it has nonetheless been recognised that it has 'successfully reshaped government's approach to technology and transformation' [20].

III. CONTEXT AND METHODOLOGY

This research paper lies at the intersection of technology (digital transformation) and history. It is primarily narrative and descriptive and does not purport to provide quantitative scientific proofs. It is particularly important for such multidisciplinary research to be placed in a firm academic context, as described in this section.

A. Context

This research programme tells the story of GDS and the 'Digital by Default' programme by compiling a narrative history from those who were involved. This includes perspectives from citizens (users), policy makers, procurement specialists, technologists, and civil servants among others. The research documents the trajectory of the initiative from its beginning in 2011 to the establishment of a mature GDS in 2019, addressing such themes as the political and social imperatives that led to GDS; the role of key individuals in the project and the challenges of introducing radical technology-driven change into central government. The emphasis is on the narrative history, rather than on interpreting underlying or hidden meaning. This means identifying common themes, events, and milestones in the GDS story as perceived by those who participated in it: the intent of the research is to allow the voices of first-hand witnesses to tell the story, and to enliven a bland statement of events with anecdote, humour and perception.

B. Theory, Research Method and Data

Although it is difficult at this stage to nominate a dominant theoretical approach, the research references the information systems (IS) historiographical constructs expounded by Land [16] and Mason et al [17]. It also follows a view of historiography that emphasises the role of individuals rather than abstract forces in history [6]; although rather than using narrative as a rhetorical device, or depending solely on anecdote, the research underpins personal experiences with empirical data. In part, the narrative follows the lines of certain broader historical and social scholarship, including the traditions of social historical research exemplified by the historians Hobsbawm [11] and Zinn [25]. From an analytical point of view, the research uses grounded theory techniques [8].

Data informing the research comprises primary and secondary written reports, emails, blogs and other contemporary and current documented sources. The bulk of the data is derived from a series of face-to-face interviews with the principal actors, conducted in a 12-week period in the last quarter of 2018. The interviews were semi-structured and relatively informal in format, and covered the interviewee's background (before GDS), and their history and involvement in GDS. The aim of the interviews was to solicit views about actual events (recollection of what happened); to understand motivations and policies (why things happened); and outcomes (what transpired). In the course of these discussions, interviewees were prompted to present their views on such topics as the technology used, the policies adopted, the problems faced, as well as circumstantial descriptions concerning such elements as the work-environment; the style and form of individual engagement; and recruitment policies.

C. Significance of Research

In 1997, a paper in MIS Quarterly, the pre-eminent journal in the field of IS research, noted that "MIS as a discipline has not yet developed a tradition of historical research" [17]. Histories, according to one scholar, "…are powerful because they both create and reinforce collective identities... Having a history is important because what is articulated as having happened in the past profoundly affects all aspects of our lives and will affect what happens in the future" [3]. This research is, in part, a response to the challenge posed by Mason, Bryant and others. It presents a view of one of the most significant (and successful) deployments of information and digital technology at scale in the world today, and documents the role played by its pioneers and participants. In doing so, it brings some balance to the academic literature, which features a disproportionate number of studies on IT failure. Further, the research will inevitably have significance in academic disciplines outside the field of IS and digital transformation. It should, for example, be relevant to those interested in organisational theory (the transformation of business enabled by digital technology), and economics and social history (the social impact of process automation in the modern era).

Finally, there is the value of the research to industry. The UK government's digital by default programme was one of those rare initiatives when something different happened: what was regarded as a dull, expensive and failure-prone domain became the centre for innovative and transformative activity, attracting the brightest and most talented people in the industry. Although there is some distance still to travel, what GDS and its originators achieved is undeniably positive for citizens, public servants, taxpayers and digital professionals in the UK and further afield. They showed that contrary to much of the evidence, implementing information technology projects in government could be done successfully with verve, flair and good deal of fun. Moreover, although the study is primarily focused on the UK, the research has global relevance and highlights similarity and specificity of digital transformation across different nations.

IV. PRIMARY EMERGING THEMES

The data highlights several consistent themes that permeate the transformation programme, from which some early observations can be made. First, the scale of the initiative dictated approach and tactics. A small team of 'outsiders' – for the most part enthusiastic and talented digital natives, many with no experience of working in the public sector – sought to influence and sometimes overturn decades of practice and settled protocol in organisations that numbered tens of thousands of seasoned, knowledgeable and competent civil servants, with annual budgets in hundreds of millions of pounds. This was no mean undertaking; rather it was a concerted attempt to use digital technology to change the way in which public services were planned, designed, procured and delivered. The GDS team were in this sense revolutionaries, and conversations with the team repeatedly draw attention to a zealous sense of mission and focus, a willingness to take risk, a tendency towards iconoclasm. This drew predictable responses from some civil servants, who felt threatened by and therefore sought to derail the introduction of change. Among the incumbent IT practitioners, the GDS approach was frequently welcomed as a refreshing and empowering programme.

Three essential elements of the GDS approach appear to be critical success factors in the digital by default programme: agile development methodologies featuring user-focused design; accelerated procurement from small, nimble providers; and the use of open-source rather than proprietary technology and standards.

While this research programme will comment on these and other success factors in due course, at this early stage it is possible to identify the use of agile development methodologies as an outstanding enabling factor. From the 1990s, PRINCE2, a generic waterfall project management methodology with an emphasis on risk management, was widely used for government-funded projects. It mattered little that PRINCE2 had failed to mitigate the risk of several high-profile IT projects, such as the London Ambulance despatch system [1], and the methodology continued to sometimes be required or expected in large government departments. GDS believed that user-centric digital services would be more effectively designed and delivered by in-house IT specialists using agile software development methodologies, rather than by using large software solutions bought off the shelf or developed by global IT service providers, such as IBM, Accenture and Oracle. This iterative, user-centred approach using Scrum was at the heart of the GDS programme and featured heavily in the Service Design Manual and associated Digital by Default Service Standard, a set of guidelines and benchmarks for government departments on development of digital services [21]. (A current version of the Digital Services Standard, now titled 'Service Manual' was published in May 2022 [24]). It appealed to developers because it was less constraining and more empowering than traditional waterfall development. Moreover, it acknowledged the inherent uncertainty in large scale development projects and sought to develop solutions collaboratively with users rather than in a technology vacuum.

As for many successful IT programmes, success was enabled by factors that had little to do with technology. In the case of GDS, a relentless focus on communication at every level proved extremely influential in dictating the pace and raining the profile of the digital by default initiatives. This ranged from formal engagement with external stakeholders through government channels to informal blogging, networking and promotion encouraged in GDS and in exemplar government departments. It mattered that Mike Bracken himself was a consummate communicator, and he deployed considerable skill in countering scepticism at high levels of government [2]. The award of the prestigious Museum Design of the Year Award 2013 for the flagship gov.uk website – a radical redesign of the online portal to UK government websites into a single domain – was more an indication of GDS's skill at communication than of its technical and design prowess [23].

Other themes, including those that illustrate programme weaknesses, will emerge from the data as analysis proceeds. Detractors of the programme have identified flaws in the GDS approach, and it is true that the organization as it exists today is different in many key aspects to the revolutionary cadre of agile developers who formed the core of GDS in the beginning. Edgar [5] identifies collaboration between government departments as a particular systemic weakness, along with a continued lack of accountability for outcomes across departments. The NAO in its 2017 assessment pointed out that "...only six of the live exemplars and two of the publicly available trials had provided an integrated service by March 2015. Full transformation and digitisation was not achieved, either for the citizen or for government." [20]

Nonetheless, even those who viewed the digital by default programme with suspicion cannot deny the impact it has had on the way in which digital transformation has shaped how UK citizens now consume public services online. The full scope of this impact is ill-defined at present and requires further study.

V. Conclusion and Future Work

This programme of research aims primarily to document the history of the UK's digital-by-default programme between 2013 and 2018, and in doing so to identify the extent to which the ambitions of the programme have been achieved. However, transformation at this scale takes a great deal of time, and in an organization as large and diverse as the UK public sector, the pace of change can be glacial. Nonetheless, the next stage of this research will attempt to assess the impact of GDS on the effectiveness of digital service provision to UK citizens by conducting a series of follow-up interviews in 2026. Although this represents a short time since the GDS programme terminated, much has happened in both political and IT domains. Notably, GDS now includes other government digital agencies such as the Central Digital and Data Office (CDDO), the Incubator for AI (i.AI) and Responsible Technology Adoption Unit. Yet, progress on wholesale transformation remains mixed and a report by the UK Public Accounts Committee [10] notes that successful digital transformation remains elusive and that the government remains far behind the private sector in its recruitment of the technology professionals needed to force change.

Research on this topic is also sparse. There is active comment in the form of blogs, such as those by Edgar and Thompson [5][22], but to date there has been no major academic study on digital policy and transformation in the UK public sector. Future work in this research programme intends to remedy this by publishing a complete account of the GDS experiment (in 2025); conducting a further round of data gathering and analysis with current stakeholders (in 2026); and publishing a comprehensive longitudinal study that addresses the ambitions and outcomes of UK government digitization over the past decades (in 2027).

References

[1] P. Beynon-Davies, "Human error and information systems failure: the case of the London ambulance service computer-aided despatch system project", Interacting with Computers, 1999, vol. 11, no. 6, pp. 699-720

[2] M. Bracken, "What we mean when we say "service transformation" – Government Digital Service", 2014, [retrieved: March 2025]

[3] A. Bryant, A. Black, F. Land and, J. Porra, "Information Systems history: What is history? What is IS history? What IS history? and why even bother with history?", Journal of Information Technology, 2013, Vol. 28, pp. 1 – 17

[4] R. Chesterman, "Queensland Health Payroll System Commission of Inquiry Report", Queensland Health Payroll System Commission of Inquiry - QHPSCI, 2013, [retrieved: May 2025]

[5] M. Edgar, "Marks out of ten – how are we doing after a decade of public digital transformation? – mattedgar | Public Sector Blogs", 2023, [retrieved: June 2025]

[6] G. R. Elton, "Second Thoughts on History at the Universities", History, 1969, Vol. 54, No. 180, pp 60–67

[7] S. Foreshew-Caine,"How digital and technology transformation saved £1.7bn last year – Government Digital Service", 2015, [retrieved: March 2025]

[8] B. Glaser and A. Strauss "The Discovery of Grounded Theory", 1967, Chicago, Aldine

[9] Guardian, "The costly trail of British government IT and 'big bang' project disasters", The costly trail of British government IT and 'big bang' project disasters | e-Government | The Guardian, [retrieved: March 2025]

[10] House of Commons Committee of Public Accounts, "Digital transformation in government: addressing the barriers to efficiency", HC 1229, Seventieth Report of Session 2022–23

[11] E. Hobsbawm, "The age of revolution: 1789-1848", 1962, New York, New American Library

[12] C. Johnson and H. Reed, "Why the Government Never Gets Tech Right", The New York Times, 2013, http://www.nytimes.com/2013/10/25/opinion/getting-to-the-bottom-of-healthcaregovs-flop.html, [retrieved: March 2025]

[13] R. Kattel and I. Mergel, "Estonia's digital transformation: Mission mystique and the hiding hand", UCL Institute for Innovation and Public Purpose Working Paper Series (IIPP WP 2018-09), 2018, https://www.ucl.ac.uk/bartlett/public-purpose/wp2018-09, [retrieved: May 2025]

[14] P. Kelly, "2024 in Review: Key Innovations in UK Public Sector Technology", 2024, [retrieved: May 2025]

[15] M. Lane Fox, "Letter from Martha Lane Fox to Francis Maude, 14 October 2010", Directgov 2010 and beyond: revolution not evolution, a report by Martha Lane Fox - GOV.UK, [retrieved: March 2025]

[16] F. Land, "The use of history in IS research: an opportunity missed?", Journal of Information Technology, 2010, Vol. 25, pp. 385-394

[17] R. Mason, J. McKenney, and, D. Copeland, "Developing an Historical Tradition in MIS Research", MIS Quarterly, 1997, Vol. 21, No. 3, pp. 257-278

[18] NAO, "Improving IT procurement", Comptroller and Auditor General HC 877 Session 2003-2004:. p. 3 extension://efaidnbmnnnibpcajpcglclefindmkaj/https://www.nao.org.uk/wp-content/uploads/2004/11/0304877.pdf, [retrieved: March, 2025]

[19] NAO, Press Release on publication of report, "The National Programme for IT in the NHS: an update on the delivery of detailed care records systems", The National Programme for IT in the NHS: an update on the delivery of detailed care records systems - NAO report, 2014, [retrieved: March, 2025]

[20] NAO, Comptroller and Auditor General, "Digital Transformation in Government", HC1059 Session 2016-17, extension://efaidnbmnnnibpcajpcglclefindmkaj/https://www.nao.org.uk/wp-content/uploads/2017/03/Digital-transformation-in-government.pdf, 2017, [retrieved: March, 2025]

[21] T. Scott, "A year in the making – the Digital by Default Service Standard – Government Digital Service", 2014, [retrieved: March, 2025]

[22] M. Thompson, "Fixing public services: Thoughts from the Labour and Conservative Conference Fringes - Exeter INDEX", 2024, [retrieved: May, 2025]

[23] UK Cabinet Office, Press Release, 2013, "GOV.UK wins Design of the Year 2013 - GOV.UK", [retrieved: March, 2025]

[24] UK Cabinet Office Publication 2022, "Service Manual - GOV.UK", [retrieved: May, 2025]

[25] H. Zinn, "A People's History of the United States", (1st ed.), 1980, Harper & Row, New York

Revisiting Process Virtualization: A Systematic Review of How Collaboration Tools Support Social Presence and Situation Awareness

Inga F. Schlömer
IT and Engineering Department
IU International University
Erfurt, Germany
e-mail: inga.schloemer@iu.org

Abstract—**Process Virtualization Theory (PVT) provides a framework for understanding the virtualization of work processes. Recent research underscores the importance of social presence and situation awareness — two critical IT characteristics that support remote interaction. Through a systematic literature review of 32 research articles, this paper examines how collaboration tools enhance virtual teamwork by fostering these IT characteristics, highlighting their role in trust, coordination, and interpersonal connection. Findings suggest that a strategic mix of synchronous and asynchronous communication strengthens both relational bonds and collective awareness. Thus, this paper extends PVT by showing how collaboration tools cultivate social presence and situation awareness, filling an important gap in digital transformation research.**

Keywords—digital transformation; virtual collaboration; process virtualization theory; collaboration tools.

I. INTRODUCTION

Virtual collaboration has become an integral part of organizational operations, driven by advancements in digital communication technologies and further accelerated by the COVID-19 pandemic. Virtual teams have evolved from a niche practice to a widespread organizational norm [1]. The transition from traditional office environments to remote and hybrid models has necessitated the virtualization of work processes, as defined by the Process Virtualization Theory (PVT) [2]. PVT assesses how physical processes translate to virtual settings.

The pandemic-induced shift to remote work challenged existing assumptions about the limitations of virtual processes, demonstrating that even knowledge work processes with high relational demands could be effectively virtualized [3]. This evolution from a temporary adjustment to a new post-pandemic digital era has opened opportunities to re-evaluate how digital tools can support not only operational efficiency but also the social and relational aspects of teamwork. Central to this discussion are the IT characteristics of social presence and situation awareness, which contribute to creating a sense of interpersonal connection and maintaining contextual understanding within remote teams.

Through a systematic literature review, this paper shows how digital communication tools enhance social presence and situation awareness in virtual collaboration, thus contributing to digital transformation research with strategies for remote work. By examining how technology facilitates virtual interactions, this research contributes to the broader discourse on optimizing digital collaboration for the evolving needs of virtual teams.

Following this introduction, Section II anchors the study in PVT and synthesizes prior work on social presence and situation awareness that motivates the review. Section III specifies the systematic review protocol — databases queried, selection criteria, and qualitative analysis — ensuring methodological rigor. Section IV reports the findings in three parts: how collaboration tools foster social presence, how they enhance situation awareness, and finally, how trust links these two mechanisms. Additionally, limitations are addressed. Section V concludes with theoretical and managerial implications and directions for future research.

II. BACKGROUND

A virtual team is defined as a group of individuals who collaborate toward a shared goal while being geographically dispersed, relying primarily on digital technologies to coordinate their work and overcome spatial, temporal, and organizational boundaries [4]. Over the past few decades, growing numbers of employees have worked fully or partially remotely, indicating a steady rise in virtual collaboration [1]. The COVID-19 pandemic, coupled with mandatory remote work policies, accelerated the shift toward both remote and hybrid team structures [5]. As a result, most organizations today exhibit some degree of virtuality, making it increasingly difficult to draw clear distinctions between virtual and non-virtual teams [6].

The virtualization of work processes is a fundamental prerequisite for enabling remote collaboration. PVT provides a theoretical framework for analyzing the digital transformation of business processes by examining the extent to which physical processes can be effectively replicated in virtual environments [2]. At the core of PVT lies the concept of process virtualizability, which determines how well a process can be executed without reliance on physical interactions between individuals or individuals and objects. This concept plays a crucial role in guiding organizations through digital transformation by identifying which processes are most suited for virtualization [7]. Four constructs determine whether a process can be effectively virtualized: sensory, relationship, synchronization, as well as identification and control requirements [2][7]. 'Sensory requirements' address the need to replicate physical experiences; 'relationship requirements' emphasize personal and social interactions; 'synchronization requirements' ensure timely, real-time or sequential execution; and 'identification and control requirements' manage identity verification and oversight mechanisms. These factors negatively affect virtualizability, meaning that as their importance increases, the feasibility of virtualization decreases [2].

PVT's core model highlights three information technology (IT) characteristics that moderate process virtualization. IT characteristics are 'representation', which ensures that virtual processes accurately simulate their physical counterparts; 'reach', which extends accessibility by enabling location-independent participation; and 'monitoring capability', which provides oversight and ensures compliance through remote activity tracking. Building upon these principles, recent research has expanded the application of PVT across various domains. Studies have examined the barriers to process virtualization in remote work environments, revealing that sensory and synchronization requirements often limit the effectiveness of virtualized processes [8]. Further research extends PVT with e-commerce attributes [9] and participant-related factors [10].

The COVID-19 pandemic has provided a unique context for re-evaluating PVT through a crisis-driven perspective [3]. The global health crisis necessitated the rapid virtualization of knowledge work processes, many of which had previously been resistant to digital transformation. As a result of this accelerated transformation, virtualizability evolved from a dependent variable to a determining factor in the fulfillment of process requirements. Organizations increasingly relied on IT characteristics to address these virtualization challenges, leveraging digital tools to simulate sensory elements, facilitate relationship-building, support synchronous interactions, and enhance monitoring capabilities. In this revised understanding of PVT, two additional IT characteristics — social presence and situation awareness — were identified, which further contribute to the effective virtualization of knowledge work processes. Social presence refers to the ability of IT to create a sense of interpersonal connection in virtual settings. The Social Presence Theory states that the degree of perceived psychological and emotional connection between individuals in a mediated communication environment influences the effectiveness and quality of interactions [11][12]. It emphasizes how communication technologies vary in their ability to convey social cues in virtual settings.

Situation awareness — essentially "knowing what is going on" [13] — centers on perceiving relevant context information, interpreting its meaning, and anticipating its future development. When shared among team members, this becomes team situational awareness [3], a collective view of conditions, implications, and likely trajectories that is vital for the relational demands of remote work.

The pandemic has challenged the notion that processes can only be virtualized to a limited extent, as the empirical reality of widespread remote work has shown that IT can indeed support the social aspects of collaboration in virtual teams. While some critiques have underscored that many recommendations overlooked the involuntary nature of pandemic-related remote work [14], now, in the post-pandemic digital era, the urgency to virtualize has receded. This transition creates an opportunity to reflect on progress made in remote collaboration and to reevaluate the potential of collaboration tools through the lens of social presence and situation awareness. Both of these IT characteristics present innovative pathways for understanding how virtual environments can foster not only operational efficiency but also the interpersonal and contextual dimensions of teamwork.

III. METHOD

To gain insights and a wider understanding of the contribution of collaboration tools to social aspects of virtual collaboration, this paper draws on existing literature. This systematic review analyses how digital communication tools shape social presence and situation awareness in virtual teams, addressing the following research questions:

RQ1: In what ways do digital collaboration tools foster social presence in remote settings?

RQ2: In what ways do digital collaboration tools enhance situation awareness in remote teams?

A. Search Strategy

The review applied the structured approach of [15] to address the research questions. The review scope was defined as a summary of previous research activities and their underlying theories on remote work, collaboration tools, and virtual team collaboration [16]. The research covered several relevant databases (ACM, EBSCO, Emerald, IEEE, Science Direct, Springer). The systematic search combined the keywords "collaboration tool," "new work," "remote work," "hybrid work," "team cohesion," "social bonding," "group cohesion," "sense of community," and "virtual team dynamics" with Boolean AND/OR operators to ensure comprehensive, relevant results. Figure 1 summarizes the four-iteration review process and the resulting study counts as proposed by [17].

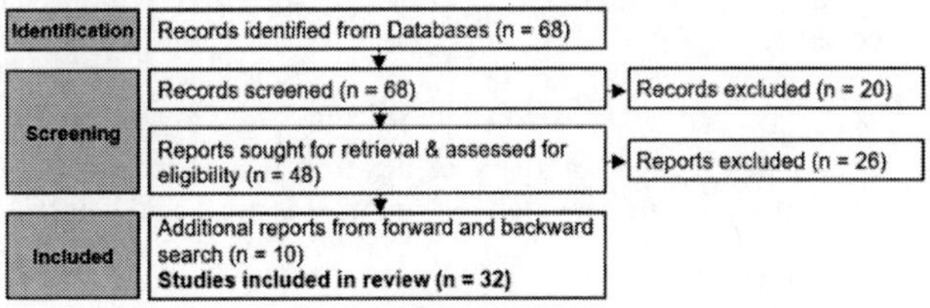

Figure 1: Review Process.

A database search using the predefined terms was followed by abstract screening based on the criteria in Table I, full-text review using the same exclusions, and forward and backward citation tracking, adding ten articles and yielding 32 eligible studies.

TABLE I: EXCLUSION CRITERIA

Exclusion Criteria	• Published before 2010. • No use of collaboration tools. • Focus on teams without a degree of virtuality. • Articles in any other language as German and English.

B. *Data Analysis*

The collected data was analyzed using qualitative content analysis [18]. Recurring themes and patterns were identified that shed light on key factors in the use and effectiveness of collaboration tools for supporting social presence and situation awareness.

Social presence is understood as the degree to which digital communication tools facilitate awareness of the other person and interpersonal relationships during interaction [11]. Accordingly, the category of 'interpersonal relationship/team cohesion' is used. In addition, the review also looks at the concepts of 'collaboration' and 'community/belonging'.

Situation awareness refers to the collective understanding of work dynamics within a team. It is promoted through the provision of information within the team and identified accordingly through the concept of 'knowledge exchange'. In addition, it is primarily shaped by 'informal communication' — accordingly, this forms a further concept.

From the analysis, 'trust' emerged as a relevant concept that is crucial for effective virtual collaboration, so this concept is also taken up in the analysis. The appendix presents the resulting concept matrix, which analyzes the literature and classifies it by research design and type of tool mentioned.

C. *Limitations*

Although this review followed a structured protocol across multiple databases, the reliance on a single researcher remains a significant limitation. Potential selection bias might have affected the breadth and inclusivity of identified studies, as different reviewers could have interpreted inclusion and exclusion criteria differently or identified additional relevant publications. Moreover, focusing on specific search terms may have overlooked research addressing remote collaboration from adjacent perspectives (e.g., organizational psychology, workplace design). Together, these factors could limit the generalizability of the findings and should be considered when interpreting the results.

IV. FINDINGS

A descriptive summary of the findings regarding social presence, situation awareness, and trust is presented below.

A. *Social Presence*

Social presence is a critical factor in virtual collaboration. Many studies emphasize that digital platforms can be designed to foster the feeling of togetherness typically experienced in face-to-face settings. Synchronous communication tools, such as video conferencing and instant messaging, have been found to be particularly effective at cultivating social presence by enabling immediate, reciprocal interaction and conveying rich social cues (e.g., facial expressions and gestures), all of which are vital for establishing and maintaining interpersonal bonds [19][20]. Immersive digital environments, such as virtual workspaces and avatars, can further strengthen this sense of connection by simulating physical co-presence, thereby enhancing engagement and team cohesion [21][22]. For instance, the platform Gather lets remote colleagues initiate spontaneous interactions by virtually approaching one another [22]. This ability for rapid, informal encounters can mitigate the isolation that often arises in remote settings [20][23][24].

The Embodied Social Presence Theory (ESPT) suggests that virtual workspaces should replicate key aspects of physical interaction to improve communication, particularly by enabling participants to interpret nonverbal signals even in digital environments [21]. Through the use of synchronous video tools and virtual reality platforms, ESPT's focus on embodied co-presence reduces ambiguity in remote interactions and reinforces interpersonal relationships.

Some authors emphasize that organizational culture and shared values can be reinforced through collaboration tools when they are used for team-building events, recognition programs, and personal updates [25]. Similarly, planned informal interactions can improve social presence by compensating for the lack of casual conversations in the corridor [26]; teams that allocate time for social check-ins tend to feel more aligned and engaged. Studies further highlight the importance of intentional, well-structured digital communication to replicate the camaraderie of co-located offices [27][28]. Frequent touchpoints, such as virtual coffee chats and informal Slack channels, help remote employees preserve a communal sense of identity [23][26]. Meanwhile, personalized introductions — including Asynchronous Semi-Guided Professional Introductions (ASGPIs) — facilitate the exchange of personal and professional information, thereby strengthening interpersonal connections [20].

It is also recognized that even asynchronous tools can support social presence by enabling indirect reciprocity and sustained connections over time, yet their overall impact is constrained by the absence of immediate interaction and emotional engagement [21]. However, studies indicate that an overreliance on asynchronous communication can lead to feelings of social isolation and a reduced sense of belonging, particularly in teams that lack prior face-to-face interactions [25]. The literature stresses that choosing the right mix of synchronous and asynchronous channels is vital for sustaining high-quality interactions [24][29]. Platforms, such as Slack, Teams, Gather, or Zoom, allow for both project-focused conversations and casual "break room" chats [30]. This multimodal approach ensures that teams can adapt their communication methods to both the complexity and urgency of tasks [19]. Well-timed, media-rich interactions, like video-based calls early in a team's lifecycle, foster personal rapport, while text-based channels and shared documents suffice for routine status updates [29][31]. This provides a direct link and a transition to situation awareness.

B. *Situation Awareness*

While social presence fosters emotional connection, situation awareness centers on the ability to stay informed about colleagues' work progress, needs, and challenges in real time, essential for coordinating team efforts and ensuring alignment. While traditional offices often rely on spontaneous observations and overheard conversations [32], remote work environments lack these spontaneous exchanges and must adopt purposeful strategies to maintain comparable levels of context [33]. The inability to observe colleagues' work activities or engage in impromptu discussions often leads to knowledge silos and reduced collaboration efficiency [34]. In addition, [35] found that virtual team members often hesitate to seek help because problems are harder to explain and responses are slower. To counteract these effects, many teams have adapted their communication practices by integrating asynchronous chat tools, such as Slack, which facilitate real-time knowledge exchange despite physical separation [26]. Tools, such as email, shared documents, and discussion forums, contribute to collaboration by supporting structured information exchange and enabling parallel collaboration [19][36].

It is underlined that knowledge sharing keeps remote teams aligned and efficient [37]. Similarly, [24] argues that social support, which includes knowledge-sharing practices, strengthens connectivity and reduces workplace stress, fostering a more cohesive understanding of team dynamics. Furthermore, [36] describes that mutual exchange of knowledge builds trust and reinforces collective competence. The authors highlight the significance of informal knowledge exchange in virtual environments, where psychological safety plays a crucial role in facilitating open discussions and information flow. For example, short, informal encounters or informal side chats during official meetings allow members to ask quick questions, seek clarifications, or exchange immediate feedback, much as they might in the physical workspace [26][34]. Additionally, these ongoing knowledge exchanges, whether over group messaging or video calls, counteract the risk of isolation and misalignment [26][31].

According to [29], well-structured check-ins and routine status updates via shared platforms help team members anticipate when others might need assistance. This transparency not only aids productivity but can also reduce stress and foster mutual trust, as teams learn to predict and fill potential gaps [27][29][38]. This more flexible backup behavior can also be enabled by "total information awareness" — circulating relevant communications to all team members, even those not directly involved [39]. Such communication practices are linked to outcomes like improved team performance [36], while consistent rules, norms, and leadership behaviors can further reinforce positive team functioning in virtual contexts [28][40][41]. However, [35] emphasizes that virtual teams must deliberately invest in relationship-building. For example, proactively introducing newcomers through informal sessions can foster familiarity even faster than in co-located teams.

C. *Trust*

Trust is a fundamental prerequisite for the effectiveness of virtual teams, closely linked to social presence and situation awareness. Occasional face-to-face meetings or richer social engagement can significantly enhance trust. Even a brief in-person kickoff fosters early trust that carries into online collaboration [42]. When in-person interaction is not feasible, virtual teambuilding events, informal chats, or open channels can help create spontaneous bonding moments, reinforcing interpersonal connections [35][43]. Then, technology must support both task-related and relational exchanges to facilitate trust [44]. Trust and team cohesion are highly interdependent: When early trust is established, cohesive collaboration develops more easily, whereas low initial trust complicates maintaining unity across geographic and temporal divides [42]. Similarly, [38] highlights that without deliberate efforts to foster socio-emotional bonds, relationships between subordinates and managers can deteriorate in purely virtual settings, further undermining trust.

In the context of social presence, shared emotional cues, authentic self-disclosure, and informal interactions foster affective trust. High-synchronicity media convey nonverbal cues that help team members assess intentions, while excessive asynchronous text communication can undermine trust due to misinterpretation [19]. A well-balanced media strategy that supports both structured collaboration and spontaneous social contact strengthens trust at the group level [30][36].

From a situation awareness perspective, low trust hampers information flow, as individuals hesitate to disclose difficulties or seek help in perceived hostile environments. Weak trust discourages transparent data sharing due to fears of appearing incompetent or misusing sensitive information [39]. Conversely, high-trust teams proactively coordinate, offer support, and monitor emerging challenges, enhancing performance in remote settings [29][42]. At the leadership level, trust mitigates the "invisibility problem" in remote work, enabling fair treatment, nonintrusive oversight, and accountability without micromanagement [14][38][45].

In sum, while social presence creates the emotional conditions under which trust thrives, situation awareness ensures that group members have enough insight into one another's actions and challenges to uphold a trustworthy, dependable workflow. Tying these two elements together, trust becomes the linchpin that channels technological affordances into truly cohesive remote teamwork

V. Conclusion and Future Work

This research demonstrates that thoughtful applied collaboration tools can replicate many of the relational and informational aspects of co-located work. Key strategies include informal virtual gatherings, immersive technologies, and personalized introductions that foster interpersonal connection [20][21][26]. Transparent communication and leadership support, through regular check-ins and structured feedback, are equally important for cultivating trust and reinforcing a supportive organizational culture [28][46]. Teams benefit from structured yet informal exchanges and real-time collaboration platforms that sustain project visibility and cohesive teamwork [26][34].

Nevertheless, technology remains only one pillar; clearly defined channel norms, active leadership, and periodic face-to-face encounters are still necessary to deepen trust and creativity, making hybrid collaboration the most resilient operating model [14][27][32][42][47][48].

Practitioners should adopt platforms that combine rich real-time interaction with asynchronous flexibility and embed visibility features — presence indicators, shared task boards, and sentiment dashboards — to increase situation awareness and social presence [27][32][49].

Tool developers should design configurable mixed-synchronicity architectures and trust-enhancing affordances, such as privacy-aware analytics and seamless transitions between immersive and text modes. This will allow teams to adjust interaction richness as projects evolve [48].

Future research opportunities lie in controlled and longitudinal experiments that go beyond description to isolate the causal effects of specific platform features on outcomes such as trust building, knowledge sharing, and team performance [29]. Comparative studies across industries and cultural contexts, supplemented by in-situ and neurophysiological measures, could further reveal boundary conditions of PVT and illuminate how social presence and situation awareness dynamically co-evolve. Advancing these agendas will yield collaboration ecosystems that not only virtualize processes but actively cultivate the human connections on which effective teamwork depends.

REFERENCES

[1] J. M. Barrero, N. Bloom, and S. J. Davis, "The Evolution of Work from Home," *Journal of Economic Perspectives*, vol. 37, no. 4, pp. 23–49, Nov. 2023, doi: 10.1257/jep.37.4.23

[2] E. Overby, "Process Virtualization Theory and the Impact of Information Technology," *Organization Science*, vol. 19, no. 2, pp. 277–291, Mar. 2008, doi: 10.1287/orsc.1070.0316

[3] A. Zeuge *et al.*, "Crisis-driven digital transformation as a trigger for process virtualization: Fulfilling knowledge work process requirements for remote work," *International Journal of Information Management*, vol. 70, 102636, Jun. 2023, doi: 10.1016/j.ijinfomgt.2023.102636

[4] J. Lipnack and J. Stamps, "Virtual teams: The new way to work," *Strategy & Leadership*, vol. 27, no. 1, pp. 14–19, Jan. 1999, doi: 10.1108/eb054625

[5] M. Sako, "From remote work to working from anywhere," *Commun. ACM*, vol. 64, no. 4, pp. 20–22, Apr. 2021, doi: 10.1145/3451223

[6] S. Zheng *et al.*, "Understanding the positive and negative effects of team virtuality: A theoretical review and research agenda," *Human Resource Management Review*, vol. 34, no. 2, 101013, Jun. 2024, doi: 10.1016/j.hrmr.2024.101013

[7] E. Overby, "Migrating Processes from Physical to Virtual Environments: Process Virtualization Theory," in *Information Systems Theory*, Y. K. Dwivedi, M. R. Wade, and S. L. Schneberger, Eds., in Integrated Series in Information Systems, vol. 28. New York, NY: Springer New York, 2012, pp. 107–124. doi: 10.1007/978-1-4419-6108-2_6

[8] Y. Feng, J. Park, and M. Feng, "What is holding back business process virtualization in the post-COVID-19 era? Based on process virtualization theory (PVT)," *Front. Psychol.*, vol. 14, Feb. 2023, doi: 10.3389/fpsyg.2023.1084180

[9] M. Barth and D. Veit, "Which Processes Do Users Not Want Online? Extending Process Virtualization Theory," *ICIS 2011 Proceedings*, Dec. 2011.

[10] B. Balci and C. Rosenkranz, "'Virtual or material, What do You Prefer?' a Study of Process Virtualization Theory," *ECIS 2014 Proceedings*, Jun. 2014.

[11] J. Fulk, J. Schmitz, and C. W. Steinfeld, "A Social Influence Model of Technology Use," in *Organizations and Communication Technology*, Newbury Park, London, New Delhi: Sage Publications, 1990.

[12] J. Short, E. Williams, and B. Christie, "The social psychology of telecommunications." John Wiley, 1976.

[13] M. R. Endsley, "Toward a Theory of Situation Awareness in Dynamic Systems," *Hum Factors*, vol. 37, no. 1, pp. 32–64, Mar. 1995, doi: 10.1518/001872095779049543

[14] S. Torres and M. A. Orhan, "How it started, how it's going: Why past research does not encompass pandemic-induced remote work realities and what leaders can do for more inclusive remote work practices," *Psychology of Leaders and Leadership*, vol. 26, no. 1, pp. 1–21, 2023, doi: 10.1037/mgr0000135

[15] J. vom Brocke *et al.*, "Reconstructing the giant: On the importance of rigour in documenting the literature search process," in *17th European Conference on Information Systems, ECIS 2009*, 2009, pp. 2206–2217.

[16] H. M. Cooper, "Organizing knowledge syntheses: A taxonomy of literature reviews," *Knowledge in society*, vol. 1, no. 1, pp. 104–126, Jan. 1988.

[17] M. J. Page *et al.*, "The PRISMA 2020 statement: an updated guideline for reporting systematic reviews," *BMJ*, n71, Mar. 2021, doi: 10.1136/bmj.n71

[18] U. Kuckartz, *Qualitative Inhaltsanalyse. Methoden, Praxis, Computerunterstützung (Qualitative content analysis. Methods, practice, computer support)*, 4., Überarbeitete Aufl. in Grundlagentexte Methoden. Weinheim: Beltz, 2018.

[19] O. Torro, H. Pirkkalainen, and H. Li, "Media synchronicity in organizational social exchange," *ITP*, vol. 35, no. 8, pp. 162–180, Dec. 2022, doi: 10.1108/ITP-06-2020-0384

[20] G. C. Muresan, S. Mititelu, J. Andres, and M. C. Schraefel, "'Should I Introduce myself?': Asynchronous semi-guided professional introductions for enhanced perceived team effectiveness in new virtual dyadic teams," *International Journal of Human-Computer Studies*, vol. 188, 103279, Aug. 2024, doi: 10.1016/j.ijhcs.2024.103279

[21] J. Yang and H. Fang, "Integrating Embodied Social Presence Theory and Process Virtualization Theory to assess business process virtualizability: The mediating role of embodied co-presence," *PLoS ONE*, vol. 19, no. 6, e0305423, Jun. 2024, doi: 10.1371/journal.pone.0305423

[22] L. Okpara, C. Werner, A. Murray, and D. Damian, "The role of informal communication in building shared understanding of non-functional requirements in remote continuous software engineering," *Requirements Eng*, vol. 28, no. 4, pp. 595–617, Dec. 2023, doi: 10.1007/s00766-023-00404-z

[23] S. Bilderback and M. D. Kilpatrick, "Global perspectives on redefining workplace presence: the impact of remote work on organizational culture," *JEET*, vol. 4, no. 1, pp. 62–72, Oct. 2024, doi: 10.1108/JEET-08-2024-0023

[24] K.-L. Tan *et al.*, "Beyond laptops and tables: unveiling Singapore's success in hybrid work through a two-wave gender multigroup analysis of compassionate leadership," *ER*, vol. 47, no. 1, pp. 148–172, Jan. 2025, doi: 10.1108/ER-02-2024-0108

[25] A. Asatiani and L. Norström, "Information systems for sustainable remote workplaces," *The Journal of Strategic Information Systems*, vol. 32, no. 3, 101789, Sep. 2023, doi: 10.1016/j.jsis.2023.101789

[26] A. Whillans, L. Perlow, and A. Turek, "Experimenting during the shift to virtual team work: Learnings from how teams adapted their activities during the COVID-19 pandemic," *Information and Organization*, vol. 31, no. 1, 100343, Mar. 2021, doi: 10.1016/j.infoandorg.2021.100343

[27] E. De Bruyne and D. Gerritse, "Exploring the future workplace: results of the futures forum study," *JCRE*, vol. 20, no. 3, pp. 196–213, Nov. 2018, doi: 10.1108/JCRE-09-2017-0030

[28] C. Mayer, T. Sivatheerthan, S. Mütze-Niewöhner, and V. Nitsch, "Sharing leadership behaviors in virtual teams: effects of shared leadership behaviors on team member satisfaction and productivity," *TPM*, vol. 29, no. 1/2, pp. 90–112, Feb. 2023, doi: 10.1108/TPM-07-2022-0054

[29] L. L. Gilson, P. Costa, T. A. O'Neill, and M. T. Maynard, "Putting the 'TEAM' back into virtual teams," *Organizational Dynamics*, vol. 50, no. 1, 100847, Jan. 2021, doi: 10.1016/j.orgdyn.2021.100847

[30] C. Miller *et al.*, "'How Was Your Weekend?' Software Development Teams Working From Home During COVID-19," in *2021 IEEE/ACM 43rd International Conference on Software Engineering (ICSE)*, May 2021, pp. 624–636. doi: 10.1109/ICSE43902.2021.00064

[31] A. Alaiad, Y. Alnsour, and M. Alsharo, "Virtual Teams: Thematic Taxonomy, Constructs Model, and Future Research Directions," *IEEE Transactions on Professional Communication*, vol. 62, no. 3, pp. 211–238, Sep. 2019, doi: 10.1109/TPC.2019.2929370

[32] M. Landowski *et al.*, "Beyond Hallway Chats ? Negotiating Content Awareness in Hybrid Work Practices," in *Proceedings of Mensch und Computer 2024*, Karlsruhe Germany: ACM, Sep. 2024, pp. 508–513. doi: 10.1145/3670653.3677523

[33] T. Losev, S. Storteboom, S. Carpendale, and S. Knudsen, "Distributed Synchronous Visualization Design: Challenges and Strategies," in *2020 IEEE Workshop on Evaluation and Beyond - Methodological Approaches to Visualization (BELIV)*, Salt Lake City, UT, USA: IEEE, Oct. 2020, pp. 1–10. doi: 10.1109/BELIV51497.2020.00008

[34] B. Viererbl, N. Denner, and T. Koch, "'You don't meet anybody when walking from the living room to the kitchen': informal communication during remote work," *JCOM*, vol. 26, no. 3, pp. 331–348, Aug. 2022, doi: 10.1108/JCOM-10-2021-0117

[35] A. Lechner and J. Tobias Mortlock, "How to create psychological safety in virtual teams," *Organizational Dynamics*, vol. 51, no. 2, 100849, Apr. 2022, doi: 10.1016/j.orgdyn.2021.100849

[36] M. Mahtta *et al.*, "A pathway to virtual team performance in the New Normal paradigm," *JOEPP*, vol. 9, no. 4, pp. 549–571, Sep. 2022, doi: 10.1108/JOEPP-11-2020-0218

[37] I. Wahl, D. Wolfgruber, and S. Einwiller, "Mitigating teleworkers' perceived technological complexity and work strains through supportive team communication," *CCIJ*, vol. 29, no. 3, pp. 329–345, Apr. 2024, doi: 10.1108/CCIJ-05-2023-0061

[38] T. D. Golden and A. Fromen, "Does it matter where your manager works? Comparing managerial work mode (traditional, telework, virtual) across subordinate work experiences and outcomes," *Human Relations*, vol. 64, pp. 1451–1475, Nov. 2011, doi: 10.1177/0018726711418387

[39] J. V. Dinh *et al.*, "Developing team trust: Leader insights for virtual settings," *Organizational Dynamics*, vol. 50, no. 1, 2021, doi: 10.1016/j.orgdyn.2021.100846

[40] E. Raguseo, L. Gastaldi, and P. Neirotti, "Smart work: Supporting employees' flexibility through ICT, HR practices and office layout," *EBHRM*, vol. 4, no. 3, pp. 240–256, Dec. 2016, doi: 10.1108/EBHRM-01-2016-0004

[41] S. A. Newman and R. C. Ford, "Five Steps to Leading Your Team in the Virtual COVID-19 Workplace," *Organ Dyn*, vol. 50, no. 1, 100802, 2021, doi: 10.1016/j.orgdyn.2020.100802

[42] R. Paul, J. R. Drake, and H. Liang, "Global Virtual Team Performance: The Effect of Coordination Effectiveness, Trust, and Team Cohesion," *IEEE Transactions on Professional Communication*, vol. 59, no. 3, pp. 186–202, Sep. 2016, doi: 10.1109/TPC.2016.2583319

[43] A. S. L. De Andrade, V. Jackson, R. Prikladnicki, and A. Van Der Hoek, "On meetings involving remote software teams: A systematic literature review," *Information and Software Technology*, vol. 175, 107541, Nov. 2024, doi: 10.1016/j.infsof.2024.107541

[44] L. S. Müller, S. Reiners, J. Becker, and G. Hertel, "Long-term effects of COVID-19 on work routines and organizational culture – A case study within higher education's administration," *Journal of Business Research*, vol. 163, 113927, Aug. 2023, doi: 10.1016/j.jbusres.2023.113927

[45] L. Chernyak-Hai and E. Rabenu, "The New Era Workplace Relationships: Is Social Exchange Theory Still Relevant?," *Ind. Organ. Psychol.*, vol. 11, no. 3, pp. 456–481, Sep. 2018, doi: 10.1017/iop.2018.5

[46] K. Tworek, "E-leadership shaped by IT adaptability through Employees' Dynamic Capabilities," *Procedia Computer Science*, vol. 225, pp. 357–365, 2023, doi: 10.1016/j.procs.2023.10.020

[47] M. Marinho *et al.*, "Happier and further by going together: The importance of software team behaviour during the COVID-19 pandemic," *Technology in Society*, vol. 67, 101799, Nov. 2021, doi: 10.1016/j.techsoc.2021.101799

[48] R. Gong and M. Hua, "Designing Multimodal User Interfaces for Hybrid Collaboration: A User-Centered Approach," in *HCI International 2023 – Late Breaking Papers*, M. Kurosu, A. Hashizume, A. Marcus, E. Rosenzweig, M. M. Soares, D. Harris, W.-C. Li, D. D. Schmorrow, C. M. Fidopiastis, and P.-L. P. Rau, Eds., in Lecture Notes in Computer Science, vol. 14054. Cham: Springer Nature Switzerland, 2023, pp. 67–82. doi: 10.1007/978-3-031-48038-6_5

[49] L. Liu, H. Van Essen, and B. Eggen, "An exploratory study of how to design interventions to support informal communication in remote work," in *Nordic Human-Computer Interaction Conference*, Aarhus Denmark: ACM, Oct. 2022, pp. 1–10. doi: 10.1145/3546155.3546673

APPENDIX

TABLE A: CONCEPT MATRIX.

Article	Classification		Concepts					
	Research Design	**Tool-Types mentioned**	**Social Presence**			**Situation awareness**		**Trust**
			Interpersonal Relationship/ Team Cohesion	***Collaboration***	***Community/ belonging***	***Knowledge exchange***	***Informal Communication***	
[14]	REV	Vid, Pl	x		x		x	x
[19]	REV + CON	VR,Vid,Ch	x	x	x			x
[20]	CON	Vid, Pl	x	x	x	x	x	x
[21]	CON	Pl	x		x			
[22]	Q	VR, Vid, Ch, Pl	x	x	x		x	
[23]	CON	Pl	x		x		x	
[24]	QU	Vid, Ch	x		x	x		x
[25]	REV	Pl, Em	x		x	x	x	x
[26]	Q	Vid, Ch, Em	x				x	
[27]	Q	Pl	x	x	x		x	
[28]	QA	ND	x	x	x			x
[29]	REV	Vid, Ch, Pl, Em					x	x
[30]	QM	Ch, NT	x				x	
[31]	REV	VR, Vid, Ch, Pl, Em	x	x		x		x
[32]	Q	VD	x				x	
[33]	Q	Vid, Ch, Pl, Ph	x	x				x
[34]	Q	Vid, Ch, Em, Ph	x		x		x	
[35]	Q	VR, Vid, Ch, Em	x			x	x	x
[36]	Q	Vid, PL	x	x		x		x
[37]	QU	Vid, Ch, Pl, Em, Ph				x		x
[38]	QU	Em, Ph, ND	x				x	x
[39]	REV + Q	Vid, Em	x	x	x		x	x
[40]	QM	ND		x	x			
[41]	CON	Vid, Ch, Pl, Em, Ph	x	x	x		x	x
[42]	REV + QU	Vid, Ch, Pl, Em	x					x
[43]	RE	VR, Vid, Ch, Pl, Em	x	x	x		x	x
[44]	Q	Vid, Ch, Pl, Em, Ph	x	x		x		x
[45]	CON	Pl						x
[46]	QU	Vid, Ch, Pl		x	x	x		
[47]	QU	Vid, Ch, Pl,	x	x			x	
[48]	CON	Vid, Ch, Pl, Em, Ph	x	x				x
[49]	Q + CON	Vid, Ch					x	
Σ *(Research Design/ Tool-Types/ Segments with concept)*	Q = 10 CON = 8 REV = 7 QU = 6 **QM = 2** **EXP = 0**	Vid = 22 Pl = 18 Em = 13 Ch= 15 Ph = 7 **VR = 5** ND = 3	85	28	36	16	106	53

Classification legend:
Research Design: Q = Qualitative, QU = Quantitative, QM = Mixed, EXP = Experiment, REV = Review/Meta-Analysis, CON = Conceptional/Design Science
Tool-Type: VR = Virtual Reality, Vid = Video, Ch = Chat, Pl = Platform-Suite, Em = e-mail, Ph = Phone, ND = not defined

What Do Young Adults Expect from Social Robots?

Zühal Erden
Mechatronics Engineering Department
Atilim University
Ankara, Türkiye
e-mail: zuhal.erden@atilim.edu.tr

Çiğdem Turhan
Software Engineering Department
Atilim University
Ankara, Türkiye
e-mail: cigdem.turhan@atilim.edu.tr

Abstract—**Personalization of social robots depends on the identification of different characteristics and preferences of the users and, thus, creating a more efficient and adoptable usage/collaboration experience. The first and most important step of the social robot design for specific user groups is determining, analyzing, and learning their preferences and habits. In this paper, the expectations of young adult users between the ages of 18-39 from social robots were investigated using structured interviews. Statistical and qualitative analysis of the obtained results reveal the importance of four dimensions in designing social robots for the specified user category: (1) Routine Task, Education and Learning Support, (2) Mental, Social and Emotional Interaction, (3) Ethics and Privacy, and (4) Physical and Behavioral Design.**

Keywords-social robot; user-centered design; young adult; design dimension.

I. Introduction

Social robots which aim to offer cognitive support and assistance to humans with meaningful interactions are seen as one of the most transformative technologies of the future [1]. With human-like features, such as speech, emotion, face, and object recognition along with other artificial intelligence-related abilities, social robots are increasingly being utilized for therapy, education, and entertainment [2], [3].

In 2008, Microsoft founder Bill Gates predicted that as robots become affordable to consumers, they will change how individuals communicate, entertain, learn, and work at home [4]. In parallel with this prediction, in 2025, Tesla founder Elon Musk projected that they aim to manufacture 500,000 humanoid robots in three years and that 10 billion humanoid robots will exist by 2040 costing 20-25 dollars [5], [6].

The recent advances in new technologies, such as Generative Artificial Intelligence and the global increase in the aging population have directly affected the interest in social robots with many studies investigating the acceptance and effects of social robots on different user groups. For example, in their research, Søraa et al. [7] examine whether older adult users are properly included in the user-centered approach to robot development. Pu et al. [8] investigate the effectiveness of social robots on the physiological and psychological outcomes of older adults with randomized controlled trials. In another study, the functional and non-functional requirements of an assistive system for the home care of elderly patients with neurological impairments have been examined [9].

Other studies focus on the utilization of social robots for children. Kanero et al. [10] review the literature on child–robot interaction for language learning in young children. In another study, the relationship formation between children and social robots is investigated [11]. Finally, the influence of a social robot modeling prosocial behavior on children is examined by Peter et al. [1].

As shown by the existing literature, social robots have gained significant attention in recent years, especially in education, healthcare, and elderly care in domestic settings [2]. Yet, the consumer interest and expectations from social robots for the other adult population groups have not been studied extensively. Further research is required to understand the human needs and interests of diverse adult population groups, as social robots are anticipated to integrate into societal frameworks for the near future. These investigations will be important to ensure that the development and deployment of these technologies align with the expectations and requirements of various demographic groups [12].

To address this gap, the present study aims to explore the requirements and expectations of the younger population in the age range of 18-39. For this purpose, structured interviews were conducted with a sample of 83 participants to identify the tasks they envision social robots performing and the features they desire such robots to possess. The differences between the genders were also investigated statistically and qualitatively. Based on the findings, the main dimensions for designing personalized social robots for young adults are explored along with their key considerations. Hopefully, the outcomes of this study will provide insight to social robot designers and developers as more social robots are developed for all age groups.

The rest of the paper is structured as follows: Section II introduces the methodology; Section III presents the quantitative analysis of the interview results; Section IV describes important qualitative findings obtained from the user interviews; Section V proposes main dimensions to design personalized social robots for young adults; finally, the work is concluded in Section VI.

II. Methodology

In this study, data was collected via structured face-to-face interviews conducted within the framework of predetermined questions. The interview questions are provided in Table 1. The first three questions are open-ended focusing on the young adults' requirements in terms of roles, tasks, and capabilities of social robots, whereas the remaining two are multiple-choice type closed questions investigating the young adults' preferences for social robots. As a result of the interviews, participants' preferences on the social robots' tasks and features are obtained.

TABLE I. THE QUESTIONS IN THE STRUCTURED INTERVIEWS

No	Question
1	What role(s)do you expect a social robot to play in your daily life?
2	What are the 3 most important tasks you want the robot to perform?
3	What are the most important features or capabilities you want the robot to have?
4	Would you like to have a social robot designed according to your personal preferences and needs?
5	Do you want the robot to recognize you or your family members?

In total, 83 young-adult people within the age range of 18-39 participated in the study and all of them were provided informed consent for the anonymous use of their data. Approval of the research was obtained from the Institutional Ethical Review Board of Atilim University. The results of the structured interviews were then statistically and qualitatively analyzed leading to the development of a conceptual framework for social robot design dimensions for young adults which will be described in detail in the following sections

III. Statistical (Quantitative) Analysis

Structured interviews were conducted on 83 participants within the age range of 18 to 39. The gender distribution of the participants is given in Table 2. In the structured interview, the participants were inquired about the tasks they would prefer the social robot to be able to perform.

TABLE II. TABLE TYPE STYLES

Gender	Count	Percentage
Male	51	61,45%
Female	32	38,55%

As illustrated in Figure 1, the two most preferred tasks were those of assistant and house chores. The assistant task was chosen by 59% of the participants representing a significant margin while the house chores task was favored by nearly half of the participants (49%). According to the responses of the participants, the constituents of the tasks can be seen in Table 3.

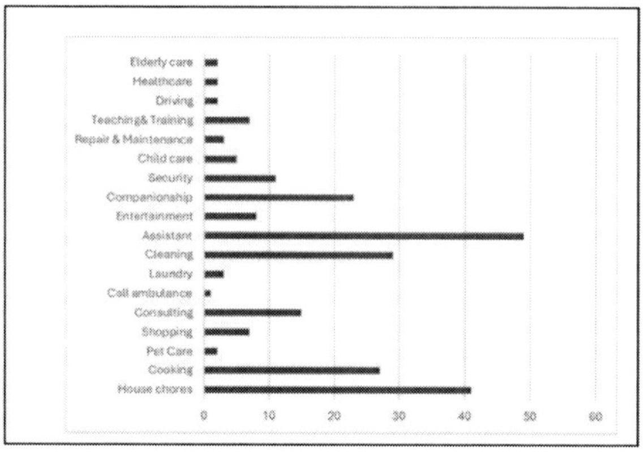

Figure 1. Task preferences of the participants.

TABLE III. CONSTITUENTS OF THE TASKS

Task	House chores	Assistant	Consulting	Teaching& Training	Cooking	Entertainment	Security
Elements	Wash dishes	Reminding	Recommendation	Diet coaching	Make coffee	Play games	Check oven
	Make bed	Alarm	Answer questions	Sports coaching	Make break-fast	Play music	Check risky places
	Tidy the house	Daily plans	Decide what to wear	Language tutoring			
	Turn off lights	Time management					
	Bring drinks	Personal care (hair, makeup)					
	Ironing	Research					
	Fold laundry	Grade homeworks					
	Carry items						

In addition, the participant responses for task preferences were statistically analyzed based on gender where they were initially converted to their percentage values to generate standardized results.

As shown in Figure 2, the assistant task is preferred by the female participants by a wide margin. Male participants showed a greater interest in tasks related to shopping, entertainment, security, and healthcare, whereas female participants demonstrated a stronger preference for tasks involving cleaning, household chores, companionship, and the care of the elderly and children.

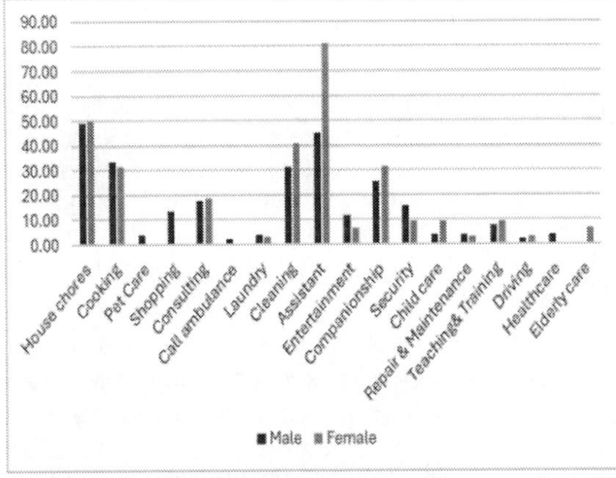

Figure 2. Task preferences according to gender.

The preferred features of social robots were also investigated in this study. As illustrated in Figure 3, the most requested features were for the social robot to talk and communicate through speech, to exhibit empathy and emotional intelligence and possess security and privacy features. The feature preferences according to gender were also investigated and the results are shown in Figure 4.

The features where there were differences in the preference of genders were as follows. Male participants were more interested in a small and quiet social robot prioritizing security and privacy, having fast and long-lasting charge, capable of multimodal interaction. On the other hand, female contributors focus more on the social robot displaying empathy and emotional intelligence with problem solving skills and quick response features.

IV. QUALITATIVE ANALYSIS

The qualitative findings obtained from the user interviews in this study are presented in this section based on all questions. The interview results revealed that young adults have expectations from social robots in three main themes: making life easier, emotional and mental support, and physical and behavioral features. These themes are explained below and sample comments obtained from the user interviews for each theme are presented as an excerpt in quotation.

A. *Support for easy life*

Young people expect social robots to make their lives easier and save them time by performing monotonous and routine tasks that they need to do. For example, while some participants stated these requests in general terms as "Doing routine tasks for me and saving me time", "Representing me in various environments" and "Making my life easier", other participants expressed them with much more specific and defined expressions, such as "Being able to do monotonous, periodically required tasks and meetings", "Entering classes and taking notes, signing for me", "Earning money for me (by doing extra work)" and "Doing homework and similar things for me". The expectations stated in this group also revealed the need for social robots to learn habits or routines and act accordingly. For example, while some participants stated their general requests as "Following personal routines" and "Learning my habits", another expressed a similar request much more clearly as "Remembering past teachings (favorite table in the restaurant)".

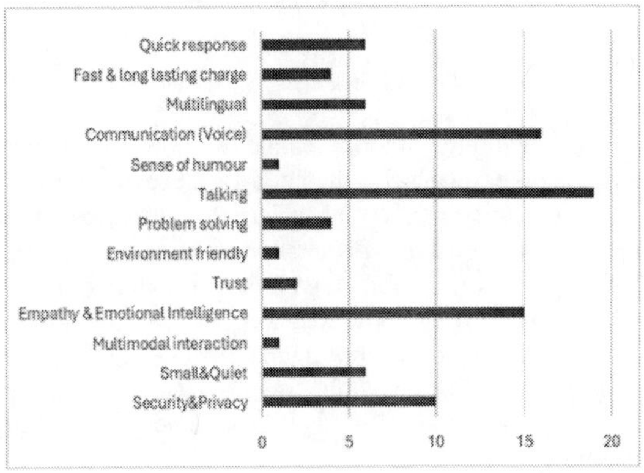

Figure 3. Feature preferences of the participants.

B. *Emotional and mental support*

Among the expectations of the participants from social robots, emotional and mental support also have an important place. In this category, all participants stated their expectations regarding the request for mental support. For example, an interesting expression used by one participant, "Let it be a second brain, like my clone", expresses this need. A similar demand is also seen in the sentence "It should be able to transfer the information it acquires to my brain by telepathic method" by another participant. Some participants stated that they expected a rather standard level of mental support with expressions, such as "Budget planning, ability to make investments", "Plan and remember instead of me" and "Make my day more productive". One participant's specific expectation from the social robot was "Helping to socialize". In this category, it is observed that there are differences in the expectations of male and female participants regarding emotional support.

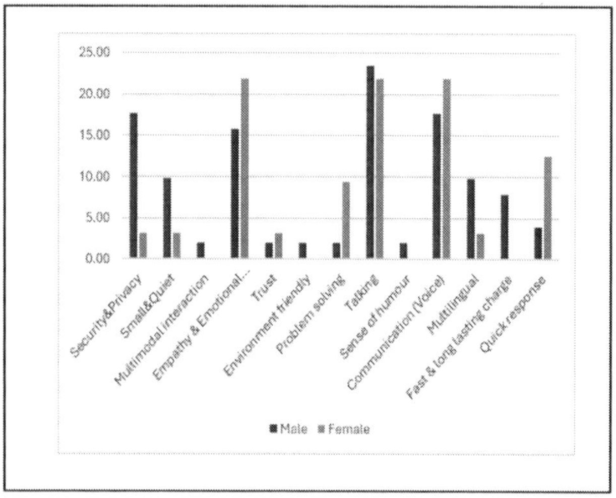

Figure 4. Feature preferences according to gender.

For example, among female participants, there is an expression emphasizing the need for "Providing mental and emotional support". Another female participant expressed the importance of emotional support from social robots and her expectation in this regard as "Providing morale and motivation". Male participants generally do not demand emotional and moral support, and some, even, have opposite expectations. For example, one of the male participants stated that a social robot should be "unemotional and have no empathy".

C. Behavioural features

Participants stated various expectations regarding the behavioral characteristics of social robots. The most requested one is that social robots work in integration and cooperation with other systems. For example, expressions, such as "Home management integrated with smart home systems", "Integration with the devices I use", or "Working in harmony with other electronic devices" used by the participants express this important expectation. Among the expectations, demands, such as "Analyzing what I say and do" and "Improving itself by learning" show that the participants generally expect social robots to be intelligent and able to learn. For example, expressions, such as "Recognizing guests" or "Being able to think" also support this expectation. Young adults expect mental support from social robots, learning many tasks, performing them autonomously, and thus making life easier. On the other hand, statements, such as "Not disturbing", "Not being too smart", and "Turning off all functions" also show that they want to control the social robots. Participants are also sensitive about the environmental friendliness of social robots. For example, while one participant said, "It completes business processes in an environmentally friendly manner," another emphasized environmental sensitivity by defining the most important features of the robot as "Empathy, trust, and being environmentally friendly." Young participants also expressed the need for intelligent, witty, and skillful social robots with expressions, such as "It should be humorous" and "It should be quick-witted, fast, and agile," sensitive to fragile social groups with the expression "It helps the disabled," and reliable with the expression "It should not perceive me or my loved ones as a threat." Some participants emphasized their expectations regarding the structure and situation-behavior of social robots by using expressions, such as "Warning and assistance in natural disasters," "Arms and legs," and "Doing sports." The comments of young adults between the ages of 18-39, who were considered as the focus group in this research, exemplified under the 3 categories above, reveal the need for a great deal of behavioral personalization of the design of social robots.

V. CONCEPTUAL STRUCTURING OF SOCIAL ROBOT DESIGN DIMENSIONS FOR YOUNG ADULTS

The data obtained from the present research reveals four main dimensions to design personalized social robots for young adults. The key considerations of each dimension that can be addressed in social robot design are depicted in Figure 5 and explained below.

A. Dimension 1: Routine task, education and learning support

One of the most important expectations of young adults from social robots is to take on routine tasks and save time for learning and self-development. Therefore, it would be useful for social robot designers to understand, classify, and prioritize the specified routine tasks in detail and consider them in designing social robots, accordingly. How social robots can improve the learning experiences of young users, how to find the most effective ways to provide personalized education or mentoring for this purpose and how to design robots accordingly, how to encourage and develop creativity and critical thinking in young people with the support of social robots can be considered as design requirements.

B. Dimension 2: Mental, social and emotional interaction

Young users expect assistant and companion roles from social robots. To meet this expectation, designers can focus on how social robots can recognize users' emotions in a natural and meaningful way, and what the most effective verbal and nonverbal communication strategies can be for interaction with young people. In addition, how social robots can support young users, especially those with anxiety or social communication difficulties, can provide an important design perspective.

C. Dimension 3: Ethics and privacy

In social robot design, issues and questions, such as what privacy and data security challenges are related to personalizing social robots for young users, how transparency and user control can be provided over the collected data, and what ethical concerns young users may raise when interacting with social robots intellectually and emotionally are important. Moreover, the recommendations of UNESCO [13] on ethical issues related to the impacts of AI technologies as well as the standards, analysis and recommendations of UN [14] on the protection of human rights in the digital space should be taken into consideration in this dimension.

D. Dimension 4:Physical and behavioural design

What the basic design principles can be for designing social robots that are both appealing to young people and do not create a perception of threat is an important issue. How the physical appearance of a social robot can affect young users' trust and cooperation has also been evaluated as a design area that needs to be studied. Additionally, how the behaviors of social robots and their multimodal interaction (speech, touch, gestures) can increase the personalization of these robots for young people are also important considerations.

VI. Conclusions

In this study, the requirements and expectations of the younger population from social robots are explored. For this aim, structured interviews were conducted with a sample of 83 participants to identify their preferences regarding the tasks and features they expect social robots to possess. In addition, the differences between the genders were also investigated statistically and qualitatively. Based on the findings, the main dimensions for designing personalized social robots for young adults are identified along with their key considerations. The results will hopefully provide insight into social robot designers and developers to reach the expectations of young adults.

Besides technical aspects, social expectations have strong potential in developing social robots in the foreseeable future. From this perspective, we will need to develop function-, behavior- and emotion-based responses into the design of these systems. It will not be surprising that social robot design will evolve in such a way that user- and context-specific approaches and behaviors will appear. Young adults are an important user group who have the ability to integrate social robots into their daily lives and collaborate with them

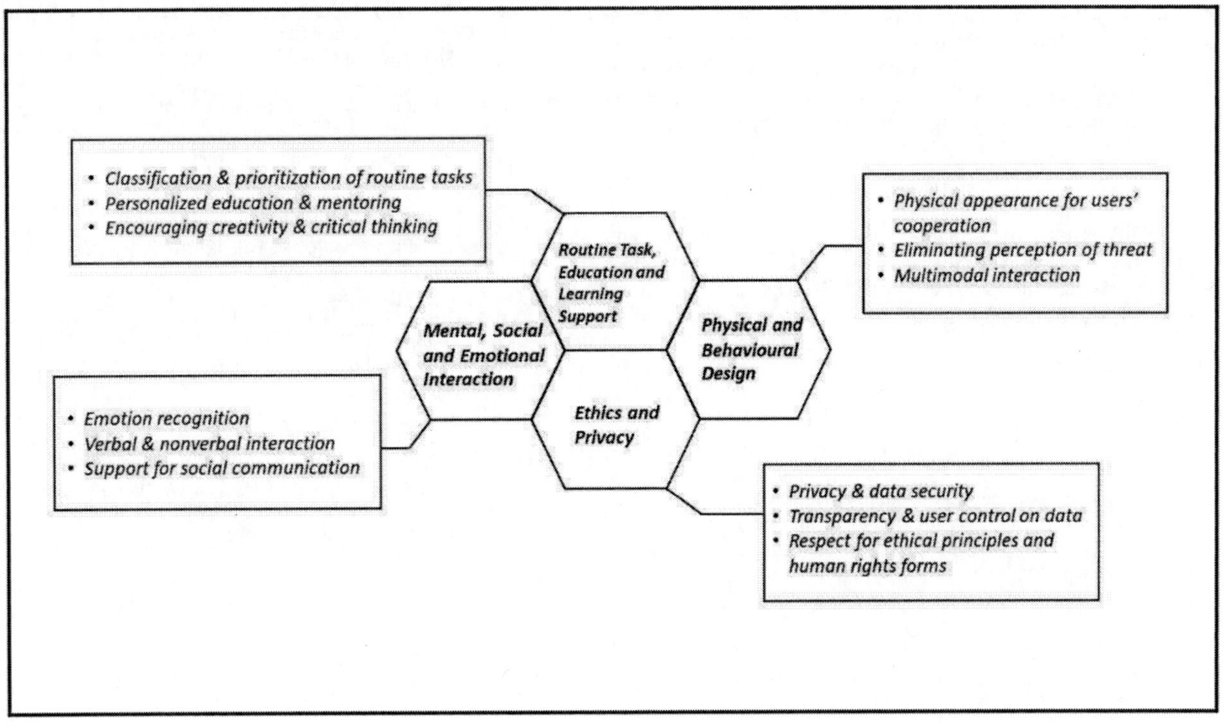

Figure 5. Dimensions and key considerations to designing social robots for young adults to gender.

One of the limitations of the study is the sample size. Data from a larger number of participants can be collected and analyzed, yielding more accurate results. Also, the respondents were mainly university students, thus the preferences of young adults with different educational backgrounds can be explored. In addition, the preference differences in young adults with and without children was not taken into account. As for future work, the expectations of various age groups, such as the elderly and children can also be investigated and compared against the findings to achieve a more personalized social robot design for all age groups. In addition, the study can be extended so as to include the ethical dimension in a systematic way from the beginning, starting with the design of interview questions, such as "Do you see any risks or harms that could arise with the integration of robots into your daily life?" or "Are there any tasks which you would not want to delegate to a robot and why?" The answers to these types of questions can shed light on the ethics and privacy dimensions giving the same importance as the other topics that were covered by the present study.

The increasing penetration of robots in our daily lives in different social environments and contexts requires not only technical but also ethical, social and normative assessments. It should be noted that robots may pose potential risks, such as reinforcing discrimination, exclusion or deepening power imbalances, especially for marginalized groups. For this reason, "ethics by design" approaches that integrate human rights principles into the design processes of robots from the very beginning are of great importance. These approaches not only ensure user safety, but also enable the development of fair, inclusive and socially responsible technologies.

ACKNOWLEDGMENT

This study was supported by the Scientific and Technological Research Council of Turkey (TUBITAK) under the Grant Number 123E653. The authors thank TUBITAK for their support.

REFERENCES

[1] J. Peter, R. Kühne, and A. Barco, "Can social robots affect children's prosocial behavior? An experimental study on prosocial robot models," Comput Human Behav, vol. 120, Jul. 2021, pp. 106712, doi: 10.1016/j.chb.2021.106712.

[2] Y. Gao, Y. Chang, T. Yang, and Z. Yu, "Consumer acceptance of social robots in domestic settings: A human-robot interaction perspective," Journal of Retailing and Consumer Services, vol. 82, pp. 104075, 2025.

[3] S. Chatterjee, R. Chaudhuri, and D. Vrontis, "Usage intention of social robots for domestic purpose: from security, privacy, and legal perspectives," Information Systems Frontiers, pp. 1–16, 2024.

[4] Bill Gates, *A Robot in Every Home*. Scientific American. [Online]. [Retrieved: May, 2025] Available from: https://www.cs.virginia.edu/~robins/A_Robot_in_Every_Home.pdf.

[5] R. Haruni, *Elon Musk's Vision: 30 billion Robots and a New Economic Dawn*. [Online]. [Retrieved: May, 2025]. Available from: https://wallstreetpit.com/122284-elon-musks-vision-30-billion-robots-and-a-new-economic-dawn/#:~:text=Musk's%20vision%20extends%20far%20beyond,20%20to%2030%20billion%20robots.

[6] Reuters. *Elon Musk: 10 billion humanoid robots by 2040 at $20K-$25K each*. [Online]. [Retrieved: May, 2025]. Available from: https://www.reuters.com/technology/elon-musk-10-billion-humanoid-robots-by-2040-20k-25k-each-2024-10-29/.

[7] R. A. Søraa, G. Tøndel, M. W. Kharas, and J. A. Serrano, "What do Older Adults Want from Social Robots? A Qualitative Research Approach to Human-Robot Interaction (HRI) Studies," Int J Soc Robot, vol. 15, no. 3, pp. 411–424, Mar. 2023, doi: 10.1007/s12369-022-00914-w.

[8] L. Pu, W. Moyle, C. Jones, and M. Todorovic, "The Effectiveness of Social Robots for Older Adults: A Systematic Review and Meta-Analysis of Randomized Controlled Studies," Jan. 09, 2019, Gerontological Society of America. pp.e37-e51, doi: 10.1093/geront/gny046.

[9] C. Di Napoli, G. Ercolano, and S. Rossi, "Personalized home-care support for the elderly: a field experience with a social robot at home," User Model User-adapt Interact, vol. 33, no. 2, pp. 405–440, Apr. 2023, doi: 10.1007/s11257-022-09333-y.

[10] J. Kanero, et al., "Social Robots for Early Language Learning: Current Evidence and Future Directions," Child Dev Perspect, vol. 12, no. 3, pp. 146–151, Sep. 2018, doi: 10.1111/cdep.12277.

[11] C. L. van Straten, J. Peter, and R. Kühne, "Child–Robot Relationship Formation: A Narrative Review of Empirical Research," *Int J Soc Robot*, vol. 12, no. 2, pp. 325–344, May 2020, doi: 10.1007/s12369-019-00569-0.

[12] V. Lim, M. Rooksby, and E. S. Cross, "Social Robots on a Global Stage: Establishing a Role for Culture During Human–Robot Interaction," Sep. 01, 2021, *Springer Science and Business Media B.V.* pp.1307-1333, doi: 10.1007/s12369-020-00710-4.

[13] UNESCO, *Recommendation on the Ethics of Artificial Intelligence*. [Online]. [Retrieved: May, 2025]. Available from: https://unesdoc.unesco.org/ark:/48223/pf0000381137

[14] United Nations, *Human Rights and Digital Technology*. [Online]. [Retrieved: May, 2025]. Available from: https://www.digitalhub.ohchr.org/

Assessing the Impact of Artificial Intelligence on Job and Task Displacement: Evidence from the Agriculture and Healthcare Sectors

Paul S. Mupfiga, Dzinaishe Mpini, Maxmillan Giyane
Department of Computer Science
Midlands State University
Gweru, Zimbabwe
e-mail: {mupfigaps, mpinid, giyanem}@staff.msu.ac.zw

***Abstract*—The rapid advancement of artificial intelligence has ignited extensive debates regarding its impact on the workforce. A widely held assertion is that artificial intelligence replaces specific tasks within jobs rather than entire occupations. This paper critically examines this assertion by exploring empirical evidence from case studies of artificial intelligence implementations in the agriculture and healthcare sectors. A stratified purposive sampling method was employed to identify 21 use cases from five continents capturing diverse perspectives from all the different economy classifications. Of these 21 cases only 5 of the cases reviewed involved artificial intelligence tools that can fully replace human jobs, and the majority of them are from high income economies. The majority of the analysed 21 cases were not displacing existing jobs but addressing previously unmet needs. In instances were job displacement occurs, there is the opportunity for up-skilling suggesting new career opportunities for the humans. This paper contributes by giving insights from empirical evidence to employment policy makers, employers and educators necessary in preparing the workforce for the future.**

Keywords-artificial intelligence; human-AI collaboration; labor market

I. INTRODUCTION

Artificial Intelligence (AI) is transforming the modern workplace, driving significant changes in productivity and efficiency in various sectors [1]. A central debate emerges from this transformation and it is on whether AI replaces specific tasks within jobs or entire jobs themselves. The result of this debate is profound in influencing policy making, workforce development, and socioeconomic stability. Despite the extensive literature on AI and job or task automation, significant gaps remain. Previous research lacks a detailed analysis of task displacement within job roles and does not provide comprehensive and sector-specific comparisons. Furthermore, there is a dearth of studies that examine the socioeconomic impacts of AI on different demographic groups and regions.

This research aims to bridge these gaps by critically analyzing the proposition that AI replaces tasks, but not jobs, and further examining the impact of AI on task and job displacement. The analysis is guided by empirical insights from implementations of AI agents in industry. The results are broken down to encompass the impact in various sectors and the resulting socio-economic implications are outlined. The findings are expected to inform policy-makers, business leaders, and workers, guiding them towards strategies that mitigate adverse effects and harness the benefits of AI driven automation.

To carefully address this overall aim, the following research questions are answered:

- To what extent does AI replace tasks within existing jobs compared to entire job roles?
- How do different sectors and industries experience the impact of AI on job displacement and task displacement?
- What are the socio-economic implications of AI-driven tasks and job displacement for the workforce?

The significance of this research lies in its practical and policy-oriented insights regarding the evolving relationship between AI and the workforce. The study provides empirical evidence that challenges the widely held belief that AI primarily leads to job displacement. The research provides a global perspective on how AI affects the workforce, offering valuable insights for both high-income and lower-income economies. Overall, this has important implications for workforce development and educational strategies.

In Section II, we present the theoretical framework underpinning our study, exploring prior research related to investigations of the impact of AI on the workforce. Section III details the research methodology which encompasses the research approach, and strategy. It further details the case selection process, as well as the data collection and analysis procedures. Section IV is a presentation of the results of this research followed by a discussion on results with the analysed prior studies. Finally, Section V details the conclusions and proposed future work.

II. LITERATURE REVIEW

In recent years, various studies have been conducted in a bid to analyse perceptions and impact of AI in the workplace and this section reviews these studies. Firstly, theoretical frameworks that shape this topic are highlighted, followed by analysis of studies grouped into themes guided by the research questions. Gaps identified are put under each theme.

A. Theoretical Framework

This research is guided by two key theories, the Task Based Approach (TBA) and the Job Polarization Theory (JPT). TBA highlights that automation impacts tasks within jobs rather than entire occupations [2]. JPT on the other hand informs that technological advancements including AI, and automation leads to the decline of middle-skill jobs while increasing demand for high-skill and low-skill jobs, thus creating a polarized labor market with a shrinking middle class and fewer middle-class occupations [3].

B. Analysis of Related Studies

1) Job Displacement versus Task Displacement: Task displacement occurs when AI automates specific activities within a job [4] whilst job displacement happens when the automation of tasks leads to the elimination of entire positions [5]. Studies on the impact of AI on job and task displacement present a clear picture of how technology influences the labor market. [6] argued that AI has the potential to perform many tasks more efficiently and inexpensively than humans. This early insight suggested the current debate on AI's role in automating routine tasks. [7] provided a comprehensive view, discussing how automation displaces tasks but also creates new opportunities, such as productivity gains and new task creation, which could potentially increase labor demand. [8] suggested that professionals with substantial skills and education in fields, such as computing, law, and medicine are less at risk, as AI augments rather than replaces their work.

[9] surveyed AI practitioners, finding that a significant portion of human tasks can be automated, with immediate potential to automate 22% of these tasks. However, their study was limited by sample bias, focusing solely on AI practitioners only from Europe, North America, and Asia, and without considering economic impacts. [10] explored the economic implications of generative AI tools like ChatGPT, highlighting the job displacement of routine job workers. [11] supported these findings by showing that while routine jobs are at high risk of automation, non-routine jobs have seen growth, underscoring the complexity of AI's impact on labor markets.

Although these reviewed studies discuss the potential of AI to automate tasks, there is a lack of detailed analysis on the specific skill level within various job roles that are most susceptible to AI. More granular studies are needed to identify which tasks within job roles are being automated. Furthermore, there is a scarcity of longitudinal studies that track the impact of AI on task displacement over time.

2) Sector Specific Impact: The impact of AI varies significantly between different sectors. [12] review that regions with a focus on technology, healthcare and creative industries may benefit from task automation and job transformation. [13] argues AI serves to enhance and optimize the work of medical professionals, highlighting the sector's resistance to full automation due to the complex and interpersonal nature of healthcare tasks.

In the manufacturing industry, the integration of AI and robotics has led to significant productivity gains. Automated systems perform tasks, such as assembly, inspection, and packaging with greater precision and efficiency than human workers. According to [14], each additional robot per thousand workers reduces the employment-to-population ratio by 0.2 percentage points and wages by 0.42%. This suggests that while tasks are automated, the overall number of jobs is also impacted.

The financial sector has embraced AI for tasks, such as data analysis, trading, and customer service. AI-driven algorithms execute trades at speeds and efficiencies beyond human ability, while chatbots handle routine customer inquiries. This has led to a reduction in the need for human traders and customer service representatives, indicating a shift towards job displacement [15].

Although there are studies focused on specific sectors, comprehensive comparative analyses across multiple sectors are limited. More research is needed to systematically compare how different industries are affected by AI in terms of both job and task displacement.

3) Skill Specific Impact: High skill jobs require cognitive and interpersonal skills and are generally less susceptible to automation [16]. These roles often involve complex problem-solving, decision-making, and creativity, areas where AI currently lags human capability. However, AI can augment these jobs, enhancing productivity and enabling workers to focus on more strategic tasks [16].

Middle-skill jobs, particularly those involving routine tasks, face significant risk [17]. The decline in middle-skill jobs contributes to job polarization and a shrinking middle class [3].

Low skill jobs, such as those in personal care and service industries, may see varying impacts. While some routine tasks can be automated, many low-skill jobs require physical presence and human interaction, which are challenging for AI to replicate. Therefore, these jobs may experience less displacement compared to middle skill jobs [17].

4) Socio Economic Impact: [18] provided qualitative insights into employee perceptions on job loss from AI and automation in New Zealand, and the study reveals a mix of no threat, potential threat, and real threat sentiments among workers from various professions. [19] echoed concerns about significant job losses due to AI, despite acknowledging potential productivity boosts and new job opportunities. [20] conducted a literature survey on worker-AI coexistence, proposing that trust issues and the need for continuous skill development are crucial for a symbiotic relationship between workers and AI. They emphasized the importance of human and conceptual skills in complementing technical proficiency, suggesting that ongoing training is essential for effective worker-AI collaboration.

[10] further illustrated the economic impact of AI tools like ChatGPT, predicting significant displacement of routine jobs while also acknowledging the potential for new high-skill job creation and increased productivity. [21] projected that AI could impact a substantial percentage of jobs in both advanced and developing economies, potentially affecting 800 million jobs worldwide by 2025.

Existing studies like those by [20] and [19] discuss broad socio-economic impacts but do not detail how different demographic groups, such as age, gender, and education level are affected. More targeted research is needed to understand the differential impacts of AI on various workforce segments. [21] and other global projections highlight the widespread impact of AI, but there is limited research on regional disparities. Understanding how AI-driven displacement varies across regions, particularly between urban and rural areas, and between developed and developing countries, is crucial.

III. Methodology

This section outlines the research design and procedures employed to investigate the impact of AI on job and task displacement. The methodology is structured to ensure a rigorous and systematic analysis of empirical evidence across diverse sectors and economic contexts.

A. Research Philosophy

The methodology for this research is grounded in a pragmatic research philosophy, which emphasizes practical problem solving. This approach is particularly suitable for exploring the impacts of AI on job and task displacement across various sectors and geographical locations. A qualitative research approach was chosen to provide in-depth insights into the impacts of AI adoption, focusing on context-specific factors rather than broad generalizations.

B. Research Strategy

The content analysis research strategy was used, and this strategy enabled systematic examination and interpretation of textual data on AI use cases across the globe. The analyzed data was from academic publications, industry reports, company websites, as well as reputable news and blog platforms. The strategy further ensured that the findings are rooted in comprehensive and credible evidence, allowing for a detailed understanding of AI's role in transforming jobs and tasks within the agriculture and healthcare sectors.

C. Case Selection

A purposive and stratified sampling technique was adopted to ensure comprehensive coverage of use cases. The purposive sampling encouraged picking the agriculture and healthcare sectors which are identified as the early adopters of AI [22]. Stratification was conducted by continent and economy type to achieve geographical and economic diversity. Continent classification adhered to [23], encompassing Africa, America, Asia, Europe, and Oceania. Economy classifications followed [24], comprising low-income, lower-middle-income, upper-middle-income and high-income economies.

D. Data Collection

Data collection was conducted through desktop research, drawing from academic journals, industry reports, reputable company websites, and blogs. Desktop research was selected due to its broad accessibility to diverse and globally distributed data sources, enabling the study to capture a comprehensive range of implemented AI use cases across sectors and regions. By relying on published academic literature, industry reports, and reputable company websites, we ensured the inclusion of validated and credible data. Peer reviewed articles provide insights on impacts which are verified. Industry reports provide insights into applied observations. Real world deployments from company websites and reputable blogs provide first hand information of AI deployments. Only implemented AI solutions were considered, excluding conceptual studies, as well as research and development efforts. Each continent was represented for healthcare and agriculture sectors, ensuring all four economy classifications were covered without repetition of countries.

To ensure a systematic search; under a particular sector, continent and economy classification, the researchers identified the countries which fall in that continent and economy classification and made a search from the Google search engine to identify AI use cases from countries that satisfy the continent and economy classification. The chosen approach ensured representativeness of AI implementations across diverse geographies and economic classifications, minimizing potential bias. Each continent and economy classification was equally represented, with no country repeated in the dataset. The used keywords included "AI powered agent for *category name* use cases in *country name*", as well as *category name* AI agent AND *country*. For example *Healthcare AI agent AND Angola*. Sticking to a systematic search protocol and following these standards ensured a methodological control allowing for replication of results.

The data assessment in this collection prioritized identifying real-world implementations of AI rather than conceptual or research and development (R&D) efforts. Conceptual studies and R&D efforts were excluded to maintain focus on observable workforce impacts. Implemented cases provided verifiable evidence of displacement. The assessment emphasized role classification, guided by the framework outlined in [25], to evaluate the nature of tasks and jobs influenced by AI technologies. Key areas of analysis included the extent to which AI replaced specific tasks within roles versus entire job roles, as well as the socio-economic implications of these changes. The data was analyzed thematically in alignment with the research questions, enabling a structured exploration of task displacement, sectoral impacts, and workforce impacts.

E. Data Analysis

Several critical factors were considered during the analysis. These included the availability of sufficient data to enable sound deductions, the identification of AI agents or classifications, and the specific roles covered by these implementations. Role classifications were examined to determine whether AI-driven technologies led to task or job displacement. Additionally, the study categorized data by economy classification, continent, and sector, ensuring representation from healthcare and agriculture across diverse geographical and economic contexts. Socio-economic impacts, such as the effect on workforce skills, were also assessed, providing a comprehensive understanding of AI's influence. This approach ensured the analysis addressed the complexities of AI adoption within varying global and sectoral environments. In reporting, findings were presented thematically, guided by the research questions. Themes included job displacement versus task displacement by skill, sector-specific impacts, and socio-economic implications. Analysis considered economy, continent, type of AI, and industry classifications to provide a comprehensive understanding of AI's impact on the workforce.

IV. Results and Discussion

This research investigated the impact of AI on job and task displacement focusing on the agriculture and healthcare sectors across the globe. A total of 21 use cases of AI agents implementations were analyzed. Tables I to III all show these analyzed use cases with extra data on the country, economy, role, and skill level. Table I shows use cases where actual job displacements happened. Table II shows use cases where task displacements occured and Table III shows where no displacements are happening. A discussion utilizing the thematic approach guided by the research questions then follows. An attempt was made to obtain both a healthcare and an agriculture use case from each continent and economy classification, but some continents did not have a country falling in a particular economy classification, hence the cases fell short from the expected 40 use cases. Additionally, in some use cases there was no sufficient information online to describe an implemented use case hence these were ignored. Sufficient data in this case encompassed AI agent implemented, and country implemented in. The 21 use cases spanned all 5 continents, with Africa (24%, n=5), Europe (24%, n=5), and the Americas (24%, n=5) equally represented, followed by Asia (19%, n=4) and Oceania (10%, n=2). Economically, cases were distributed across all World Bank classifications: low-income (10%, n=2), lower-middle-income (24%, n=5), upper-middle-income (33%, n=7), and high-income economies (33%, n=7). Sectorally, healthcare cases predominated (57%, n=12) over agriculture (43%, n=9), reflecting AI's earlier adoption in medical applications while still capturing significant agricultural implementations. This stratified distribution ensures our findings account for diverse development contexts and implementation environments.

Table I
SUMMARY OF USE CASES RESULTING IN JOB DISPLACEMENT

Use Case	Role	ISCO Skill Level	Economy
Robotti. Sweden Self-driving robot used for tasks, such as seedbed preparation, sowing, and mechanical weed control in agriculture. [26]	Agriculture Assistant	3	upper-middle-income
John Deere CP770. United States of America Automated cotton harvesting machine that uses AI to optimize harvesting process and improve yield quality. [27]	Agriculture Assistant	2	high-income
Agrist Robot. Japan AI-powered robots to harvest crops like cucumbers and tomatoes autonomously. [28] [29]	Agriculture Assistant	2	high-income
YV01. France Autonomous vineyard spraying robot addressing both labor shortages and environmental compliance. [30]	Agriculture Assistant	2	high-income
Oxin Tractor. New Zealand AI-driven autonomous tractor used for tasks like plowing, seeding, and weeding. [31]	Agriculture Assistant	2	high-income

A. *Job Displacement versus Task Displacement*

Table I shows where total job displacements are occurring and this is more prevalent in high-income economies and in the agriculture sector. High-income economies accounted for 80% (4 of 5) of full job displacement cases, while low- and lower-middle-income economies exhibited zero instances of complete job replacement. In high-income countries, advanced automation is prevalent, as seen with the John Deere CP770 Cotton Picker in the United States of America, which automates cotton harvesting, and the Robotti in Sweden, which performs sowing and weed control tasks. Such technologies illustrate [6] argument that AI has the potential to execute tasks more efficiently than humans and hence in the end may replace humans.

Table II shows where task displacements are happening and task displacement is more prevalent in the healthcare sector. Upper-middle-income economies led in AI complementation (50%, 7 of 14 cases). Low-income cases focused on unmet needs (90% augmentation). The findings reflect AI technologies automate repetitive and routine tasks, enhancing efficiency and accuracy while preserving the need for human involvement in complex decision-making, empathy, and critical thinking. In healthcare, AI-driven systems like the Automated X-ray Imaging Device in Sudan automate routine processes, such as image interpretation and inquiries. This aligns with [2] argument that automation tends to impact specific tasks within occupations rather than eliminating entire roles. AI technologies automate repetitive and routine tasks, enabling greater efficiency and accuracy, while retaining the need for human involvement in roles requiring complex decision-making, empathy, or critical thinking.

Table III shows where no displacement is happening, but where AI is helping complement human labor. contributing to socio-economic growth and of the analyzed cases these cases where there is no displacement are the majority. Systems, such as Robin the Robot in Armenia augment human capabilities, particularly in tasks requiring professional judgment or emotional intelligence. Whilst high-income countries employ advanced systems like the John Deere CP770 Cotton Picker

Table II
SUMMARY OF USE CASES RESULTING IN TASK DISPLACEMENT

Use Case	Role	ISCO Skill Level	Economy
Automated X-ray Imaging Device. Sudan Portable AI system that screens for tuberculosis (TB) by interpreting X-ray images. [32]	Radiologist	4	low-income
Sophie Bot. Kenya AI powered chatbot offering answers to sexual and reproductive health questions. [33] [34] [35]	Sexual Health Educator	2	lower-middle-income
Tele-health Learning Robot. Cambodia A tele-health robot that enhances health education and tele-consultations in low-resource settings. [36]	Health Educator	3	lower-middle-income
LaLuchy Robotina. Mexico Robot to alleviate loneliness and assist COVID-19 patients by enabling virtual communication. [37] [38] [39]	Healthcare Assistant	2	upper-middle-income
Panafricare Clinic AI Agents. Sychelles AI systems to manage patient records, prescribe medication, and assist in clinical examinations. [40]	Healthcare Assistants	2	high-income
Medicine Delivery Robot. Singapore Voice-activated robot to deliver medications in hospitals. [41]	Assistant Nurse Clinician	2	high-income

in the United States to replace human labor, low- and middle-income countries use these AI systems like MkhulimaGPT in Rwanda and uMudhumeni in Zimbabwe to enhance human productivity. The shortage of this critical staff is addressed by emergence of AI systems. This corroborates with [14] who indicates that AI can create new opportunities, particularly in resource-constrained settings, by augmenting human productivity.

In the healthcare sector, AI-driven systems displace routine and repetitive tasks. For instance, the automated X-ray imaging device in Sudan automate image interpretation and routine inquiries. These examples highlight [2]'s observation that routine tasks are more susceptible to automation. However, high-tech systems like Robin the Robot in Armenia enhance

Table III
SUMMARY OF USE CASES RESULTING IN NO DISPLACEMENT

Use Case	Role	ISCO Skill Level	Economy
Radify AI. South Africa AI system that diagnose medical images. [42] [43] [44]	Radiologist	4	upper-middle-income
Robin the Robot. Armenia Companionship robot providing emotional support to pediatric patients. [45] [46] [47]	Healthcare Assistant	2	upper-middle-income
FoxTac. Ukraine Robotic stretchers for safe medical evacuations in conflict zones. [48] [49]	Healthcare Assistant	2	upper-middle-income
Montreal's Scale AI. Canada AI platforms which optimize hospital operations across Canada. [50] [51]	Hospital Administrator	4	high-income
Mazor X Stealth Platform. Australia Robotic surgery platform that assists spine surgeons. [52] [53] [54])	Surgeon Assistant	4	high-income
MkhulimaGPT. Rwanda Smart chatbot which gives farming advice. [55] [56]	Agriculture Extension Worker	2	low-income
uMudhumeni. Zimbabwe Smart chatbot which poses as an agricultural extension worker. [57] [58]	Agriculture Extension Worker	2	lower-middle-income
Plantix. Bangladesh Mobile application for crop disease diagnosis using photos. [59] [60]	Agriculture Extension Worker	2	lower-middle-income
Anton Tech. Botswana AI platform that uses drones to monitor both plant diseases and soil quality. [61] [62]	Agricultural Assistant	2	upper-middle-income
Jeevn AI. Argentina Expert system which provides personalized farming advice. [63]	Farm Advisory Assistant	2	upper-middle-income

professionals' capabilities, consistent with [2] and [8] assertion that tasks demanding human intelligence and professional skills, such as those involving substantive decision-making or emotional intelligence, are less likely to be affected. In the agriculture sector on the other hand, task displacement varies significantly by economic context.

The extent of displacement also correlates with the economic classification of countries. In low-income countries, AI supports workers by automating routine tasks, allowing them to focus on higher-value activities. In high-income countries, the potential for full automation leads to more significant task displacement in sectors like agriculture. For example, the YV01 autonomous vineyard spraying robot in France and the Agrist Harvesting Robot in Japan replace manual labor in specific agricultural tasks. [3] notes that technological advancements often cause a decline in middle-skill jobs, which rely on routine manual tasks, while increasing the demand for high-skill jobs requiring expertise and creativity. Simultaneously, these advancements can also increase demand for very low-skill jobs that involve tasks difficult to automate, such as caregiving or maintenance.

Overall, the analysis underscores that AI technologies are reshaping tasks within jobs rather than eliminating entire roles. As [2] noted, routine, repetitive, and physically demanding tasks are more prone to automation, while roles requiring human intelligence, creativity, or emotional interaction remain largely unaffected. This distinction is critical for understanding how AI impacts labor markets, as it necessitates targeted upskilling programs to help workers adapt to evolving job requirements. Moreover, [14] highlights the potential for AI to create entirely new opportunities, further mitigating the risk of complete job displacement.

Furthermore, the integration of AI across different economic contexts reflects varied strategies. Low-income countries utilize AI for augmentation, emphasizing human-AI collaboration, while high-income countries adopt AI for efficiency and cost savings, leading to more comprehensive task automation. This is consistent with [3]'s observation that technological advancements can lead to polarization in labor markets, increasing demand for both high-skill and very low-skill jobs while eroding middle-skill roles.

B. Sector Specific Impacts

A notable pattern emerges when comparing sectors; while AI in healthcare often complements human expertise, AI in agriculture leans more towards displacing specific tasks in high-income countries. In healthcare, 67% of cases (8 of 12) involved task displacement without job loss. In the agriculture sector, the research showed higher job displacement rates (44%, 4 of 9 cases) concentrated exclusively in high-income contexts.

The disparity stems from differences in tasks and the economic context of adoption. Healthcare tasks requiring empathy, judgment, or professional skills are less amenable to full automation, aligning with findings by [2], [3] and [8]. In contrast, routine and physically intensive tasks in agriculture are more prone to automation, particularly in wealthier nations with greater access to advanced technologies.

Across both sectors, the economic classification of countries influences AI deployment strategies. In low-income economies, AI technologies are primarily used for augmentation, allowing workers to focus on higher-value activities. For example, advisory chatbots in agriculture and tele-health robots in healthcare supplement human roles without replacing them. In high-income countries, however, AI's potential for full task automation leads to greater task displacement, as seen in autonomous tractors and surgical robots.

C. Skill Specific Impact

In healthcare, expert systems, such as automated X-ray imaging devices reduce dependence on specialized radiologists in remote regions while encouraging healthcare workers to develop skills in AI-assisted diagnostics. Chatbots like Sophie Bot provide healthcare consultation and sexual education support, enhancing digital literacy among healthcare providers and patients. Robotic platforms, such as the Mazor X Stealth Robotic Surgery Platform, augment surgeons' capabilities, requiring professionals to undergo specialized training to operate these advanced systems. Similarly, robots like Robin the Robot and FoxTac, used in pediatric care and healthcare assistance, necessitate that staff learn to integrate robotic technologies into their workflows.

In agriculture, AI applications have reshaped skill requirements for farmers and technicians. Tools like Plantix and Anton Tech use computer vision and machine learning for crop health diagnostics, encouraging farmers to adopt data-driven practices. Robotic systems, such as the Agrist Harvesting Robot and Oxin Autonomous Tractor, reduce the need for manual labor while increasing demand for skilled operators and maintenance technicians. These technologies not only improve productivity but also require workers to develop technical literacy and familiarity with AI-powered systems. For example, initiatives like MkhulimaGPT and uMudhumeni empower agricultural extension workers with improved knowledge in disease management and digital tools.

These examples highlight that AI disproportionately affects low- and middle-skill jobs, leading to job polarization and a shrinking middle class [3]. While AI enhances the efficiency and precision of various tasks, it also creates a pressing need for workforce re-skilling and up-skilling to align with the evolving demands of AI-driven industries. This dual impact underscores the importance of targeted educational initiatives and sector-specific training programs to mitigate the socio-economic disruptions caused by AI automation and ensure equitable access to opportunities in the new labor market.

D. Socio Economic Impacts

The analysed use cases reveal contrasts in AI's impact across economic classifications. Job displacement is heavily concentrated in high-income economies (80%). In contrast, low- and lower-middle-income economies observed zero cases of full job replacement. This reflects AI's role in augmentation. Task displacement dominates lower-middle-income economies (33.3%), where AI automates repetitive tasks. An example is Plantix disease diagnosis in Bangladesh. High-income economies also show significant task displacement (33.3%), but alongside job losses. No displacement is most prevalent in upper-middle-income economies (50%), where AI complements labour. Low-income economies (10%) lag in adoption due to infrastructure gaps.

Furthermore, the socio-economic implications of AI adoption vary widely across sectors and economic classifications. In healthcare, AI improves accessibility and efficiency, particularly in low-income countries where resources are limited. For example, automated X-ray imaging devices in Sudan address critical gaps in healthcare services. However, the integration of AI requires workforce adaptation, as professionals must learn to work with new technologies. In agriculture, AI's economic impact is profound, with advanced automation in high-income countries leading to significant cost savings and productivity gains. However, in low-income countries, AI tools primarily support farmers, fostering productivity without displacing workers.

In healthcare, AI adoption has significantly improved efficiency and accessibility, particularly in low-income economies where resource constraints are severe. For instance, Sudan's automated X-ray imaging devices for Tuberculosis diagnosis demonstrate how AI addresses critical healthcare gaps. However, the integration of AI necessitates workforce adaptation.

Similarly, in agriculture, AI innovations, such as MkhulimaGPT in Rwanda and uMudhumeni in Zimbabwe have empowered smallholder farmers with actionable insights, improving productivity and resilience. However, in high-income economies like the United States and Sweden AI tools, such as John Deere's CP770 Cotton Picker and Robotti automate labor-intensive tasks, displacing low-skill jobs. These examples highlight AI's dual impact: fostering efficiency and innovation while also necessitating workforce realignment to more technical and conceptual roles.

V. Conclusion and Future Work

The research shows that AI reshapes tasks within jobs by automating repetitive processes while preserving human roles in complex decision-making and critical thinking, with deployment strategies differing between high- and low-income countries. In healthcare, AI automates routine tasks but relies on human expertise for roles requiring empathy and judgment, while in agriculture, task displacement is more pronounced in high-income countries due to advanced automation. AI adoption transforms workforce skills, with middle-skill jobs most affected, creating a need for re-skilling and technical literacy, especially in AI-assisted diagnostics and data-driven agricultural practices. Socio-economic impacts vary by sector and economic classification, with AI improving efficiency in low-income countries while driving automation and productivity gains in high-income regions, highlighting the need for strategic adaptation to mitigate disruptions and promote equitable development.

The findings lead to the conclusion that AI is fundamentally transforming the nature of work by displacing tasks rather than entire jobs, with sectoral and economic variations shaping its impact. In both healthcare and agriculture, AI enhances efficiency and productivity by automating repetitive and routine tasks while leaving roles that require human judgment, empathy, and creativity largely intact. The degree of task displacement is influenced by the economic context, with high-income countries leveraging advanced automation technologies to replace labor-intensive tasks, while low- and middle-income countries adopt AI tools to augment human efforts and improve productivity. This underscores the deep relationship between AI deployment and socio-economic contexts, where resource availability and task complexity determine the extent of automation and augmentation. Moreover, the increasing reliance on AI has heightened the need for workforce re-skilling and up-skilling, particularly for middle-skill roles, to address the socio-economic challenges posed by task displacement and job polarization. Overall, while AI offers significant opportunities for innovation, accessibility, and efficiency, particularly in low-income regions, its integration requires strategic adaptation to ensure equitable development and mitigate potential workforce disruptions.

Based on the research findings, several recommendations can be made to address the challenges and maximize the benefits of AI adoption across sectors and economic contexts. First, policymakers and stakeholders should invest in targeted education and training programs to equip workers with the skills necessary to adapt to AI-driven changes. Emphasis should be placed on re-skilling and up-skilling initiatives for middle-skill workers who are most vulnerable to task displacement, with a focus on technical literacy, data-driven decision-making, and AI-assisted processes. Second, governments and organizations in low- and middle-income countries should prioritize the development and deployment of AI tools that augment human efforts rather than replace them, ensuring inclusive growth and minimizing socio-economic disruptions. Partnerships between the private sector, academia, and international organizations can help foster innovation and improve access to AI technologies in undeserved regions.

This research was limited in that it only analyzed case studies from the agriculture and healthcare sectors only. Further research should focus on granular, longitudinal studies for each sector to gain a better understanding of the long-term trends and impacts of AI on job displacement and creation. Furthermore, while the study reveals important socio-economic patterns in AI-driven displacement, the analysis was limited in examining granular demographic impacts, such as gender and age. These factors likely mediate how different workforce segments experience AI adoption. Future research should prioritize these granular demographic impacts and analyzing how AI adoption affects vulnerable subgroups across economic contexts. This enables targeted policy interventions.

References

[1] J. Bughin *et al.*, "Artificial intelligence the next digital frontier", McKinsey & Company, Brussels, Tech. Rep., 2017.

[2] D. H. Autor, F. Levy, and R. J. Murnane, "The skill content of recent technological change: An empirical exploration", *The Quarterly journal of economics*, vol. 118, no. 4, pp. 1279–1333, 2003.
[3] D. H. Autor, "Why are there still so many jobs? the history and future of workplace automation", *Journal of economic perspectives*, vol. 29, no. 3, pp. 3–30, 2015.
[4] C. B. Frey and M. A. Osborne, "The future of employment: How susceptible are jobs to computerisation?", *Technological forecasting and social change*, vol. 114, pp. 254–280, 2017.
[5] J. Bessen, "Automation and jobs: When technology boosts employment", *Economic Policy*, vol. 34, no. 100, pp. 589–626, 2019.
[6] N. J. Nilsson, "Artificial intelligence, employment, and income", *AI magazine*, vol. 5, no. 2, pp. 5–5, 1984.
[7] D. Acemoglu and P. Restrepo, "Artificial intelligence, automation, and work", in *The economics of artificial intelligence: An agenda*, University of Chicago Press, 2018, pp. 197–236.
[8] Q. Wang, X. Liu, and K. Huang, "Displaced or augmented? how does artificial intelligence affect our jobs: Evidence from linkedin.", in *Fortieth International Conference on Information Systems*, 2019, pp. 1–10.
[9] R. Gruetzemacher, D. Paradice, and K. B. Lee, "Forecasting extreme labor displacement: A survey of ai practitioners", *Technological Forecasting and Social Change*, vol. 161, p. 120 323, 2020.
[10] A. Zarifhonarvar, "Economics of chatgpt: A labor market view on the occupational impact of artificial intelligence", *Journal of Electronic Business & Digital Economics*, vol. 3, no. 2, pp. 100–116, 2024.
[11] R. Tiwari, "The impact of ai and machine learning on job displacement and employment opportunities", *International Journal of Engineering Technologies and Management Research*, vol. 7, no. 1, pp. 1–8, 2023.
[12] T. Berger and B. Frey, *Digitalisation, jobs and convergence in Europe: Strategies for closing the skills gap*. Oxford Martin School Oxford, 2016, vol. 50.
[13] F. Jiang *et al.*, "Artificial intelligence in healthcare: Past, present and future", *Stroke and vascular neurology*, vol. 2, no. 4, 2017.
[14] D. Acemoglu and P. Restrepo, "Robots and jobs: Evidence from us labor markets", *Journal of political economy*, vol. 128, no. 6, pp. 2188–2244, 2020.
[15] M. Arntz, T. Gregory, and U. Zierahn, "The risk of automation for jobs in oecd countries: A comparative analysis", OECD Publishing, Paris, Tech. Rep. 189, 2016. DOI: 10.1787/5jlz9h56dvq7-en.
[16] E. Brynjolfsson and A. McAfee, *The second machine age: Work, progress, and prosperity in a time of brilliant technologies*. WW Norton & Company, 2014.
[17] M. Goos, A. Manning, and A. Salomons, "Explaining job polarization: Routine-biased technological change and offshoring", *American economic review*, vol. 104, no. 8, pp. 2509–2526, 2014.
[18] D. Brougham and J. Haar, "Smart technology, artificial intelligence, robotics, and algorithms (stara): Employees' perceptions of our future workplace", *Journal of Management & Organization*, vol. 24, no. 2, pp. 239–257, 2018.
[19] A. Ansari and A. Ansari, "Consequences of ai induced job displacement", *International Journal of Business, Analytics, and Technology*, vol. 2, no. 1, pp. 4–19, 2024.
[20] A. Zirar, S. I. Ali, and N. Islam, "Worker and workplace artificial intelligence (ai) coexistence: Emerging themes and research agenda", *Technovation*, vol. 124, p. 102 747, 2023.
[21] A. S. George, "Bracing for the coming ai tsunami: Preparing the global workforce for displacement and inequality in the age of accelerating technological advancement", *Partners Universal Innovative Research Publication*, vol. 2, no. 3, pp. 126–146, 2024. DOI: 10.5281/zenodo.11668571.
[22] K. McElheran *et al.*, "Ai adoption in america: Who, what, and where", *Journal of Economics and Management Strategy*, vol. 33, no. 2, pp. 375–415, 2024.
[23] P. Markert, A. Adhikari, and S. Das, "A transcontinental analysis of account remediation protocols of popular websites", *arXiv preprint arXiv:2302.01401*, 2023.
[24] World Bank, "World bank country and lending groups", 2024, [Online]. Available: https://datahelpdesk.worldbank.org/knowledgebase/articles/906519-world-bank-country-and-lending-groups (visited on 04/04/2025).
[25] International Labour Organisation, "International standard classification of occupations (isco)", 2024, [Online]. Available: https://ilostat.ilo.org/methods/concepts-and-definitions/classification-occupation/ (visited on 04/04/2025).
[26] Lantmännen, "Lantmännen in unique robot project as part of the farming of the future", 2021, [Online]. Available: https://www.lantmannen.com/about-lantmannen/newsroom/press-releases/2021/lantmannen-in-unique-robot-project-for-the-farming-of-the-future/ (visited on 04/18/2025).
[27] John Deere, "Cp770 cotton picker", 2024, [Online]. Available: https://www.deere.com/en/harvesting/cotton/cp770-cotton-picker/ (visited on 04/18/2025).
[28] Agrist, "Robot", 2024, [Online]. Available: https://agrist.com/products/robot (visited on 04/18/2025).
[29] K. Funaki, "Focus: Use of ai-based robots on the rise in japanese agriculture", 2023, [Online]. Available: https://english.kyodonews.net/news/2023/11/1b953d6db421-focus-use-of-ai-based-robots-on-the-rise-in-japanese-agriculture.html (visited on 04/18/2025).
[30] Ymedia, "The yanmar spraying robot – making work in the vineyard safer and more sustainable", 2024, [Online]. Available: https://www.yanmar.com/global/about/ymedia/article/spraying-robot.html (visited on 04/18/2025).
[31] Oxin by Smart Machine, "Meet oxin, the autonomous and multi-tasking robotic tractor", 2024, [Online]. Available: https://www.oxin.nz/ (visited on 04/18/2025).
[32] United Nations Development Programme, "Harnessing artificial intelligence for health", 2024, [Online]. Available: https://www.undp.org/stories/harnessing-artificial-intelligence-health (visited on 04/05/2025).
[33] Artificial Intelligence for Development, "Building responsible ai for global health", 2024, [Online]. Available: https://ai4d.ai/project/building-responsible-ai-for-global-health/ (visited on 04/05/2025).
[34] SophieBot, "Sophiebot - artificial intelligence to answer your questions on sexual reproductive health, try her out today", 2024, [Online]. Available: https://www.sophiebot.ai/ (visited on 04/05/2025).
[35] Villgro Africa, "Ai innovator spotlight: Sophie bot", 2024, [Online]. Available: https://villgroafrica.org/ai-innovator-spotlight-sophie-bot/ (visited on 04/05/2025).
[36] Health Volunteers Overseas, "Robot enriches telehealth learning in cambodia", 2021, [Online]. Available: https://hvousa.org/blog/robot-enriches-telehealth-learning-in-cambodia/ (visited on 04/05/2025).
[37] Medical Press, "Robot eases loneliness of mexican virus patients", 2020, [Online]. Available: https://medicalxpress.com/news/2020-08-robot-eases-loneliness-mexican-virus.html (visited on 04/12/2025).
[38] A. France-Presse, "Robot eases loneliness of mexican virus patients", 2020, [Online]. Available: https://www.abs-cbn.com/classified-odd/08/30/20/robot-eases-loneliness-of-mexican-virus-patients (visited on 04/12/2025).
[39] International Social Security Association, ""laluchy robotina", the humanoid robot: Robotic therapist programme for mental

health", 2020, [Online]. Available: https://www.issa.int/gp/242717 (visited on 04/12/2025).

[40] Sychelles Nation, "The health trends of 2022", 2021, [Online]. Available: https://www.nation.sc/articles/11915/the-health-trends-of-2022 (visited on 04/12/2025).

[41] C. Lok, S. Seah, and J. A. Baker, "Robots that deliver medication, voice-activated devices: Hospitals tap technology to improve patient care", 2023, [Online]. Available: https://www.channelnewsasia.com/singapore/tech-ai-healthcare-ttsh-smart-ward-cgh-ae-emergency-robots-3634801 (visited on 04/12/2025).

[42] EnvisionIT, "Raddify for mammograms", 2024, [Online]. Available: https://www.radify.ai/for-mammograms/ (visited on 04/18/2025).

[43] A. Njanja, "South africa's envisionit deep ai gets $1.65m to expand access to medical imaging", 2023, [Online]. Available: https://techcrunch.com/2023/02/23/south-africas-envisionit-deep-ai-gets-1-65m-to-expand-access-to-medical-imaging/ (visited on 04/18/2025).

[44] Daba Finance, "South africa's envisionit deep ai partners with pharma giant bayer", 2024, [Online]. Available: https://dabafinance.com/en/news/south-africas-envisionit-deep-ai-partners-with-pharma-giant-bayer (visited on 04/18/2025).

[45] J. Kart, "Robin the robot comforts kids in hospitals, can help with covid-19", 2020, [Online]. Available: https://www.forbes.com/sites/jeffkart/2020/06/17/robin-the-robot-comforts-kids-in-hospitals-can-help-with-covid-19/ (visited on 04/12/2025).

[46] R. Melkumyan, "The making of robin: A robotic friend for pediatric patients", 2024, [Online]. Available: https://evnreport.com/creative-tech/the-making-of-robin/ (visited on 04/15/2025).

[47] J. Mahakian, "Investigating the use of an autonomous robot assistant toimprove the wellbeing of institutionalized older adults inarmenia", in *Alzheimer and Dementia*, 2022.

[48] R. Manuel, "Ukraine oks robotic stretchers for military distribution", 2024, [Online]. Available: https://thedefensepost.com/2024/09/10/ukraine-military-robotic-stretchers/ (visited on 04/15/2025).

[49] Ukrainska Pravda, "Medical evacuation robots tested in ukraine", 2024, [Online]. Available: https://www.pravda.com.ua/eng/news/2024/02/29/7444397/ (visited on 04/15/2025).

[50] M. Brady, J. Coco, and K. McDonald, "Implementing robots to support nursing home staff and socialize with residents", 2022, [Online]. Available: https://digital.wpi.edu/downloads/tb09j879b (visited on 04/12/2025).

[51] D. Daniel, "With montreal's scale ai, hospitals across canada are testing new ai applications", 2024, [Online]. Available: https://www.canhealth.com/2024/11/01/with-montreals-scale-ai-hospitals-across-canada-are-testing-new-ai-applications/ (visited on 04/12/2025).

[52] Medtronic, "Mazor - robotic guidance system for spinal surgery", 2024, [Online]. Available: https://www.medtronic.com/ca-en/healthcare-professionals/products/spinal-orthopaedic/spine-robotics/mazor-x-stealth-edition.html (visited on 04/16/2025).

[53] Warringal Private Hospital, "Mazor x stealth edition", 2024, [Online]. Available: https://www.warringalprivate.com.au/Our-Services/Mazor-X-Stealth-Edition (visited on 04/16/2025).

[54] A. Gamal *et al.*, "Clinical applications of robotic surgery platforms: A comprehensive review", *Journal of Robotic Surgery*, vol. 18, no. 1, 2024.

[55] MkulimaGPT, "About MkulimaGPT", 2024, [Online]. Available: https://mkulimagpt.com/about-1 (visited on 04/16/2025).

[56] Africa News, "Rwanda: An ai platform for small holder farmers", 2024, [Online]. Available: https://www.africanews.com/2023/09/28/rwanda-an-ai-platform-for-small-holder-farmers/ (visited on 04/16/2025).

[57] Farm Hut, "Discover our wholesome features", 2024, [Online]. Available: https://www.farmhutafrica.com/features (visited on 04/17/2025).

[58] V. Makuvaro *et al.*, "Constraints to crop production and adaptation strategies of smallholder farmers in semi-arid central and western zimbabwe", *African Crop Science Journal*, 2017.

[59] P. Kendra, "Agriculture and climate change: Call "plantix — your crop doctor" for help", 2022, [Online]. Available: https://agrilinks.org/post/agriculture-and-climate-change-call-plantix-your-crop-doctor-help (visited on 04/17/2025).

[60] I. Samal, T. K. Bhoi, A. K. Pradhan, and D. K. Mahnta, "Plantix app: A success story of artificial intelligence in plant protection", *Van Sangyan*, 2023.

[61] B. Kanana, "Botswana startup pioneers ai and drone use in agriculture for sustainable farming", 2024, [Online]. Available: https://www.cryptopolitan.com/botswana-pioneers-drone-use-in-agriculture/ (visited on 04/17/2025).

[62] Anton Tech, "Project anton, powered by anton tech", 2024, [Online]. Available: https://www.anton.co.bw/ (visited on 04/17/2025).

[63] Fermonaut, "Revolutionizing agriculture: Introducing jeevn ai by farmonaut technologies", 2024, [Online]. Available: https://farmonaut.com/precision-farming/revolutionizing-agriculture-jeevn-ai-your-personal-farm-advisor-2/ (visited on 04/17/2025).

On the Protection of Face Recognition Embeddings

Gábor György Gulyás
Vitarex Stúdió Ltd
Budapest, Hungary
email: gabor@gulyas.info

***Abstract*—Face recognition technologies rely on face embeddings, numerical representations of biometric features, which are increasingly used in security and commercial applications. However, the privacy risks associated with storing and processing these embeddings are significant, particularly under strict regulations, such as the GDPR and the AI Act. This paper investigates two main techniques for protecting face embeddings: Locality-Sensitive Hashing (LSH) and Homomorphic Encryption (HE). Through a case study using random projections and the Labeled Faces in the Wild dataset, we show that while LSH allows great reduction in data sizes and offers efficient approximate matching, it provides weak resistance to re-identification attacks. In contrast, HE enables computation directly on encrypted data and offers a more secure, though computationally expensive, alternative. We evaluate recent HE-based approaches and propose optimizations.**

Keywords-Face Recognition; Biometric Templates; Privacy; Security.

I. INTRODUCTION

Face recognition technologies are rapidly becoming integral components of modern smart city infrastructures and daily digital interactions. From secure access control in buildings and devices to personalized services in businesses, the ability to reliably identify individuals through facial biometrics offers both convenience and efficiency. At the core of these systems lie face embeddings — mathematical representations of facial features - serving as the fundamental units for recognition of individuals.

As their use becomes more widespread, security and privacy of face embeddings emerge as critical concerns. Unlike passwords or tokens, biometric data is inherently sensitive and immutable: once compromised, it cannot be revoked or changed. Hence, there are strict provisions under both the GDPR [1] (General Data Protection Regulation) and the AI Act [2] (Artificial Intelligence Act). Protecting face embeddings from exposure, inversion, and misuse is therefore essential to maintain user trust and ensuring the long-term viability of face recognition systems.

What are face embeddings? Briefly, they are our facial fingerprints; embeddings belonging to a specific person uniquely describe that individual, but differ notably from the embeddings of other individuals. State-of-the-art face recognition systems are predominantly based on deep learning, particularly Convolutional Neural Networks (CNNs). These models learn to extract compact and discriminative feature vectors (known as face embeddings) that capture the unique identity of individuals while remaining invariant to variations in pose, lighting, and expression. Face recognition technologies use various deep learning architectures, and their vector structure usually consists of float values with a variable length, typically having 128-512 dimensions.

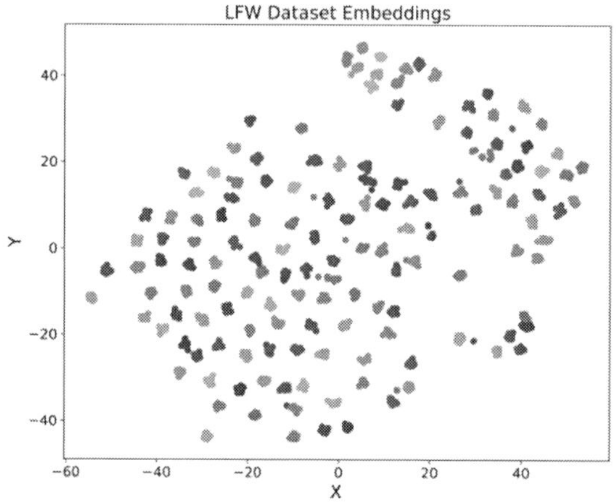

Figure 1. Individuals' embeddings (with at least 10 embeddings per individual) visualized from the LFW dataset [3].

We provide an example of the behavior of embeddings in Figure 1, where we visualize embeddings of individuals from the Labeled Faces in the Wild (LFW) dataset [3], using TSNE [4] (t-distributed stochastic neighbor embedding). It is clearly visible that each individual's embeddings cluster together but separately from others.

This paper investigates how state-of-the-art technical security measures can protect face embeddings [5]; in particular, we analyze Locality-Sensitive Hashing (LSH) and Homomorphic Encryption (HE). LSH offers a transformation with information loss to map embeddings into distance-preserving hashes that can still support approximate matching. HE, on the other hand, provides strong cryptographic guarantees by enabling computation on encrypted data without ever revealing the plaintext embeddings.

We examine the effectiveness of LSH through an experiment on random projection using the LFW dataset. Our results show that while LSH can preserve identity similarity for efficient matching, it offers limited resistance to re-identification under adversarial conditions. To address these shortcomings, we investigate HE as a cryptographic alternative that allows secure computation on encrypted embeddings.

The rest of this paper is organized as follows. In Section

II, we introduce LSH and evaluate its security and utility in the context of face embeddings. Section III presents HE, we review relevant literature and compare the effectiveness of recent approaches, also concerning face recognition. Finally, Section IV concludes the paper with a summary of our findings and outlines directions for future research.

II. Locality-Sensitive Hashing

LSH is a technique used to reduce the dimensionality of data while retaining the ability to efficiently perform approximate searches of the nearest neighbor. Unlike traditional cryptographic hash functions, which aim to maximize randomness and unpredictability, LSH functions are designed so that similar inputs (e.g., according to cosine distance) are more likely to be hashed to nearby buckets. This property makes LSH particularly useful for tasks such as face recognition, where exact matches are rare, but similar embeddings need to be quickly identified.

A. Related Work

Works on face hashing derive their own features to create embeddings. One of the first works on hashing faces introduces Local Feature Hashing (LFH), a face recognition method designed for scalability and robustness in large-scale, real-world applications [6]. LFH combines local image descriptors with p-stable distribution-based Locality Sensitive Hashing (pLSH) to achieve fast and Accurate Approximate Nearest Neighbor (ANN) searches.

Another, more recent work, explores the effectiveness of various LSH techniques to improve the performance compared to previous LFH methods [7]. Due to the increasing volume of facial images on social networks and databases, reducing the system response time is critical. The authors propose an unsupervised face recognition pipeline using local feature extraction, PCA (Principal Component Analysis) for dimensionality reduction, and several LSH variants for efficient indexing and similarity search. Their method is evaluated on three facial image datasets, and hashing function evaluated concerning their impact, scalability, and responsiveness. Their work suggests future research into combining LSH with deep learning.

B. Deep Learning and LSH

Since embeddings are structured simply as float vectors, random projection [8] seems to be a suitable LSH technique for dimension reduction. Therefore, random projection is a technique to reduce the dimensionality of high-dimensional data while approximately preserving the pairwise distances between points. Its core idea is based on the Johnson–Lindenstrauss lemma, which states that a small set of points in a high-dimensional space can be projected into a lower-dimensional space in such a way that the distances between the points are nearly preserved.

Mathematically, given a data vector $x \in R^d$, we multiply it by a random matrix $R \in R^{k \times d}$, where $k \ll d$, to obtain a lower-dimensional representation $x\prime = Rx$. The entries of R are typically sampled from a Gaussian distribution $\mathcal{N}(0,1)$ or a sparse distribution with similar properties. This method is computationally efficient and preserves the structure of the data well enough for many applications.

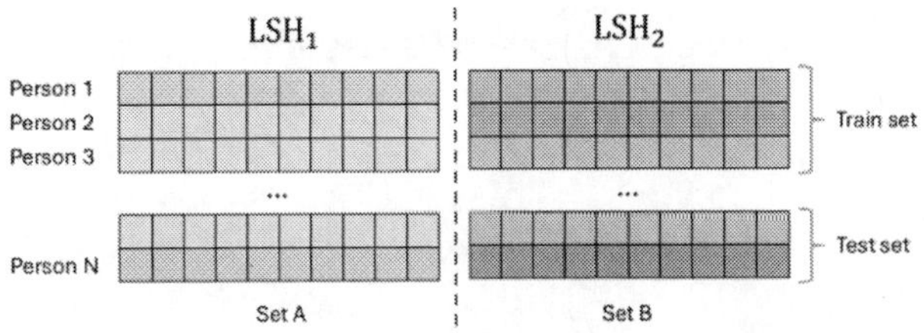

Figure 2. Our methodology: each profile (rows) were split half, then we used different LSH hashes to map their embeddings from 2048 bits to 64 bits.

C. Evaluation

In this section, we evaluate random projection for face recognition embeddings. Our methodology is as follows. Using a subset of the LFW dataset [3], we evaluated whether identity-preserving similarity can be maintained after applying random projections (with different key matrices) that significantly reduce the dimensionality of the embeddings. One could imagine that using a method with such information loss (e.g., shrinking embeddings only to their $1/32$), would prevent matching identities.

We first selected a subset of the LFW dataset by filtering for individuals with at least 40 available face embeddings, then we randomly sampled exactly 40 embeddings, ensuring balanced coverage across individuals. Then these embeddings were split into two disjoint sets of 20, simulating two independent profiles of each person. This resulted in a dataset of 19 people.

To simulate an LSH scenario using random projection, we generated two independent random matrices $R_A \in R^{4 \times 128}$ and $R_B \in R^{4 \times 128}$, with entries sampled from a standard Gaussian distribution $\mathcal{N}(0,1)$. These matrices were used to map each set of embeddings to a 64-bit binary hash, effectively reducing the 128-float (i.e., 2048 bits) representation to a compact binary code. We denote these LSH_1 and LSH_2, and the resulting hashed profiles are set A and B, respectively (see in Figure 2).

This setup allows us to analyze the linkability properties of randomly projected embeddings across two independent LSH spaces (assuming not knowing the projection matrices). Furthermore, this evaluation models practical scenarios where an attacker may try to correlate different embedding databases. Hence, the underlying questions is: is using LSH secure under the condition that an attacker cannot access the projection matrix?

The baseline approach could be to guess the mapping between embeddings $e_1 \in |A|$, $e_2 \in |B|$. The probability of a correct mapping is $1/19 \sim 5.2\%/$. A more sophisticated attack would be to map an embedding to the person to which it is more similar using cosine similarity: this naive algorithm also leads to a re-identification rate of 5.2%.

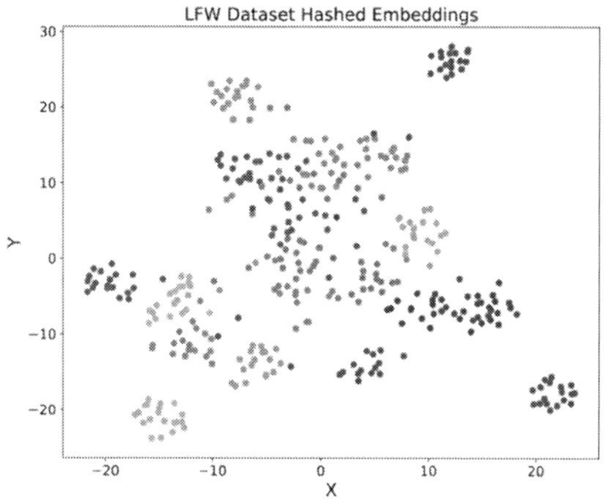

Figure 3. Hashed subset of the LFW dataset with only 20 embeddings per individual. Despite the significant loss of information, the hashing preserved differences between identities, while embeddings belonging to the same person are still clustered.

The underlying problem is identical to a re-identification situation. The core component of re-identification algorithms is the similarity metric that determines if two pieces of information (e.g., profile descriptors) are related or not. Only changing the similarity metric without touching the rest of the algorithm can yield significantly better results [9].

In our next step, we conducted a classification experiment using XGBoost (eXtreme Gradient Boosting), a gradient-boosted decision tree model. We constructed a binary classification task where the input consisted of embedding pairs, and the labels indicated whether the pair belonged to the same identity (positive class) or to different identities (negative class). Training and test data structures are illustrated in Figure 2.

Due to the inherent class imbalance in pairwise face verification tasks, where negative pairs typically outnumber positive ones (e.g., 4104 vs 228 in our experiment), we applied class-balancing techniques during training. Specifically, we assigned higher importance to the underrepresented class and reinforced the model's sensitivity to the minority class. The model was trained on the train set of embedding pairs and evaluated on a similar disjoint test set (with a $80:20$ train-test ratio). With this setup, we have achieved an overall 89.87% accuracy, with a recall of 91% for non-matching hashed embedding pairs (4104 cases), and 68% for matching ones (228 cases).

This leads us to the conclusion that while LSH is an efficient tool for reducing data volume while preserving utility, but offers weak utility.

III. Homomorphic Encryption

The previous conclusion on LSH leads us to the need to look for cryptographic solutions. This brings us to investigate HE, which is an emerging cryptographic technique that enables computation on encrypted data without requiring decryption. In the context of face recognition, this means that sensitive biometric embeddings can remain encrypted while still supporting operations, such as similarity comparison. This capability is especially valuable for privacy-preserving applications, where biometric data must be processed by untrusted systems or outsourced to third-party cloud services - or simply just for compliance reasons.

Formally, a HE scheme allows specific algebraic operations (e.g., addition or multiplication) to be performed on ciphertexts such that, when decrypted, the result matches the operation as if it had been performed directly on the plaintexts. Fully Homomorphic Encryption (FHE) schemes support arbitrary computations on encrypted data, while Partial Homomorphic Encryption (PHE) schemes restrict the type of operations. The first working FHE solution was published in 2009 [10].

Although HE offers strong privacy guarantees, their use in face recognition systems has been limited due to computational overhead and complexity. However, recent advancements in the efficiency and usability of HE libraries have opened new possibilities for secure biometric matching, making it a promising direction for embedding protection in real-world deployments. In the following, we provide a literature survey on new results.

Mi et al. [11] propose a privacy-preserving face recognition method that transforms facial data extracted from images in a way that conceals the subject's identity, while still enabling accurate recognition. Their approach demonstrates strong recognition performance and improved privacy compared to earlier transformation-based techniques. However, one notable limitation is that, in the event of a data breach, the transformed representations can still be partially inverted—allowing the recovery of visual cues, such as skin tone or hair color. Leaking such personal attributes can still lead to re-identification as demonstrated in [12], therefore any meaningful reconstruction or inference by an attacker must be prevented.

A recent study by Serengil et al. [13] presents an encryption-based face recognition approach in which most of the computation—including face detection and matching—is carried out directly in the encrypted domain. This design ensures a high level of security by minimizing exposure of sensitive data. The authors report that the system achieves both high accuracy and practical performance. While their method is sound, significant improvement needs to be done to reduce runtime efficiency. We have checked their approach by running our own simulations (with a different HE library), and we believe speedups of 4-8x could be possible, depending on the configuration – which we leave for future work.

A similar technique had been introduced before by Boddeti [14], who applies similar cryptographic optimizations to enable secure face recognition. However, their method has only been evaluated on isolated datasets in experimental settings. As a result, its applicability in real-world scenarios remains uncertain.

In summary, HE represents a compelling solution for protecting face recognition embeddings, offering strong theoretical guarantees and the ability to perform computations on encrypted face recognition embeddings. While prior work has laid important foundations, many of the proposed systems either fall short in terms of efficiency or have yet to be validated in realistic, large-scale scenarios.

IV. Conclusion and Future Work

As face recognition technologies become increasingly embedded in everyday digital infrastructure, the need for robust protection of biometric data, and specifically face embeddings, grows ever more urgent. In this paper, we examined the security and privacy challenges associated with storing and processing face recognition embeddings, with a particular focus on two technical approaches: LSH and HE.

Our evaluation of LSH, including a random projection-based case study, revealed that while LSH can efficiently reduce data size (up to $1/32$) and preserve similarity for approximate matching, it provides no privacy protection against re-identification attacks. In contrast, HE offers a higher level of security by enabling computations to be carried out on encrypted embeddings. While existing HE-based face recognition systems demonstrate promising results in terms of privacy and accuracy, many still need future work on the practical side.

Future work should build on existing results by doing extended evaluations to larger and more life-like and diverse datasets, explore integration with secure hardware enclaves, and investigate hybrid schemes that combine LSH and encryption for a balanced trade-off between efficiency and security. Additionally, adapting these techniques to real-time video analytics remains a promising direction for achieving scalable, redundant, privacy-preserving biometric recognition for smart cities and enterprise applications.

Acknowledgement

The author is grateful for Csaba Kiss, Dániel Kuknyó, Gergely Erdődi for their support provided while carrying out this work.

Project entitled "GDPR compliant anonymous facial recognition for analytics and improving security", with no. 2021-1.1.4-GYORSÍTÓSÁV-2022-00076 has been implemented with the support provided by the Ministry of Culture and Innovation of Hungary from the National Research, Development and Innovation Fund, financed under the 2021-1.1.4-GYORSÍTÓSÁV funding scheme.

References

[1] *Regulation (eu) 2016/679 of the european parliament and of the council of 27 april 2016 on the protection of natural persons with regard to the processing of personal data and on the free movement of such data, and repealing directive 95/46/ec (general data protection regulation)*, https://eur-lex.europa.eu/eli/reg/2016/679/oj, Accessed: 2025-04-11, 2016.

[2] *Regulation (eu) 2024/xxxx of the european parliament and of the council laying down harmonised rules on artificial intelligence (artificial intelligence act) and amending certain union legislative acts*, https://eur-lex.europa.eu/legal-content/EN/TXT/?uri=CELEX:52021PC0206, Accessed: 2025-04-11, 2024.

[3] G. B. Huang, M. Mattar, T. Berg, and E. Learned-Miller, "Labeled faces in the wild: A database forstudying face recognition in unconstrained environments", in *Workshop on faces in'Real-Life'Images: detection, alignment, and recognition*, 2008.

[4] L. Van der Maaten and G. Hinton, "Visualizing data using t-sne.", *Journal of machine learning research*, vol. 9, no. 11, 2008.

[5] S. M. S. Ahmad, B. M. Ali, and W. A. W. Adnan, "Technical issues and challenges of biometric applications as access control tools of information security", *International journal of innovative computing, information and control*, vol. 8, no. 11, pp. 7983–7999, 2012.

[6] Z. Zeng, T. Fang, S. Shah, and I. A. Kakadiaris, "Local feature hashing for face recognition", in *2009 IEEE 3rd International Conference on Biometrics: Theory, Applications, and Systems*, IEEE, 2009, pp. 1–8.

[7] M. Dehghani, A. Moeini, and A. Kamandi, "Experimental evaluation of local sensitive hashing functions for face recognition", in *2019 5th International Conference on Web Research (ICWR)*, IEEE, 2019, pp. 184–195.

[8] E. Bingham and H. Mannila, "Random projection in dimensionality reduction: Applications to image and text data", in *Proceedings of the seventh ACM SIGKDD international conference on Knowledge discovery and data mining*, 2001, pp. 245–250.

[9] G. G. Gulyás, B. Simon, and S. Imre, "An efficient and robust social network de-anonymization attack", in *Proceedings of the 2016 ACM on Workshop on Privacy in the Electronic Society*, 2016, pp. 1–11.

[10] C. Gentry, "Fully homomorphic encryption using ideal lattices", in *Proceedings of the forty-first annual ACM symposium on Theory of computing*, 2009, pp. 169–178.

[11] Y. Mi *et al.*, "Privacy-preserving face recognition using trainable feature subtraction", in *Proceedings of the IEEE/CVF Conference on Computer Vision and Pattern Recognition*, 2024, pp. 297–307.

[12] I. Fábián and G. G. Gulyás, "De-anonymizing facial recognition embeddings", *Infocommunications Journal*, vol. 12, no. 2, pp. 50–56, 2020.

[13] S. Serengil and A. Ozpinar, "Cipherface: A fully homomorphic encryption-driven framework for secure cloud-based facial recognition", *arXiv preprint arXiv:2502.18514*, 2025.

[14] V. N. Boddeti, "Secure face matching using fully homomorphic encryption", in *2018 IEEE 9th international conference on biometrics theory, applications and systems (BTAS)*, IEEE, 2018, pp. 1–10.

Greater Effectiveness in Citizen Participation in Smart Cities

A Legal Perspective on Adapting Procedures to Complexity, Uncertainty, and Ambiguity

José Miguel Lucas
Faculty of Law
University of Coimbra
Coimbra, Portugal
e-mail: josemiguellucas@gmail.com

Abstract—**Despite the growing emphasis on citizen participation, we agree with the authors who defend that the current mechanisms still often suffer from (i) low utilisation, (ii) limited adherence, and (iii) participant dissatisfaction, highlighting a gap between normative frameworks and their practical effect. To address these challenges, this work combines a targeted literature review with an argumentative legal analysis to propose a specific approach to citizen participation in smart cities, aligning public law with good governance and sustainability and envisioning efficient and equitable decision-making. More precisely, this work proposes a legal-technical framework to enhance citizen participation in municipal decision-making, drawing inspiration from Klinke and Renn's risk governance framework. Still, unlike the authors' risk-centric policy definition, the current study focuses on municipal decisions (excluding contracts, regulations, and administrative acts such as licensing), addressing some of their challenges, including complexity (multi-factor issues), uncertainty (data gaps), and ambiguity (value conflicts). The proposed solution is based on (i) adapted/tailored participation procedures and (ii) targeted engagement of participants, including underrepresented groups (to ensure inclusivity), all driven by (iii) impact criteria (e.g., economic value, the population affected, social significance) to categorise decisions and guide participation, supported by (iv) smart city technologies, like artificial intelligence-driven platforms (e.g., with semantic analysis), to streamline bureaucracy and enable scalable, inclusive, and transparent participation.**

Keywords - smart cities; citizen participation.

I. Introduction

This first section introduces the identified problem and the proposed solution, outlining the research's methodology.

A. The identified problem

We argue that current municipal decisions – especially those that are strategic/impactful/sensitive decisions that may shape municipal priorities through significant citizen participation – require greater sustainability (encompassing environmental, social, and economic/governance dimensions) and alignment with the principle of good governance. To achieve this, citizen participation, recognised as both a right and a principle, must be a key consideration. In that vein, in 2020, the Organisation for Economic Co-operation and Development (OECD) collected evidence and data that support the idea that citizen participation in public decision-making can deliver better policies, strengthen democracy, and build trust [1]. However, in 2022, Chen et al. [7, p. 141] indicated that, regarding future research, little had been written about the effectiveness of these measures, specifically the extent to which citizen involvement and dynamisation have contributed to social equity and quality of life.

According to some studies, specific mechanisms directly related to citizen participation (such as citizens' conferences, deliberative surveys or citizen consultations), despite being normatively enshrined in their respective legal systems, have rarely been used, have not had excellent adherence or have been unsatisfactory for participants (e.g. [2], [3], [4], [5], [6] and [7]), appearing more important in theory than in practice. This discrepancy, referred to by Delicado [5] as the "participation fallacy" and by Arnstein [6] as "tokenism", reveals a critical gap between the normative value of participation and its practical effectiveness.

B. Purpose and description of the solution

This article aims to develop a legally grounded, technology-enabled framework for citizen participation in smart cities that may overcome the "participation fallacy" by (i) adapting/tailoring participation procedures and (ii) targeting engagement of diverse participants, including underrepresented groups (to ensure inclusivity), all driven by (iii) strategic/impact/sensitive criteria (e.g., economic value, the population affected, social significance) to categorise decisions and guide participation, supported by (iv) smart city technologies, like artificial intelligence (AI) driven platforms (e.g., with semantic analysis), to streamline bureaucracy and enable scalable, inclusive, and transparent participation.

These ideas were inspired by the 2011 work of Klinke and Renn [8], who, based on previous works and in the 2005 white paper from IRGC (International Risk Governance Council) [9], proposed an adaptive and integrative risk governance model to address contemporary risk challenges, expanding the classic risk analysis model (assessment, management, communication) with additional steps (pre-estimation, interdisciplinary risk estimation, risk characterisation, evaluation, and management) and emphasising multi-actor involvement. That work's focus was on designing a flexible, inclusive governance process to handle risks characterised by complexity, scientific uncertainty and socio-political ambiguity.

Complexity, according to Klinke and Renn [8], arises in decisions with intricate technical or scientific components where cause-and-effect relationships are difficult to predict (e.g., tech policy). The scope is narrow, targeting experts or specialised stakeholders (e.g., engineers, scientists, or industry representatives). The depth demands deep technical analysis, focusing on data-driven or evidence-based contributions rather than broad public opinion.

Regarding uncertainty, according to the referred authors, it occurs when outcomes are unpredictable, but values, priorities, or local knowledge are critical (e.g., environmental Planning and urban redevelopment). The scope targets institutional actors, interest groups, and informed stakeholders (e.g., Non-Governmental Organisations (NGOs), local businesses, community leaders), who are key to surfacing these elements. It is balanced, combining stakeholder insights with technical input, with a focus on values and local context.

Regarding ambiguity, according to the referred authors, it arises in decisions involving moral, political, or value-based conflicts where a broad consensus is required (e.g., zoning disputes and social equity policies). The scope is broad and open to all citizens, ensuring diverse perspectives and legitimacy. It is deliberative, focusing on dialogue and consensus-building rather than technical detail. The general public, citizens, and civil society would be best suited to resolve these value clashes.

Beyond that idea (considering others, such as adaptive and integrative capacity and the governance decision tree), we would like to highlight the spectrum that goes from linear risk problems (as a category with low complexity, uncertainty, and ambiguity, making it suitable for routine risk handling) to those situations which require risk-informed, precaution-based, or discourse-based management. Consequently, stakeholder involvement would vary depending on the risk type. Linear risks (instrumental processing) would involve (only) governmental actors; complex risks (epistemic processing), experts; uncertain risks (reflective processing), stakeholders; and, for ambiguous risks (participative processing), the public.

While inspired by this risk governance theory, our proposed framework is not intended to reform legal structures but to serve as a best-practice, regulatory-level tool adaptable by municipalities within existing legal norms."

C. *Research questions*

To guide this investigation, this study poses the following explicit research questions:

a) Are participation procedures more critical for strategic/impactful/sensitive decisions compared to linear, routine decision-making processes?

b) How can Klinke and Renn's risk governance framework (especially regarding complexity, uncertainty, and ambiguity) be adapted to design effective citizen participation models?

c) How can administrative procedures be adapted to enhance citizen participation in smart cities?

d) How can smart city technologies support tailored participation by enhancing citizens' engagement, inclusivity, and decision-making?

D. *Difficulties, obstacles and challenges*

Regarding the challenges of the proposed solution, it is necessary to clarify that, unlike Klinke and Renn's risk-centric model, the current work focuses on municipal decisions (excluding contracts, regulations, and administrative acts, such as licensing) during policy implementation, enhancing participation and governance effectiveness, thereby emphasising the impact of these decisions. By adapting the authors' concepts of complexity, uncertainty, and ambiguity to the municipal context, this approach ensures that participation is tailored to the decision's impact and to its inherent challenges, making governance more responsive and inclusive.

In summary, the authors' framework will serve as a starting point, while our focus will be on impact-driven participation. We will propose six impact-based criteria as the core framework for assessing decisions while offering complexity, ambiguity, and uncertainty as supplementary tools to refine participation strategies when needed. They help municipalities address decisions that go beyond simple impact assessment, ensuring participation is effective in challenging cases. Unlike the six impact-based criteria, complexity, ambiguity and uncertainty are not required for every decision. They are applied selectively, maintaining the simplicity of the original framework while adding depth where necessary.

As such, the aforementioned theory can be applied to municipal decision, recognizing that these decisions differ from risk governance and national risk scenarios, but often share similar characteristics that affect how participation should be structured.

For instance, municipal decisions often involve complex situations with multiple technical components, interdependent systems, or specialised knowledge (e.g. deploying a city-wide sensor network may require technical workshops or cross-departmental collaboration alongside citizen input).

Local governance may also face long-term or unpredictable outcomes (e.g., future population growth and the effects of climate change), especially where data are incomplete. For example, a public transport investment plan might use scenario-based consultations, roundtables or phased feedback to adapt to emerging trends.

Furthermore, as we will see bellow, municipal decisions may also involve sensitive socio-cultural issues, ethical dilemmas, cultural sensitivities, or conflicting stakeholder values. For instance, a zoning change sparking community debate might require deliberative forums (such as citizen assemblies) or mediation to align perspectives, mirroring socio-political ambiguity.

Regarding the difficulties in implementing effective citizen participation, we identify those that we consider more relevant. First, low engagement stems from citizens' lack of awareness, trust, or perceived influence, exacerbated by opaque processes or inadequate feedback loops [2] and [10].

Second, inclusivity barriers – such as digital divides, low digital literacy, or exclusion of marginalised groups – hinder broad participation, particularly in smart cities [4].

Third, administrative rigidity in public law frameworks often employs one-size-fits-all procedures, overlooking the diverse nature of decisions (e.g., complex technical projects versus value-laden policy choices) [10].

Fourth, although the features of smart cities are becoming increasingly noticeable, their widescale implementation is uneven globally and in terms of technology application. Resource constraints challenge municipalities, such as designing tailored processes or deploying advanced technologies (e.g., AI platforms), which require significant investment and expertise [4].

Fifth, our proposal implies the definition of tiers, which should still be defined in concrete by municipalities (nevertheless, we suggest defining values, for instance, considering that a decision is strategic/impactful/sensitive if any quantitative criterion reaches Tier 3 or above or the qualitative criterion is triggered).

E. *Importance of the problem*

As to the importance of the problem, the "participation fallacy" is a critical issue for democratic governance and smart city development, with far-reaching implications.

Legitimation is a broader democratic function: participation increases the acceptability and sustainability of decisions, especially where multiple participants and conflicting interests are involved. Thus, participation should not be symbolic or limited to information provision. It must empower citizens to shape outcomes. To overcome these challenges, we advocate for regulatory frameworks that ensure inclusiveness, clarity, and effective and practical implementation. Participation gains legitimacy and adherence when citizens understand how their input will be used. Legal norms and especially municipal regulations must enable not just the right to be heard but also the duty of the administration to respond and justify. It is essential to reach those who need it most, particularly through inclusive technology and enhanced digital literacy.

Ineffective participation erodes public trust, weakens policy legitimacy, and risks suboptimal outcomes as citizens' preferences and local knowledge remain untapped [6]. For municipalities, addressing this gap is crucial to meeting the mandates of good administration and democratic legitimacy. Neglecting this problem risks social exclusion, policy resistance (e.g., in contentious zoning decisions), and missed opportunities to leverage smart city technologies for inclusive governance, rendering it a pressing scientific and practical challenge.

F. *Limitations*

Our proposed approach has several limitations. First, it relies on municipal capacity to implement sophisticated technologies and regulatory frameworks, which may be challenging for smaller or resource-constrained cities [4]. Second, the proposed tiered criteria (e.g., economic value, population affected) require local adaptation, risking inconsistency across jurisdictions due to subjective interpretations [10]. Third, digital inclusion remains a challenge, as reliance on smart city technologies (which often adopt top-down solutions) may exclude citizens with low digital literacy or access, potentially undermining inclusivity [5]. Fourth, this study has a legal perspective and is strictly limited in scope. It does not address forms of political participation or seek to explore in detail the ethical or philosophical underpinnings of democratic theory. Finally, the exploratory nature of the research lacks empirical validation, necessitating future testing to confirm the framework's effectiveness in diverse smart city contexts.

G. *Methodology*

Regarding the methodology, this work employs an exploratory, qualitative approach that combines a targeted literature review with an argumentative legal analysis to propose a specific approach to citizen participation in smart cities. Scientific articles were collected from reputable library databases, including EBSCO, IEEE, ResearchGate, repositorium.sdum.uminho.pt, and Google Scholar, as recommended by Callahan [11].

Rather than aiming for an exhaustive summary of all literature – a hallmark of scientific systematic reviews – this work prioritises pertinent sources that either bolster the proposal or illuminate counterarguments, aligning with the qualitative research principles outlined by Jaeger and Halliday [12], Cardano [13], and Günther [14]. This selective approach reflects a core tenet of legal scholarship, where persuasion takes precedence over comprehensiveness, allowing the analysis to construct a compelling case rather than merely describe the field. References follow the IEEE style, as per the conference guidelines. Zotero and Grammarly software were used.

H. *IARIA context*

We defend that both problem and solution are aligned with the topics of the International Academy, Research and Industry Association (IARIA) Annual Congress on Frontiers in Science, Technology, Services, and Applications, especially regarding smart cities (systems), understood as " *an innovative city that uses ICTs and other means to improve quality of life, efficiency of urban operation and services, and competitiveness, while ensuring that it meets the needs of present and future generations concerning economic, social, environmental as well as cultural aspects*" [15]. Moreover, we have already established that there should be a legal concept of smart cities that is more focused on citizens' rights [16].

I. *Structure*

This work is structured as follows: the current Section I (Introduction) outlines identified problem, the proposed solution, and methodology. Section II (Research) includes the definition of the impact criteria for decision categorisation, details the tailored procedures (inspired by Klinke and Renn's framework, targeted participants' engagement and the role of smart city technologies. Lastly, Section III (Conclusions) synthesises findings, advocating for legal reforms to achieve substantive participation.

II. RESEARCH

This section develops a framework for effective citizen participation in smart cities, exploring four key ideas: decision impact criteria, tailored procedures, targeted citizen engagement, and the role of technology.

A. Definition of criteria for strategic/impactful/sensitive decisions

Rather than directly transplanting risk typologies into urban governance, our proposal for a framework selectively draws on the concepts of complexity, uncertainty, and ambiguity, as well as their consequences. In our proposal, their role is to fine-tune participation design in situations where impact-based criteria alone may not fully reflect a decision's full significance.

Balancing efficiency and democracy poses a dilemma: overly broad participation in minor decisions wastes resources, while insufficient engagement in strategic/impactful/sensitive issues undermines legitimacy. Thus, we defend the advantages of prioritising higher participation (citizen power) for strategic/impactful/sensitive decisions [6] and [17] and a standardised yet flexible framework (e.g., a municipal regulation) that defines participation levels based on decision impact according to different criteria (thus avoiding case-by-case discretion). Inspired by several authors ([1], [6], [10], [17] and [18]), we defend the existence of six criteria: economic value, number of people affected, territorial area impacted, duration of impacts, risk of irreversible effects and qualitative factors as a "safety valve" (socio-cultural sensitive decisions).

Each of the quantitative criteria, without a hierarchical order, has a predefined tiered system (e.g., tiers 1–5) that ensures consistency and efficiency. We consider that (i) the municipality must define the values of each tier in concrete, according to its reality, and (ii) the tiers may need to be adapted by the municipality according to the matter at stake (e.g., specific NGOs, marginalised communities).

As a theoretical exercise, we propose some values that we consider reasonable for each tier. Regarding the first criterion (economic value), we suggest it should be measured according to the average value of the most expensive public contract awarded in the last 5 years, from ≥ 5% (Tier 1) to ≥ 80% (Tier 5). It measures the financial scale of a decision relative to municipal budgets. Due to their strategic nature, high-cost decisions (e.g., major infrastructure projects) likely require broader or more targeted participation.

The second criterion is the number of affected people (from < 0.5% (Tier 1) to > 50% or national/inter-municipal impact (Tier 5)). This criterion resonates with the emphasis on engaging those most affected. Decisions affecting large populations (e.g., urban redevelopment) may warrant broader participation to ensure legitimacy and transparency. Still, the low threshold for Tier 1 (<0.5%) may exclude niche but critical groups (e.g., minorities), thereby risking the exclusion of vulnerable participants, thus highlighting the need for the sixth (quantitative) factor alongside percentages.

The third criterion is the territorial area affected (< 0.1% (Tier 1) to > 50% or national/inter-municipal impact (Tier 5)). Despite the high impact, small but densely populated areas (e.g., urban centres) may fall into lower tiers, suggesting a need for density-weighted adjustments.

The fourth criterion is impact duration (< 1 week (Tier 1) to > 5 years (Tier 5)), which highlights long-term decisions which require participation to ensure sustainability and legitimacy. Still, the 5-year threshold for Tier 5 may be too short for some strategic decisions (e.g., climate adaptation plans spanning decades).

The fifth criterion, irreversibility of the effects (may vary from "none" (Tier 1) to "systemic damages" (Tier 5)) aligns with the mention of sustainability and risk governance. Still, the subjective nature of "systemic damages" may lead to inconsistent municipal classifications.

The sixth criterion is a qualitative flag for strategic/impactful (e.g., decisions shaping city identity or long-term vision) or socio-cultural sensitive decisions (which involve value conflicts, public controversy, or stakeholder polarisation, often requiring broad engagement to legitimise outcomes) that may not score high in all criteria but still require broad participation due to their systemic or value-sensitive nature (e.g., a policy shift with moderate costs but high symbolic importance) and their impact on marginalised groups.

Lastly, once the criteria are established, participants and mechanisms should be assigned according to each criterion and tier. In case of conflicting criteria (e.g., high territorial impact but low cost), a decision is strategic/impactful if any criterion reaches Tier 3 or above, as this ensures high-impact decisions trigger appropriate participation. To ensure participation is genuine and impactful, municipalities should adopt evaluative indicators such as (i) representativeness of participants (e.g., demographic match to affected population); (ii) transparency of decision influence (e.g., percentage of proposals integrated into final decisions); and (iii) satisfaction and trust metrics (e.g., post-process surveys). These indicators may be integrated into ex-post reviews of participatory processes or public reports.

B. Tailored procedures (Klinke and Renn's framework)

Further to the previous section, we propose a tiered participation matrix in which tailored mechanisms are linked to each criterion's impact level (Tiers 1–5). The intention is that this structure encourages municipalities to adopt flexible and hybrid approaches, particularly where decisions are considered strategic/impactful/sensitive. Hybrid formats (e.g., combining citizens' assemblies with digital feedback tools) are particularly recommended for higher tiers to enhance both inclusivity and effectiveness.

Similarly, in 2019, Simonofski [17] presented CitiVoice Frameworks, a governance tool designed to help define a citizen participation strategy and as a comparison and creativity tool for evaluating several cities and designing new means of participation.

In sum, we defend that municipal participation could benefit by shifting to tiered procedures, leveraging smart city technologies and grounded in administrative law (proportionality, transparency, inclusivity). First, considering that the administrative procedures include several stages that could be adapted, namely: (i) mechanism selection, (ii) notification, (iii) hybrid organisation, (iv) deliberation/voting, and (v) feedback. Secondly, considering the different tiers mentioned above. Once again, it should be the municipalities to choose the mechanisms they want to apply. Still, as a theoretical exercise, we propose some values that we consider reasonable for each tier.

Regarding the first criterion, low-cost decisions (Tier 1) could rely on digital forms or passive input tools. Moderate investments (Tiers 2–3) could utilise surveys, focus groups, or participatory budgeting methods. High-value decisions (Tiers 4–5) may require structured deliberation, such as expert roundtables, citizen assemblies, or hybrid forums that combine online and in-person engagement.

Regarding the second criterion, when few are affected (Tier 1), basic notifications or opt-in feedback could be sufficient. As impact grows (Tiers 2–3), engagement could include community meetings and targeted outreach. For large-scale effects (Tiers 4–5), we propose city-wide consultations, representative panels, and multilingual or minority-focused forums to ensure inclusion.

Regarding the third criterion, small-scale spatial issues (Tier 1) could be addressed through geo-tagged tools or apps. We defend that district-level actions (Tiers 2–3) may merit neighbourhood councils, workshops, or participatory mapping. Broader territorial impacts (Tiers 4–5) may call for hybrid assemblies, inter-municipal forums, and cross-district stakeholder planning.

Regarding the fourth criterion, short-term decisions (Tier 1–2) could benefit from simple tools such as Frequently Asked Questions (FAQs), chatbots, or commentable documents. Mid- to long-term plans (Tiers 3–4) should include phased feedback loops, foresight tools, or scenario-based consultations to inform decision-making. Strategic long-term decisions (Tier 5) require civic foresight panels and multi-stage hybrid processes.

Regarding the fifth criterion, reversible actions (Tier 1–2) could FAQs tools or feedback from NGOs. As permanence increases (Tiers 3–4), risk-mapping, ethical reviews, and stakeholder deliberations may become necessary. For systemic or irreversible effects (Tier 5), citizen–scientific panels or bioethics conferences with high transparency are recommended.

Lastly, regarding qualitative triggers, participatory mechanisms could be activated even at lower tiers. These could include storytelling workshops, civic mediation, citizen juries, or cultural forums. At higher levels, hybrid methods (e.g., deliberative assemblies and digital engagement) tend to foster dialogue, trust, and legitimacy.

C. Targeted participation

Participation should be directed and open to all, but especially to those affected and most in need. Also drawing inspiration from Klinke and Renn [8], we defend targeted engagement as *(i)* defining in abstract the most relevant/affected stakeholders (such as local communities, interest groups, or experts), *(ii)* especially those that could be affected or interested and encouraging their participation (avoiding generic or ineffective engagement and notifications), and (iii) providing a platform allowing citizens to select their areas of interest (e.g., urban mobility, environmental policies) and preferred participation methods (e.g., online surveys, in-person workshops).

Regarding the first criterion, low-cost decisions (Tier 1–2) could involve only internal staff or residents. As the financial scale increases (Tiers 3–5), participation could include representatives from businesses, NGOs, budgetary oversight bodies, technical experts, and afterwards general public, ensuring a fair distribution of public resources and legitimacy in high-cost investments.

Regarding the second criterion, we can sustain that minimal population impact (Tier 1) needs only passive notification. As more people are affected (Tiers 2–3), resident associations, interest groups, and schools should be involved. At Tiers 4–5, participation should expand to the general public, marginalised groups, and civil society organisations, reflecting the diversity of those impacted.

Regarding the third criterion, decisions with a narrow spatial scope (Tier 1–2) could involve residents or neighbourhood associations. Mid-tier impacts (Tier 3) typically may require district-level stakeholders, while significant territorial changes (Tier 4–5) necessitate cross-district, inter-municipal, or even regional collaboration involving planners and public institutions.

Regarding the fourth criterion, short-lived decisions (Tier 1–2) may require little engagement beyond direct users. Longer-term decisions (Tiers 3–4) could include policy researchers, institutional actors, or technical experts. Strategic, long-duration policies (Tier 5) could benefit from multi-generational forums, future scenario experts, and cross-sector stakeholders.

Regarding the fifth criterion, for reversible issues (Tier 1–2), one could consult frontline staff or local NGOs. Irreversible decisions (Tiers 3–5) would require the involvement of environmental professionals, ethicists, scientific advisors, and national NGOs, and afterwards general public, ensuring that long-term, possibly irreversible harms are carefully deliberated.

Regarding the sixth criterion, affected communities, cultural leaders, and conflict mediators should be involved in the process. At the highest sensitivity (Tier 5), participation should include minority communities, civil rights organisations, and possibly reconciliation forums, and afterwards general public, depending on the issue's moral and historical weight.

Defining stakeholders can inadvertently exclude groups or marginalise less vocal citizens if the process is not transparent or inclusive. Allowing citizens to choose their areas of interest increases their sense of agency and satisfaction, as they feel their input is relevant and valued (with feedback loops and transparency). A platform could facilitate participation by showing how selected inputs are used and by offering multiple participation methods (e.g., online surveys, in-person assemblies, or asynchronous feedback) to accommodate diverse needs (e.g., elderly citizens preferring in-person interactions, while younger ones prefer digital). This approach reduces barriers such as digital literacy or geographic constraints. A digital platform also risks excluding those with low digital literacy. Therefore, municipalities should preferably combine digital platforms with offline methods (e.g., kiosks and in-person sessions) and involve mediators to reach marginalised groups. Besides, identifying and engaging stakeholders requires resources and expertise to map relevant groups accurately, which could strain municipal capacities. Indeed, developing a platform (that allows citizens to choose interests and participation methods) is technologically and administratively complex. It may require robust infrastructure, data protection compliance, and a user-friendly design with personalised options, as well as ongoing maintenance, updates, and user support, which can be resource-intensive for smaller municipalities. To mitigate this, municipalities could pilot the platform in phases, starting with specific decision types (e.g., participatory budgeting) and using existing smart city infrastructure to reduce costs. Municipalities could also plan and prioritise strategic/impactful/ sensitive decisions to optimise resources.

Allowing citizens to select topics might result in over-representation of popular or controversial issues (e.g., cycle paths) while neglecting less visible but critical ones (e.g., waste management), potentially undermining balanced decision-making. Furthermore, we are also aware that if citizens could choose their areas of interest, less "exciting" or complex topics (e.g., technical infrastructure policies) might attract fewer participants, reducing the effectiveness of those decisions, which we suggest could benefit from expert input. As a mitigation measure, stratified sampling or weighted representation could be employed in stakeholder selection and platform algorithms to ensure diversity, as suggested by the need for inclusiveness.

D. Impact of technology in smart cities

The OECD [6] has catalogued effective deliberative practices across jurisdictions, revealing that well-designed citizen assemblies, participatory budgeting, and e-consultations can increase legitimacy. Technology in smart cities holds significant potential to enhance citizen participation in municipal decision-making by simplifying interfaces and providing officials and citizens with training on the effective use of technology. One way to address the aforementioned structural barriers is through real-time data analytics and/or smart governance platforms (e.g., mobile apps, online forums), which can make participation more accessible by reducing barriers such as physical access or time constraints, thereby increasing utilisation.

By fostering trust through transparent governance and clear communication, smart cities can encourage sustained participation. Smart cities can also enhance satisfaction by aligning solutions with citizens' needs (e.g., addressing urban issues such as mobility or safety) and involving them in the co-design of services through feedback loop mechanisms, thereby addressing dissatisfaction and encouraging adherence. Moreover, it helps in public awareness campaigns and reduces information asymmetry (namely by leveraging passive participation, e.g. to inform campaigns), thereby increasing governance responsiveness.

However, most examples show that effectiveness depends less on the tool's form than on its adaptation to local sociopolitical conditions and clarity of purpose [6]. Furthermore, inclusivity can be bolstered through accessibility features (e.g., user-friendly interfaces, anytime/anywhere information access, and flexible scheduling and targeted notifications), making participation more convenient and visible, thereby increasing engagement and hybrid mechanisms. Still, technocentric approaches risk exacerbating dissatisfaction if they neglect marginalised groups or fail to address privacy concerns effectively. To mitigate this risk, laws should mandate clear interfaces and accessibility standards for these platforms to ensure inclusivity, especially for groups with low digital literacy.

The intervention of AI may be particularly transformative, especially in treating the vast information provided during (qualitative) participation (for example, pairing AI semantic analysis with feedback loops to validate the input impact of large-scale citizen participation, notably from social media or e-consultations), offering a pathway to more informed, inclusive, and resilient municipal governance.

To ensure inclusive and trustworthy use of technology, municipalities adopting AI-enabled platforms for participation, beyond complying with legal rules, should incorporate basic legal safeguards. These include: (i) mandatory accessibility standards (e.g., multi-language support, mobile usability, offline alternatives); (ii) participatory guarantees; and (iii) transparency obligations, requiring that AI-supported analysis be explainable in plain language to participants. These safeguards do not require statutory reform but may be embedded in local regulations or contractual requirements.

III. CONCLUSIONS AND FUTURE WORK

Our preliminary analysis supports the hypothesis that legal frameworks for citizen participation must evolve to reflect the differentiated impact of certain administrative decisions and the available technological means. This evolution requires new regulatory models and an institutional willingness to shift from a symbolic to a substantive model of public engagement.

We consider that participation procedures are more critical for decisions that are strategic/impactful/sensitive than for linear, routine decision-making processes. Drawing inspiration from Klinke and Renn's risk governance framework, we may recommend or demand different types of stakeholders. In that vein, we also defend that there should be tailored participation procedures (minimal for routine decisions and extensive for high-impact ones). Moreover, municipal regulation should establish administrative procedures that can be adapted to local realities and the aforementioned impact criteria rather than the current one-size-fits-all procedures.

Smart cities, guided by principles of good governance, inclusive administration, and legal foresight, can lead this transformation by leveraging technologies to support tailored participation, facilitating adaptable procedures, enhancing stakeholder engagement, and utilising AI-driven semantic analysis of diverse inputs. The application of these technologies must be compliant and subject to regulation.

Finally, regarding future work, beyond further analysis regarding the mechanisms of participation and relevant concepts (e.g. stakeholders), as referred to, the exploratory nature of the research lacks empirical validation, necessitating future testing to confirm the framework's effectiveness in diverse smart city contexts.

References

Report:

[1] OECD (Organisation for Economic Co-operation and Development), "Innovative Citizen Participation and New Democratic Institutions: Catching the Deliberative Wave". Paris: OECD Publishing, 2020. Accessed: Jun. 29, 2025. [Online]. Available: https://www.oecd.org/en/publications/innovative-citizen-participation-and-new-democratic-institutions_339306da-en/full-report.html

Article in a journal:

[2] L. Boussaguet, 'Participatory mechanisms as symbolic policy instruments?", Comparative European Politics, vol. 14, no. 1, pp. 107–124, Jan. 2016, doi: 10.1057/cep.2015.12.

Article in a journal:

[3] P. L. Colenci, C. M. de Oliveira, and F. P. Oliveira, "A diagnosis of the effectiveness of citizen contribution in municipal public management (Um diagnóstico da efetividade da contribuição cidadã na gestão pública municipal)", CEDOUA - Revista do Centro de Estudos de Direito do Ordenamento, Urbanismo e Ambiente, vol. 18, no. 36, pp. 9–25, Jan. 2015.

Article in a journal:

[4] J. L. Fernández-Martínez, P. García-Espín, and M. Jiménez-Sánchez, "Participatory Frustration: The Unintended Cultural Effect of Local Democratic Innovations", Administration & Society, vol. 52, no. 5. pp. 718–748, 2020. doi: 10.1177/0095399719833628.

Article in a website:

[5] A. Delicado, "The fallacy of participation in environmental matters (A falácia da participação em matéria ambiental)", Plataforma Barómetro Social. Accessed: Jun. 29, 2025. [Online]. Available: http://www.barometro.com.pt/2018/08/20/a-falacia-da-participacao-em-materia-ambiental/

Article in a journal:

[6] S. R. Arnstein, "A Ladder Of Citizen Participation", Journal of the American Institute of Planners, vol. 35, no. 4, pp. 216–224, Jul. 1969, doi: 10.1080/01944366908977225.

Article in a journal:

[7] S. Davidson, "Spinning the Wheel of Empowerment", Planning, no. 3, pp. 14–15, Apr. 1998, Accessed: Jun. 29, 2025. [Online]. Available: https://sarkissian.com.au/wp-content/uploads/sites/13/2009/06/Davidson-Spinning-wheel-article1998.pdf

Article in a journal:

[8] A. Klinke and O. Renn, "Adaptive and integrative governance on risk and uncertainty", Journal of Risk Research, vol. 15, no. 3, pp. 273–292, 2011, doi: 10.1080/13669877.2011.636838.

Report:

[9] IRGC (International Risk Governance Council), "Risk governance: Towards an integrative approach", Geneva (Switzerland), White paper No. 1, 2005. Accessed: Jun. 29, 2025. [Online]. Available: https://irgc.org/wp-content/uploads/2018/09/IRGC_WP_No_1_Risk_Governance__reprinted_version_3.pdf

Report:

[10] OECD (Organisation for Economic Co-operation and Development), "Exploring New Frontiers in Citizen Participation in the Policy Cycle", in OECD Global Forum on Building Trust and Reinforcing Democracy. Milan (Italy): OECD Publishing, 2024. doi: 10.1787/77f5098c-en.

Article in a journal:

[11] J. L. Callahan, "Writing literature reviews: a reprise and update", Human Resource Development Review, vol. 13, no. 3, pp. 271–275, Sep. 2014, doi: 10.1177/1534484314536705.

Article in a journal:

[12] R. G. Jaeger and T. R. Halliday, "On confirmatory versus exploratory research", Herpetologica, vol. 54, pp. S64–S66, 1998, Accessed: Jun. 29, 2025. [Online]. Available: http://www.jstor.org/stable/3893289

[13] M. Cardano, "Qualitative research manual - the contribution of argumentation theory" (Manual de pesquisa qualitativa - A contribuição da teoria da argumentação). Petropolis. Brasil: Editora Vozes, 2017.

Article in a journal:

[14] H. Günther, "Qualitative research versus quantitative research: Is this the question? (Pesquisa qualitativa versus pesquisa quantitativa: Esta é a questão?)", Psicologia: Teoria e Pesquisa, vol. 22, no. 2, pp. 201–209, Aug. 2006, doi: 10.1590/S0102-37722006000200010.

Report:

[15] UNECE (United Nations Economic Commission for Europe), "Guidelines for the development of a Smart Sustainable City Action Plan". 2018. Accessed: Jun. 29, 2025. [Online]. Available: https://unece.org/fileadmin/DAM/hlm/documents/Publications/Guidelines_for_SSC_City_Action_Plan.pdf

[16] J. M. Lucas, "Legal concept of smart cities and regulation of dashboards in the governance dimension (to ensure a holistic vision) (Conceito jurídico de cidades inteligentes e regulamentação de dashboards na dimensão de governação (para assegurar uma visão holística)", in Cidades inteligentes e Direito, Governação digital e Direitos - desafios futuros globais, Coimbra: Gestlegal, 2023, pp. 369–396. Accessed: Jun. 29, 2025. [Online]. Available: https://gestlegal.pt/loja/cidades-inteligentes-e-direito-governacao-digital-e-direitos/

Article in a journal:

[17] A. Simonofski, E. S. Asensio, and Y. Wautelet, "Citizen Participation in the Design of Smart Cities: Methods and Management Framework", in Smart Cities: Issues and Challenges, Amsterdam (Netherlands); Oxford (UK); Cambridge (USA): Elsevier, 2019, pp. 47–62. doi: 10.1016/B978-0-12-816639-0.00004-1.

Article in a journal:

[18] T. Chen, J. Ramon-Gil-Garcia, and M. Gasco-Hernandez, "Understanding social sustainability for smart cities: The importance of inclusion, equity, and citizen participation as both inputs and long-term outcomes", Journal of Smart Cities and Society (SCS), vol. 1, no. 2, pp. 135–148, Jun. 2022, doi: 10.3233/SCS-210123.